读客文化

商务文化

|中英双语版|

万物简介
数字是什么

［英］彼得·希金斯　著

邱明峰　译

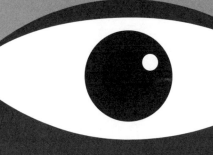

NUMBERS:
A VERY SHORT INTRODUCTION

浙江科学技术出版社

著作合同登记号 图字：11-2022-045

Numbers: A Very Short Introduction
Copyright:© Peter M. Higgins 2011
Numbers: A Very Short Introduction was originally published in English in 2011.
This translation is published by arrangement with Oxford University Press. Dook Media Group Ltd
is solely responsible for this translation from the original work and Oxford University Press shall
have no liability for any errors, omissions or inaccuracies or ambiguities in such translation or for any
losses caused by reliance thereon.

图书在版编目（CIP）数据

万物简介.数字是什么：汉文、英文 /（英）彼得·
希金斯 (Peter M. Higgins) 著；邱明峰译 . —— 杭州：
浙江科学技术出版社，2023.3
书名原文：Numbers：A Very Short Introduction
ISBN 978-7-5739-0296-2

Ⅰ.①万… Ⅱ.①彼…②邱… Ⅲ.①科学知识－普
及读物－汉、英②数学－普及读物－汉、英 Ⅳ.① Z228
② O1-491-49

中国版本图书馆 CIP 数据核字 (2022) 第 177319 号

书　　名　万物简介：数字是什么
著　　者　［英］彼得·希金斯
译　　者　邱明峰

出　　版　浙江科学技术出版社　　　　网　　址　www.zkpress.com
地　　址　杭州市体育场路 347 号　　联系电话　0571-85176593
邮政编码　310006　　　　　　　　　印　　刷　三河市龙大印装有限公司
发　　行　读客文化股份有限公司

开　　本　880mm×1230mm 1/32　　印　　张　10.75
字　　数　172 000
版　　次　2023 年 3 月第 1 版　　　　印　　次　2023 年 3 月第 1 次印刷
书　　号　ISBN 978-7-5739-0296-2　　定　　价　59.90 元

责任编辑　卢晓梅　　责任校对　张　宁
责任美编　金　晖　　责任印务　叶文炀

序

　　这本小书致力于用每个人都熟悉的语言，来解释人们所遇到的各种数的定义和它们的行为。数使我们能够将万事万物进行比较。数无处不在，任何对数缺乏理解的人都会在现代世界不知所措。然而，应该意识到，虽然我们已对数习以为常，但它们并非物理实在，而是我们从自己周围的世界抽象出来的概念。为了对它们如何运行给出一个清晰的图像，我们把它们从其他事物中分离出来单独考虑。

　　本书并非算术温习教程，也不会谈太多有关数的历史。写它的目的是解释数本身以及它们所展现出的行为。看一眼目录就会发现，这本书的前半部分主要关心普通计数用的数，而在后半部分，我们将走出这一范畴，探索从商业和科学中自然产生的问题。这一过程中，对自由计算的需求最终带着我们逐步走进复数的世界。复数是处理大部分数字相关事务的主要框架。这听起来可能有点吓人，不过请放心，真正困难的工作已经有人替你完成了。

现代数的系统并非像大礼包一样从天而降，而是经过若干世纪的发展而来的。人们曾在很长一段时间内迷惑不解。这种情况源于两个根本原因：第一是缺乏一套高效的表示数的方法以便操作；第二则是哲学上的困扰，即如何解释各种不同数的类型以及它们是否有意义。如今，我们对自己在做什么已经有把握得多了，在跟数打交道的时候无须再忧虑这些，因而我们能够在本书这样短的篇幅内给数的世界描绘一幅完整的图画。这并不是说所有的谜团都已被解开——事实远非如此，你读下去之后就会发现。

彼得·希金斯

科尔切斯特，英格兰，2011

目录

附英文原文

01

如何不去考虑数

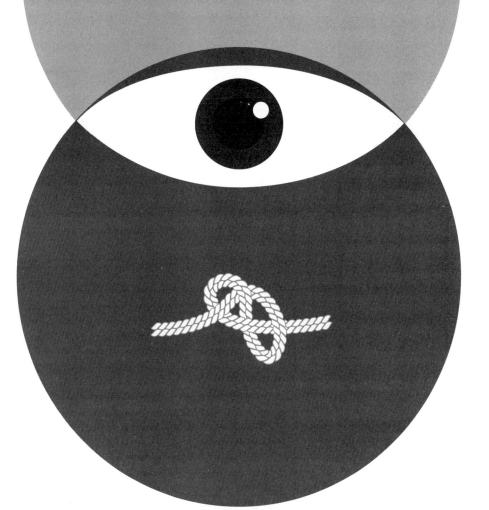

我们已经习惯看见写下来的数，也习惯从中提取出某种意义。然而，一个数字（比如6）同它所代表的那个数并不是同一个东西。就像在罗马数字中，我们会把六[1]这个数写作 Ⅵ，但是我们意识到这与用现代记号写下的6代表了同一个数，它们都对应6根算筹（ⅠⅠⅠⅠⅠⅠ）的那一类集合。让我们先花一点点时间考虑一下表示和思考数的不同方法吧。

有时候，我们会在无意识的情况下解决一些关于数的问题。例如，假设你正要组织一次会议，想要保证每个人都拿到一份议程。你可以将每份议程逐个标上与会者的名字首字母。只要议程没用完，你就知道份数是足够的。这样你就解决了问题，而没有用到算术或者直接数数。这里数依然在发挥作用，它们使我们得以将一个集合同另一个集合进行精确比较，即便这两个集合的组成元素有着截然不同的性质。就像上述例子里，一个集合包含了人，而另一个集合则由纸张组成。数让我们可以比较两个集合的大小。

1

2

在上例中，你不需要费神去数有多少人将要出席，因为没有必要知道——你的问题是判断议程的份数是否不少于出席人数，而具体的数目无关紧要。但如果你要为 15 个人买午饭，你就需要真正数一数人数了。当然，要计算这顿饭的全部开销，就一定得使用算术，哪怕是用计算器求和来得出精确的数值。

现代数字系统让我们能以一种有效且统一的方式来表示数，这方便我们将一个数和其他数做比较，以及在计数问题中进行所需要的算术操作。日常生活中，我们在所有的算术中使用十进制，换句话说，我们十个十个地数数。这么做的原因是偶然的：我们恰好有十根手指。需要明确的是，让数的系统如此有效的原因并非我们对**底数**（base number）的选择，而是我们在数的表示中使用了**位值进位法**（positional value），即一个数字的值取决于它在数字串中出现的位置。比如，1984 是 4 份 1 加上 8 份 10，再加上 9 份 100，再加上 1 份 1000 的缩写。

当我们把数写成特定形式的时候，我们想表达什么？理解这一点很重要。在这一章，我们将要考虑数代表了什么，发现不同的计数方法，认识一类非常重要的数（素数），并且介绍一些找到它们的简单技巧。

人们是如何学会数数的

这里值得我们花上一点时间来弄明白构造一套计数系统所需的两个重要阶段。让我们以十进制为例：我们会给孩子们规定两项基本任务，背诵字母表和学习数数。这两个过程表面上看是相似的，却有着本质的不同。英语基于26个字母，每个字母对应一个发音，供我们念单词用。总的来说，英语发展的结果是这门语言可以用26个符号来书写。如果不给字母表一个顺序，我们就没法编纂字典。然而，字母表并没有天生的排序。我们所采用并且都曾在学校吟诵过的 a，b，c，d，…看起来实在很随意。诚然，常用的字母一般出现在字母表的前半部分，但这也只是大致的规律，而非铁律。比如，常用字母 s 和 t 就很晚才被点名。相比之下，用以计数的数，或者叫**自然数**[1]（natural number），如1，2，3，…一旦出现便已经排好了序。例如，符号3用来表示跟在符号2后面的那个数，因此必须列在2的下一位。在一定程度上，我们可以给每个数赋予一个新的符号。但为了处理永无止境的数，我们迟早得放弃不断引入新名字，而只能开始把它们

---

1 我国的自然数包含 0，而本书所说的自然数不包含 0。

按批次分组。按10个来分组代表发展出了一个坚实的数字系统的第一阶段，这个方法在古今中外几乎都是一样的。

但是各个文明在细节上却有很多不同。罗马系统除了按10分组外，同样也喜爱用5分组。他们使用特殊符号V和L，来分别代表5和50。古希腊系统则直接使用了十进制。他们用某些字母来代表数，有时候加上上画线来告诉读者这个符号应被解读为一个数，而不是平常的词语中的一个字母。比如，π代表80，而γ代表3，于是他们可以写下πγ来代表83。与我们的现代数学符号相比，它看起来好像同样高效，也确实相差不多，但它们是不一样的。希腊人仍然没能运用进位系统，因为他们每个符号的值都是固定不变的。具体来说，γπ还是只能表示同样的数——3＋80。而如果我们将83的数字顺序颠倒，会得到一个不同的数——38。

在**印度－阿拉伯数字系统**（Hindu-Arabic number system）中，数的第二个阶段得以实现。其主要思想是让一个符号的值依赖于它在字符串中出现的位置。这使我们可以只使用一套固定的符号来表示任何数。我们最终选择了由0，1，2，…，9这十个数字组成的数字系统。这套常用的数字系统被称为**十进制**（base ten）。当然，我们完全可以用一个更大或者更小的基本符号集来建立我们的数字系统。我们甚至可以使用两个数字去建立数字系统，比如0和1。这被称为**二进制**（binary system），在电脑运算中经常被用到。需要明确的是，具有革命性的不是对底数的选择，而是这样一种思想：使用位置来传达额外的信息，从而确定数的值。

例如，当我们写下一个数，比如1905，每个数字的值取决于其在数字串中的位置。这里有5份1，9份100（即10×10），以及1份1000（即$10 \times 10 \times 10$）。符号0被用作一个占位符，这很重要。在1905这个例子中，十位并没有贡献，但我们不能忽略它而只写作195，因为那代表了一个完全不同的数。事实上，每个数字串都代表了一个不同的数，正因为如此，海量的数才可能用很短的字符串表示出来。比如，用不超过10位的字符串便可以给地球上每个人分配一个独特的号码，这样，这个巨大集合中的每一个体都有了个人代号。

不同的古代社会在书写数时使用了不同的底数，但这远不能弥补一个事实，即几乎所有文明都缺少一套真正的进位制系统，更谈不上使用零来作为占位符。在古代的所有民族中，巴比伦文明的数字系统是最为接近位值进位法的系统，考虑到他们的古老程度，这实在让人赞叹。然而，他们没有彻底拥抱那个不那么自然的数——0。比如，我们用0来区分830和83，而古巴比伦人刻意回避了在数字串末尾使用这样一个表示空的符号。

意识到0确实是数，这需要跨越一个概念上的障碍。0确实并非一个正数，但它依然是一个数，如果不将它以一种完全自洽的方式吸纳进来，我们的数字系统就是残缺不全的。约公元6世纪，印度迈出了这关键的最后一步。现代的数字系统被称为印度–阿拉伯数字系统，正因为它是从印度经由阿拉伯传到了欧洲。

有或没有小数的生活

将以10为底的位值进位法思想推广到非整数部分，就可以得到我们现在所熟知的完整十进制数字系统。比如，当我们写下3.14的时候，小数点后的1表示一份$\frac{1}{10}$。类似地，后面的4代表$\frac{4}{100}$。这种两位小数形式的数我们已经很熟悉了，因为我们在处理十进制货币的时候，最小单位——取决于具体情况——不是美元、英镑或欧元，而是便士或美分。后者是其主币的百分之一。十进制小数算术是以10为底数的系统的自然推广。在实际应用中，它代表了执行普通加法运算的最佳方法。虽然有这些优点，十进制方法的诞生却并非一蹴而就。一开始它只在数学精英们的小圈子里得到运用，直到16世纪后半叶才最终进入商业结算并被大众使用，甚至在这之后，按照非十的幂次来组织数的方法依然在用。英国直到1971年才采用了十进制货币。而部分英语地区依然顽固地使用码、英尺和英寸[1]。若要捍卫英制单位，我们可以辩解说它们是根据人体的尺寸量身定制的。我们的手大约有6~8英寸长，而我们的身高大约是5~6英尺。我们将周围的物体制作得与我们的身体尺寸相似，自然可以方便地用英尺和英寸来丈量它们。但是，如果让1英尺等于10英寸，整个系统也可以很好地运作，还更方便我们用以10为底数的计算方法来处理问题。

6

为一个数字系统选底数有点像为一张地图选比例尺，这并非基于对象内在的性质，而是类似于赋予它一个坐标系，作为控制用的工具。我们对底数的选择本质上是任意的，面对自然数集1，2，3，4，…的时

1　1码＝3英尺＝36英寸。

候，排他性地使用底数10让我们戴上了有色眼镜。只有掀起这层面纱，我们才能面对面地看清数到底是什么。当我们说起一个数，例如四十九，人们的脑海中都会浮现出两个字符4和9。某种程度上，这对我们谈论的那个数来说不太公平，因为我们毫不犹豫地将四十九转换成了 $(4×10)+9$。我们也可以同样轻松地用另一种方式来诠释这个数：$49 = (4×12)+1$。实际上，在十二进制中，四十九正是被写作41，这里数字4代表4份12。当然，四十九这个数最显著的特征是它是 $7×7$ 的积。这一特点在七进制中十分明显，此时四十九这个数会被表示为100，这里的1代表一份 $7×7$。

我们一样有权利为我们的数字系统选择另一个底数，例如12。玛雅人使用了12，而巴比伦人用了60。某种程度上，60是一个计数基底的好选择，因为60有很多因数，它是可以被1到6之间所有数整除的最小的数。不过，选择一个60这样相对大的数作为底数也有缺点，就是需要引入60个不同的符号来表示从0~59的所有数。

如果一个数是另一个数的整数倍，则称第二个数是第一个的**因数**[1]（factor）。比如，6是42的一个因数；

1　或称因子、约数，英文也可以写作 divisor。

但8不是28的一个因数，这是因为28含有三个8还余 　　7
4。数字系统的底数拥有众多因数会是一个很方便的性
质。这就是为什么相对于我们的数字系统来说，底数选
择12也许比10更好，因为12的因数是1，2，3，4，6和
12，而10只能被1，2，5和10整除。

　　数字系统的有效性，加上我们对它高度熟悉，给
了我们一种虚假的信心，同时也带来了一定的局限。
我们会更愿意使用单个的数，而非一个算术表达式。
例如，大多数人情愿谈论5969，而不是47×127，即
使这两种表示方式代表了同一个东西。仅在"求出
最终答案"5969之后，我们才觉得我们"有"了这个
数，从而可以正视它。然而，这里面包含着一丝虚妄的
成分，因为我们只是将这个数写成了多个10的几次幂
的和。若将这个数分解为一系列因数的乘积，从这个等
价形式中，我们反而可以更好地推断它一般意义上的构
造和其他的性质。确切地说，5969这个标准形式能让我
们将它和其他以同样方法表示的数直接比较大小，但并
不能展现出这个数的全部特性。分解为因数的形式可能
有用得多。在第4章中，你会发现其中的一个原因，即
一个数的十进制表示可能掩盖了关键的因数。

　　古人比我们多拥有的一项优势是，他们并未被
十进制的思想所束缚。谈到数的规律时，他们会自

然地想到一个数可能拥有或缺乏某些特殊的几何性质。比如，10和15这样的数是**三角形数**（triangular number）。这可以通过图像展现在我们面前，正如十瓶制保龄球中排成三角形的球瓶，以及斯诺克台球中15个红球摆成的三角。但如果只用十进制展示这些数，这样的画面就不会出现在我们眼前。我们要放下十进制的思维定势，告诉自己只有从很多不同角度来思考数，才能重新获得古代人天然就拥有的自由。

8

这样，把我们自己解放出来之后，我们可能会选择重点关注一个数的**因数分解**（factorization）——把数写成一些更小的数的积。因数分解揭示了一个数内部构造的相关信息。通常，我们仅将数看作科学和商业的仆人。如果我们花一点点时间专门研究数本身，而不与其他任何事物做关联，就能发现很多原来隐藏着的信息。单个数的性质可能会在自然界中以有序的模式展现出来，这比单纯的三角形或方形来得更微妙，比如，向日葵螺旋形的头状花序代表的斐波那契数。我们将在第5章中介绍这种类型的数。

素数数列概览

数的荣耀中有一项是如此显而易见，以至于很容易被忽视——它们每一个都是独一无二的。每个数都有自己的结构——如果你喜欢的话，可以称之为个性。单个数的个性非常重要，这是因为当一个特定的数出现时，它的特征会反映在它所描述的集合的结构中。当我们执行加法和乘法这些基本的数的运算时，数之间的关系也会显现出来。显然，任何比1大的自然数都可以表示成更小的数的和。但是，当我们开始将数相乘，我们很快注意到有些数从来都不会在我们得到的乘积里出现。这些数就是**素数**[1]（prime number）。它们代表了乘法的构成要素。

一个素数是一个像7，23或103这样的数。它有且仅有两个因数——1和它本身。我们并不把1看作一个素数，因为它只有1个因数。那么，第一个素数便是2。这也是仅有的偶素数。接下来的3个素数3，5和7都是奇数。大于1而又不是素数的数称为**合数**（composite number），因为它们由一些更小的数复合而成。数$4 = 2 \times 2 = 2^2$是第一个合数；9是第一个奇合

9

---

1 英文也可以写作 prime。

数，$9=3^2$也是一个**平方数**（square number）；$6=2×3$是我们第一个真正意义上复合的数，因为它由两个不同的大于1的因数复合而成。而$8=2^3$是第一个**立方数**（cube number），立方数是指等于某个数的3次幂的数[1]。

　　紧接着个位数的是我们选择的底数$10=2×5$，它本身就是特殊的，而且还是三角的，因为$10=1+2+3+4$（回想一下十瓶制保龄球）。接下来我们有一对**孪生素数**（twin primes）11和13，它们是由12隔开的两个相邻的奇数，且同为素数。考虑到数值的大小，12显得有很多因数。的确，12是第一个所谓的**盈数**[2]（abundant number），因为它的**真因数**（proper factor）——严格小于它自身的因数——之和超过了这个数本身：$1+2+3+4+6=16$。数$14=2×7$可能看起来并没有什么特别的，但这实在是一条悖论，作为第一个不特别的数本身就是一件特别的事。到了$15=3×5$，我们又遇到了一个三角数，并且它是第一个等于两个真因数之积的奇数。数$16=2^4$不仅是一个平方数，还是第一个四次幂数（在1以后），这使得它十分特别。17和19是另一对孪生素数。对于18和20，以及

1　这里指的立方数从2的立方开始，因为$1=1^3$。

2　又称丰数或过剩数。

更多数的独有性质，我就留给读者朋友自己去观察了。对每一个数，你都可以说它是特别的。

回到素数，它们中的前20个是：2，3，5，7，11，13，17，19，23，29，31，37，41，43，47，53，59，61，67，71。

显然，在数列的开始部分，素数是十分常见的，因为小的数没有多大可能会有因数分解。在这之后，素数越来越稀少。比如，只有一组连续3个奇素数：3，5，7。这三者的组合是独一无二的，因为每3个奇数就会出现1个3的倍数，所以这种情况再也不会发生。此外，素数出现频率减少的过程是十分松散的，还非常不规律。比如，30~40之间只有两个素数，即31和37，但刚过100就会有两个"相继的"孪生素数对，即101，103和107，109。

素数在数千年来一直深深吸引着人们[1]，因为它们无穷无尽（我们在下一章会证明这个说法），在自然数中现身的方式又神出鬼没。它们性质中神秘莫测的这一面在现代**密码学**（cryptography）中被加以运用，来保护互联网上的机密信息。这将是第4章的话题。

10

1　最近的例子是孪生素数猜想，传奇美籍华裔数学家张益唐在2013年取得重大进展，引起轰动。

素性检验：素数整除性测试

为了找出不大于某个数（比如100）的所有素数，最容易想到的方法是把所有数写下来，再寻找并画掉里面的合数。基于这一思想的标准方法叫作**埃拉托斯特尼筛法**[1]（Sieve of Eratosthenes）。方法如下：首先圈出2并画掉列表里2的倍数（即其他偶数）。然后回到开始，圈出第一个尚未被画掉的数（即3），画掉剩下数表里它的所有倍数。重复这一过程足够多遍，剩下没有被画掉的就是素数。即便它们中一些被圈出来了，而另一些没有。例如，图1展示了对不大于60的数运用筛法的过程。

11 　　② ③ 4̸ ⑤ 6̸ ⑦ 8̸ 9̸ 1̸0̸ 11 1̸2̸ 13 1̸4̸ 1̸5̸
　　1̸6̸ 17 1̸8̸ 19 2̸0̸ 2̸1̸ 2̸2̸ 23 2̸4̸ 2̸5̸ 2̸6̸ 2̸7̸ 2̸8̸ 29 3̸0̸
　　31 3̸2̸ 3̸3̸ 3̸4̸ 3̸5̸ 3̸6̸ 37 3̸8̸ 3̸9̸ 4̸0̸ 41 4̸2̸ 43 4̸4̸ 4̸5̸
　　4̸6̸ 47 4̸8̸ 4̸9̸ 5̸0̸ 5̸1̸ 5̸2̸ 53 5̸4̸ 5̸5̸ 5̸6̸ 5̸7̸ 5̸8̸ 59 6̸0̸

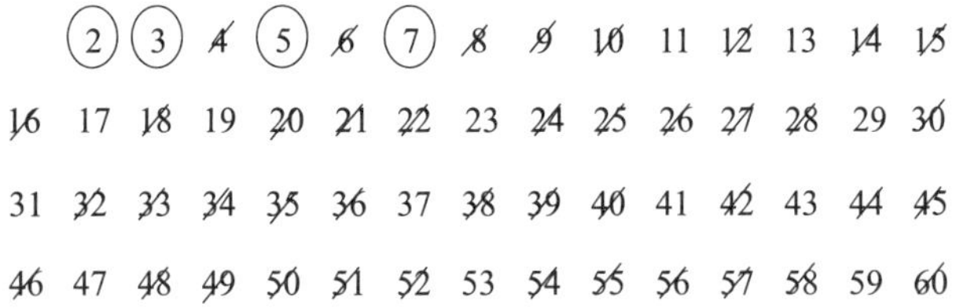

图 1　素数筛：没有被画掉的数即为60以内的素数

1　又称埃氏筛或素数筛，简称筛法。埃拉托斯特尼（公元前276—公元前194），古希腊数学家、地理学家。

你怎么知道什么时候该停止筛选呢？重复这一过程，直至圈到一个数，大于整张表中最大数的平方根。比如，当你在不大于120的数中筛选素数时，需要筛掉2，3，5和7的倍数。接着当你圈出11，就可以停下了，因为$11^2=121$。此时，你已经圈到了第一个大于你的最大数（这里是120）的平方根的数，剩下的素数虽未被触及，但所有的合数都已经被画掉，它们都是2，3，5或7的倍数。

不难看出为什么列表中最大数n的平方根决定了需要筛选的遍数。任何列出的合数m都至少有一个素因数，它最小的素因数必小于n的平方根，因为两个或两个以上大于$\sqrt{n}$的数的积大于n（并且因此也大于m）[1]。

素性问题的另一面是：任一给定数n是素数还是合数。为了确定这一点，我们可以用小于$\sqrt{n}$的素数逐个除n，如果n不能被所有这些数整除，则其为素数，否则不为素数。鉴于这个原因，对于小素数，如2，3，5，7，…了解一些简单的整除性测试方法会很便捷。下文将介绍一些简单的方法。

检测能否被2或5整除很容易，因为这两个素数是

12

---

1 当解释有关任意数的性质的时候，数学家们会用符号为讨论的对象赋予名称。对于数，这些名字通常都是小写字母，如m和n；两个数的积$m×n$经常简写为mn。——作者注

我们的底数10的素因数。要看出这一点，你只须查看待检数 n 的最后一位：当且仅当个位为偶（即0，2，4，6或8）时 n 可以被2整除，当且仅当 n 最后一位为0或5时它含有因数5。不管数 n 有多少位，判断 n 是否为2或5的倍数，我们都只须检查最后一位。对于不能整除10的素因数，我们需要多做一点工作。尽管如此，仍然有一些整除性测试方法，比计算完整的除法更快捷。

一个数能被3整除，当且仅当其各位数字之和能被3整除。例如，数 $n = 145\,373\,270\,099\,876\,790$ 的各位数字之和是87，而 $87 = 3 \times 29$，因此 n 可被3整除。当然，我们还可以将这个测试应用于数87，然后继续在每一阶段都求出各位数字之和，直到结果显而易见。对于给出的例子这样做，可以得到以下数列：

$$145\,373\,270\,099\,876\,790 \to 87 \to 15 \to 6 = 2 \times 3。$$

你会发现，这里列出的所有整除性测试方法都如此快捷，你可以相对轻松地处理有几十位的数，甚至比手持式计算器能处理的最大的数还要大上数十亿倍。

下面要给出不大于20的剩下的所有素数的整除性测试方法，因为它们都属于同一个类型。虽然它们成立的原因不那么明显，但是这些方法应用起来都很简单。即便这里没有收录论证，想证明它们的正确性并不是特别困难。

让我们从给定一个数 n 是否能被 7 整除开始。将 n 的最后一位数字乘以 2 得到一个数，n 移除最后一位数字之后的结果再减去这个数。当 n 是 7 的倍数时，新的数也恰好会是 7 的倍数。我们重复这一过程，直到结果变得显然。例如，设 $n=3465$，5 乘以 2 得 10，因此我们从 346 减去 10，得 336；接着再做一次，将 6 乘以 2 得 12，从 33 减去 12 得 21=3×7，因此 n 可以被 7 整除。如果你忘记了 7 的乘法表，我们可以再次进行，从 2 中减去 2 倍的 1 得 0，而 0 可以被 7 整除，因为 $\frac{0}{7}=0$。（可以用 0 除以一个非 0 的数，但反过来的话——除以 0 则没有意义。）甚至大如好几千万的数也可以用这个方法简单地处理。在本例和之后的例子中，我们仅仅列出**算法**（algorithm）在每个阶段输出的数。算法是指用来解决一类特定问题的一个机械的过程。正如我们这里用到的方法：

$$n=27\,916\,924 \rightarrow 2\,791\,684 \rightarrow 279\,160$$
$$\rightarrow 27\,916 \rightarrow 2779 \rightarrow 259 \rightarrow 7。$$

因此 n 可以被 7 整除。每执行一次指令循环，我们都至少能减少一位数，因此执行循环的次数大约与初始数的长度相同。

13

为了检测 n 是否有因数 11，将原数的最后一位移除，再从新数中减去原数的最后一位，依此重复。比如，我们的方法揭示了下面这个数是 11 的倍数：

$$4\ 959\ 746 \rightarrow 495\ 968 \rightarrow 49\ 588$$

$$\rightarrow 4950 \rightarrow 495 \rightarrow 44 = 4 \times 11。$$

检测能否被 13 整除，将原数最后一位移除，再用新数加上原数最后一位的 4 倍，接着用类似于 7 和 11 的方法，不断重复。比如，13 是下面这个数的一个素因数：

$$11\ 264\ 331 \rightarrow 1\ 126\ 437 \rightarrow 112\ 671$$

$$\rightarrow 112\ 71 \rightarrow 1131 \rightarrow 117 \rightarrow 39 = 3 \times 13。$$

接下来是 17 和 19。对于 17，我们将原数最后一位移除，再用新数减去原数最后一位的 5 倍，重复操作直到可判断整除性；对于 19，我们将原数最后一位移除，再用新数加上原数最后一位的 2 倍，重复操作直到可判断整除性。例如，我们来检测 18 905 是否能被 17 整除：

$$18\ 905 \rightarrow 1865 \rightarrow 161 \rightarrow 11，$$

因而它不是 17 的倍数。但对于 19，整除性测试给出了另一种结论：

$$18\ 905 \rightarrow 1900 = 100 \times 19。$$

拥有了这一组测试，你现在就可以检查不大于 500

14

的所有数的素性，因为$23^2=529$超过了500，因此19是你需要考虑的最大的素因数。例如，为了确定247的性质，我们只需要检查它是否能被不大于13的素因数整除，因为下一个素数的平方，$17^2=289$超过了247。通过对13的测试，我们发现$247\to(24+28)=52\to13$，这是一个13的倍数$(247=19\times13)$。

素数相乘可以得到**无平方因数的数**（square-free number），要想构造关于这些数的整除性测试，可以叠加并行其素数因子的整除性测试。比如，对于$42=2\times3\times7$，一个数n能被42整除，当且仅当n可以通过2，3和7的三项整除性测试。但是，对于那些有平方数因数的数，像$9=3^2$，则不能由此得到。顺便说一句，9是n的因数，当且仅当9也是n的各位数字之和的因数。

你也许会问：数千年以来，那些聪明的数学家们难道还没有想出更好、更精妙的检测素性的方法？答案是有的。2002年，我们发现了一个相对快速的判断一个给定的数是否为素数的方法。不过，如果给定的数恰好是一个合数，那么这个所谓的"**AKS素性测试**"（AKS primality test）并不能给出该数的因数分解。虽然原则上说找到一个给定数的素因数的问题可以通过试错来解决，但实际操作中，这对于很大的整

15

数依然难以实现。正因为此，它构成了很多互联网加密方法的基础。我们会在第4章回到这个话题。在那之前，我们会在接下来的两章中更近距离地认识一下素数和因数分解。

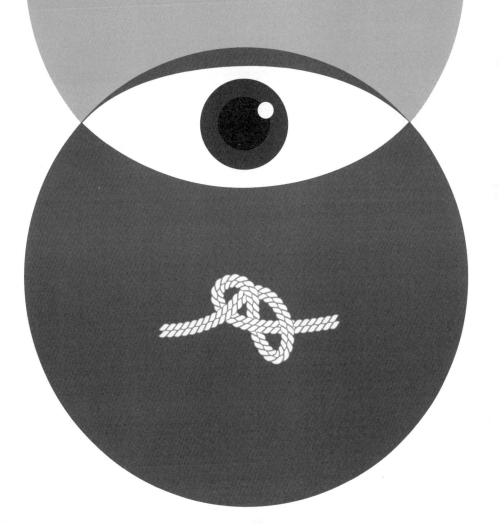

02

永无穷尽的素数

镶嵌在数的拼图中的素数

我们怎样才能确定素数不会越来越稀少，最终逐渐消失殆尽呢？你可能会认为由于有无穷多自然数，而每一个都可以被分解为素数的乘积（这一点我们一会儿仔细解释），那么必然得有无穷多个素数才能承担这一工作。虽然这个结论是正确的，但它并不能从上述观察中得出。这是因为如果我们从有限个素数开始，仅使用这些给定的素因数，我们就能制造出无穷多不同的数。确实如此，任何单个素数都有无穷多个幂次。比如，素数 2 的幂分别为 2，4，8，16，32，64，…因而完全可以设想：只有有限多的素数，每个数都是那些素数的幂的乘积。更糟的是，我们能构造出一个给定数的任意长度的幂数列，或它的任意多倍数列，却没法用同样的手段构造出一个由不同素数组成的无穷数列。对于素数，我们还是得去搜寻，到底怎么才能确定它们不会绝迹？

在这一章结束的时候，我们便会对这一点确定无疑了。首先，请你注意素数的一个值得一提的简单

17   "规律"——除了2和3以外的每一个素数，都与一个6的倍数相邻。换句话说，在这两个数之后的每一个素数，都是像$6n\pm1$这样的形式，这里n是某个确定的数。（记住$6n$是$6\times n$的缩写，符号"$\pm$"的意思是加或减。）原因很好理解，每个数都一定可以写成以下6种形式中的一种：$6n$，$6n\pm1$，$6n\pm2$，$6n+3$，因为没有数与6的某个倍数距离超过3。例如，$17=(6\times3)-1$，$28=(6\times5)-2$，$57=(6\times9)-3$。事实上，这6个形式的数是循环出现的，这意味着当你写下任意6个连续的数，6种形式每个都会出现且仅出现1次。在这之后它们会一遍又一遍地循环出现，并且出现的顺序总是相同的。很显然$6n$和$6n\pm2$形式的数都是偶数。而任何形如$6n+3$的数都可以被3整除。因此，除了2和3，只有形如$6n\pm1$的数可能是素数。如果$6n\pm1$两者都是素数，这种情况恰好对应于孪生素数：比如$(6\times18)\pm1$给出一对数107和109，我们在第1章中提到过它们。你可能会猜测每对$6n\pm1$中至少有1个是素数——这对于100以下的素数来说的确是对的，但往后不远就存在着第一个例外：$(6\times20)-1=119=7\times17$，$(6\times20)+1=121=11\times11$。当$n=20$时，这两个数都不是素数。

    素数之所以重要，主要是因为每个数都可以写成一系列素数的乘积，并且这么做的方法本质上只有一种。为了找到这个特别的分解，我们只须用某种方法分解这个给定的数，接着继续分解在因数中出现的合数，直到这样的分解不能再继续为止。比如，我们可以说120＝2×60，接着继续将合数因数60分解：

$$120 = 2 \times 60 = 2 \times (2 \times 30) = 2 \times 2 \times (2 \times 15)$$
$$= 2 \times 2 \times 2 \times 3 \times 5。$$

18

我们说120的**素因数分解**（prime factorization）为$2^3 \times 3 \times 5$，当然我们也可以用另一种途径得到这个结论。比如：

$$120 = 12 \times 10 = (3 \times 4) \times (2 \times 5)$$
$$= [3 \times (2 \times 2)] \times (2 \times 5)。$$

但如果将素因数从小到大重新排列，我们依然得到了与之前相同的结果：$120 = 2^2 \times 3 \times 5$。

至少在上面这个例子中分解的唯一性是真的。你可能或多或少已经熟悉数的这一性质，但是如何保证这个结论适用于每一个数？任何数都可以分解为素数的乘积，这已经足够清楚了。但是，一般来说有不止一种办法可以完成这个任务。那么我们如何确定这个过程总能给出相同的最终结果呢？这是一个重要的问题，因此我将花上一点儿时间概述一下推理的过程，从而使我们能绝对信赖这个结论的正确性。这个结果来自素数的一个特殊性质，我们叫它**欧几里得性质**（Euclidean property）：假设有一个由两个或更多数相乘得到的积，如果一个素数是该乘积的一个因数，那么它也是构成这个乘积的某个因数的因数。比如，7是$8 \times 35 = 280$（也可以看作乘积$280 = 7 \times 40$）的一个因数，同时我们注意到7也是35的一个因数。这个性质刻画了素数的特征，因为没有合数能够保证同样的结论成立。例如，我们可以看出6是$8 \times 15 = 120$（也可以看作$120 = 6 \times 20$）的一个因数，6却不是8或15的因数。

素数总是拥有以上性质，这一事实可以用被称为**欧几里得算法**[1]（Euclidean algorithm）的推理来证明。我们将在第4章解释这个算法。如果我们暂且相信这个结果，那么就不难解释为什么不存在一个数拥有两个不同的素因数分解。假设存在拥有两个不同素因数分解的数，那么就存在一个最小的这样的数，让我们用n表示它。n有两种素因数分解。当把n的素因数从小到大排列的时候，这两个分解不相同。我们要证明这是矛盾的，因而假设一定为假。

倘若n的这两种分解有一个共同的素数p，我们可以从两个中都消去p，从而得到一个更小的数$\dfrac{n}{p}$的两种

19

1　在中国一般称之为辗转相除法。

不同的素因数分解。由于 n 已经是最小的有两种相异素数分解的数，这是不可能的。因此，n 的不同分解中含有的素数集合必定没有交集。现在，取 n 的一种分解中的一个素数 p。因为这个素数 p 是 n 的一个因数，可以推断 p 也是第二种分解的一个因数。所以，根据欧几里得性质，p 是第二种分解中某个素数 q 的一个因数。然而，由于 p 和 q 均为素数，这仅在 $p = q$ 时是可能的。但是我们已经排除了这种情况，因为 n 的这两种分解没有共同素因数。于是我们发现了矛盾，说明这样的 n 是不可能存在的。综上得证，任何数的素因数分解都是唯一的。

值得一提的是，如果我们把数 1 包括在素数里，素因数分解的唯一性将不再成立。这是因为我们可以将 1 的任意幂次方乘上一个分解式，最后的积保持不变。这表明 1 和素数们有着本质上的不同。基于此，把 1 排除在素数的定义之外是正确的。

欧几里得：素数的无穷性

让我们回到这个问题：我们怎么知道素数无穷无尽，没有办法找到最大的素数？如果有人声称 101 是最大的素数，你即刻便能反驳他，因为你可以证明 103

没有因数（除了1和103以外），因此103是一个更大的素数。接下来你的朋友可能会承认自己大意了，他应该说103是所有素数中最大的。这时候你还可以指出107也是一个素数，从而再次表明他错了。然而你的朋友可能还是执迷不悟，他搬出你们所知的最大的素数。他甚至可能退一小步，承认自己并不知道最大的素数是多少，却继续说他很确定有这么一个数。

20　　解决这个问题最好的方法是：对于任何假想的有限的素数集合，证明我们都能给出一个不在这个集合中的新的素数。比方说，如果有人号称在某个位置存在一个最大的奇数。你可以反驳说，假如n是奇数，那么$n+2$是一个更大的奇数，因而不可能有一个最大的奇数。然而，这个方法对于素数来说可就不那么简单了——给定一串有限的素数，我们没有办法使用这个集合来造出一个素数，并且表明它比集合中所有的数都大。那么，或许真的有一个最大的素数？我们怎么才能知道那位固执的朋友是不对的呢？

　　欧几里得是知道的。约公元前300年，希腊有个数学家叫亚历山大里亚的欧几里得（Euclid of Alexandria）。他就是一切作为定语使用的词"欧几里得"（Euclidean）本人。从给定一个集合p_1，p_2，…，p_k（其中每个p_i表示一个不同的素数），他也没能找到生成一个新的素数的途径，于是他退回一步，找到了一个更加微妙的论证方法。他证明了在某个给定的数的范围内，总是存在一个或更多的新素数（但他的论据并不足以让我们在那个范围内精确地定位素数）。

他的证明如下：设 p_1，p_2，$\cdots$，p_k 为前 k 个素数。考虑比所有这些素数的积还大 1 的数 n，即 $n=p_1p_2\cdots p_k+1$。n 要么是一个素数，要么可以被一个小于它自身的素数整除。如果是后一种情况，这个素因数不可能是 p_1，p_2，$\cdots$，p_k 中的任意一个。因为假设 p 是 p_1，p_2，$\cdots$，p_k 中任意一个数，将 n 除以 p 会有余数 1。于是可推知 n 的任何素因数都会是一个新的素数，并且比 p_1，p_2，$\cdots$，p_k 里面所有的素数都大，但不超过 n 自己。特别是，由此可知不存在任何包含所有素数的有限的列表，因而素数数列会不断延续下去，永不终结。欧几里得关于素数无穷性的证明是永恒不朽的，是数学中最受敬仰的证明之一。

虽然欧几里得的推理没有确切地说明在哪里能找到下一个素数，但现在我们对素数出现的频率已经有了深入的理解。例如，如果我们任意取两个没有公因数的数，比如 a 和 b，并考虑数列 a，$a+b$，$a+2b$，$a+3b$，$\cdots$，德国数学家约翰·狄利克雷（Johann Dirichlet，1805—1859）证明这样一个数列包含无穷多个素数。

21

（当然，如果 a 和 b 有公因数——比方说 d，这就没有希望成立了。因为如此一来，列表里每一个成员都是 d 的倍数，因而不是素数。）当 $a=1$，$b=2$ 时，我们得到由奇数组成的数列。由欧几里得的证明，我们知道它包含无穷多素数。实际上，通过对欧几里得的方法进行一些十分简单的改进，还可以证明其他一些特殊情况，比方说以下形式的数列：$3+4n$，$5+6n$，$5+8n$（n 依次取 1，2，3，…），它们各自都含有无穷多素数。但是，要证明狄利克雷的一般结论就非常难了。

另一个可以简单陈述的结果是，对于任意给定的数 $n(n \geqslant 2)$，至少存在一个素数大于 n 但小于 $2n$。这在历史上被称为**伯特兰猜想**[1]（Bertrand's postulate），它可以用非常基本的数学知识来证明，虽然这个证明本身有些取巧。我们可以使用下面列出的素数，对取值不大于 4000 的 n 验证这个论断。首先观察到这个列表中位于打头的素数 2 之后的每个数都小于前一个数的 2 倍：

2，3，5，7，13，23，43，83，163，317，631，1259，2503，4001。

---

1 该猜想由伯特兰提出，后由切比雪夫证明，故称"伯特兰–切比雪夫定理"。约瑟夫·伯特兰（Joseph Bertrand），法国数学家。巴夫尼提·列波维奇·切比雪夫（Pafnuty Lvovich Chebyshev），俄罗斯数学家。

对于每个不大于4000的n，取上表中不超过n的最大素数p，它的后面一个素数q即位于$n<q<2n$的范围中。这就保证了伯特兰－切比雪夫定理对于不大于4000的所有n都是成立的。例如，当$n=100$，$p=83$，那么$q=163<2×100$。再使用一条巧妙的论证，这个论证涉及**中央二项式系数**（central binomial coefficient，将在第5章中介绍），还可以证明这个定理对大于4000的n也是正确的。

然而，我们不用走太远，就又会发现似曾相识却尚未解决的问题。举例来说，没有人知道是不是在两个连续的平方数中间总存在着一个素数。另一个观察是似乎存在足够的素数，从而可以保证每个大于2的偶数n总可以写成两个素数之和（**哥德巴赫猜想**，Goldbach's conjecture）。对于n小于10^{18}的情况，这个结论已经被直接验证。自然，我们可能会寄希望于沿着伯特兰－切比雪夫定理的思路找到一个证明。在大于某个给定的整数N时，基于对素数分布的已有知识，我们试图证明：对于任何偶数$2n \geqslant N$，至少存在一对素数p，q，构成方程$p+q=2n$的解。这个途径迄今还没能成功，不过这些思路产生了一些弱一点的结果。比如，1939年之后我们知道了：每个足够大的奇数是至多三个素数的和；每个偶数是不超过300 000个素数的和。但要想完整地证明哥德巴赫猜想，似乎还有很长的路要走。

还有一个简单的结果，颇有一些上面介绍的这类论断的味道。它说的是：存在一个小于40亿的数 n，有10种不同的方法，可以将它写成4个不同的立方数之和。已知 $1729=1^3+12^3=9^3+10^3$ 是最小的能用两种方法写成两个立方数之和的数。不过，要想知道一个数 n 存在，我们并不一定非要确定它的大小。有时候可以明确地知道一个问题有解，而不是精准地找到一个解。

在这个例子中，我们先指出如果取4个不同的数，它们都不大于一个固定的数 m，那么求它们的立方和，结果将小于 $4m^3$。同时，倘若 $m=1000$，那么通过简单的计算就可以发现，选4个不同的数求其立方和，所有可能的情况已经超过了 $4m^3 \times 10$ 种。由此可推出存在某个数 $n \leq 4m^3 = 4\,000\,000\,000$ 一定可以写成4个立方数的和，且至少有10种不同的写法。具体的计算涉及二项式系数（将在第5章中介绍），但并不困难。

卡尔·弗里德里希·高斯（Karl Friedrich Gauss，1777—1855）是19世纪引领世界的德国数学家和物理学家。素数分布的全景图像可以用他的观察来概

23

括：对不大于数 n 的素数的个数 $p(n)$，可以由 $\frac{n}{\ln n}$ 近似地给出，并且这个近似随着 n 的增大而越来越精确。例如，如果我们取 n 为 100 万，比值 $\frac{n}{\ln n}$ 告诉我们在这一阶段，大约每 12.7 个数中就会有一个素数。高斯对其中某些细节还给出了更精确的观察结果。他的猜想直到 1896 年才被证明。这里提到的对数函数是所谓的**自然对数**（natural logarithm），它的值不是以 10 为底的幂的指数，而是以一个特殊的数 e 为底的幂的指数。e 大约等于 2.718。关于这个著名的数 e，我们在第 6 章中会听到更多的故事。

数论中最著名的悬而未决的问题是黎曼猜想[1]（Riemann Hypothesis），要阐述它必须用到**复数**（complex number）——我们还没有介绍到。在这里提到它，是因为可以通过素因数分解的唯一性，重新表述这个问题的对象，使得新的提法中出现了一个包含所有素数的无穷乘积。借助这个表述我们发现，这个猜想表明，素数整体上的分布符合一条规律，那就是在大范围内，素性的出现是随机的。当然，某个数是否为素数不是一个随机事件。猜想里说的是，就很大的范围而言，素性是随机显现的，没有任何其他的规律或者

---

1 格奥尔格·弗雷德里希·波恩哈德·黎曼（Georg Friedrich Bernhard Riemann），德国数学家。

结构可循。很多数论学家衷心希望，在其有生之年，这条有150年历史的猜想能有个定论。

素数是一个极其自然的数列，以至于我们会无法抗拒地去搜寻它们的规律。然而，不存在有关素数的真正有用的公式。也就是说，没有已知的规则能够生成所有的素数，甚至无法计算出一个完全由不同的素数组成的数列。存在一些形式简洁的公式，但几乎没有实用价值，要计算其中一些的值甚至需要素数相关的知识，因此本质上它们算是作弊。形如n^2+n+41的表达式称作**多项式**（polynomial），这一个多项式能够产生极其大量的素数。例如，让n依次取值1，7和20，会分别得出素数43，107和461。确实，输入$n=0$到$n=39$，这一表达式的输出都是素数。但当取$n=41$时，这个多项式就令我们大失所望了，因为结果会有因数41。并且，对于$n=40$也失败了，因为

$$40^2+40+41=40(40+1)+41$$
$$=40\times41+41=(40+1)41=41^2。$$

可以轻而易举地证明，一般而言没有某个多项式能给出一个素数的公式，即便允许表达式中存在高于2的幂次也不行。

的确有可能设计出仅用一两句话描述的素性检验的方法。但是，想要它们有用，还需要再快

捷一点，至少在某些情况下得快于第1章中描述的直接验证方法。一个有名的结论叫作**威尔逊定理**（Wilson's theorem）。它的表述使用到了一类叫作**阶乘**（factorials）的数，我们将在第5章里再次与它相见。数$n!$读作"n的阶乘"，就是所有不大于n的正整数的乘积。比如，$5!=5\times4\times3\times2\times1=120$。威尔逊定理便是一条极其简洁的陈述：当且仅当$p$是$1+(p-1)!$的一个因数时，数$p$为素数。

证明这个结果不是很困难，实际上，其中的一个证明方向是很明显的：如果p是合数，比如$p=ab$，那么由于a和b都比p小，它们都会是$(p-1)!$的因数，因而p也是这个阶乘的一个因数。由此推出，当我们用$1+(p-1)!$除以p时，会得到余数1。（$a=b$的情况需要多考虑一点点。）这很容易让人想起欧几里得对素数无穷性的证明。于是可知，如果p是$1+(p-1)!$的一个因数，那么p必为素数。反过来的结论证明起来会难一点：如果p是素数，那么p是$1+(p-1)!$的一个因数。但这才是定理真正令人惊讶的方向。读者朋友可以轻松地验证一些特殊情况，比如，素数5确实是$1+4!=1+24=25$的一个因数。

威尔逊定理所做的，是将判定p是否为素数的问题，从一系列除法问题（检验被所有不超过$\sqrt{p}$的素

25

数除）转化为一个单独的除法问题。然而，被除数 $1+(p-1)!$（即使对于很小的 p）也是巨大的。虽然威尔逊定理是一条简明的规则，但它在识别特定素数上并没有进入实际应用。举个例子，用威尔逊定理检验 13 是素数，要求我们验证 13 是 $1+12! = 479\ 001\ 601$ 的因数。（如果使用第 1 章中 13 的整除性测试，读者朋友可以验证威尔逊是对的！）拿这个对比一下仅检验 13 既不能被 2 也不能被 3 整除的工作量吧。虽然威尔逊定理在素数检验中没什么价值，但比装饰价值还是要强一点，它可以用来证明其他理论结果。

最后，基于定义，阶乘含有很多因数。我们可以利用这一点证明，不存在仅含素数的**算术数列**[1]（arithmetic sequence），或者说仅含素数且形如 a，$a+b$，$a+2b$，$a+3b$，…的数列。因为可以证明相邻素数的间距可以任意地大，而前述数列相邻元素之差始终固定为 b。想要理解这一点，考虑由 n 个连续整数构成的数列：

$$(n+1)!+2,\ (n+1)!+3,\ (n+1)!+4,\ \cdots,$$
$$(n+1)!+n+1。$$

这些数每个都是合数，因为第一个可以被 2 整除

---

1 即等差数列。

（两项都含有因数2），第二个可以被3整除，下一个可以被4整除，以此类推，直到最后一个——含有因数$n+1$。因而对于任意给定的n，我们都有一串由n个连续整数组成的数列，其中的每一个数都不是素数。

　　在下一章中，我们将不再聚焦于具有最少因数的数（素数），而是转向拥有很多因数的数。不过我们会发现，它们和一些非常特殊的素数之间存在着令人惊讶的联系。

26

03

完美的和不那么完美的数

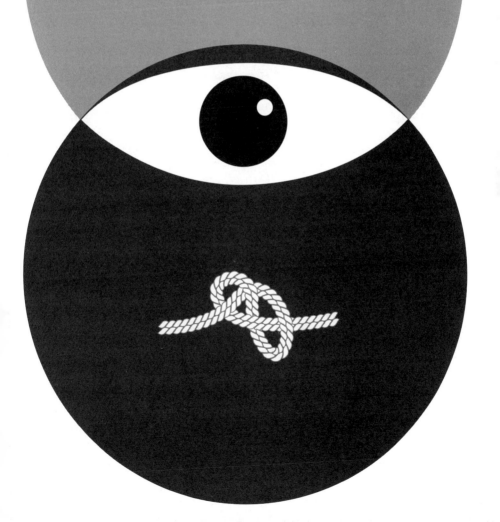

数的完美性

对于取值小的数，我们通常能轻易找到特殊的 27
性质来刻画它们，比如，3是唯一等于之前所有数
之和的数，而2是仅有的偶素数（这使得它成为最
怪异的素数）。6这个数有个独一无二的性质，它
既是所有小于自身的因数的和，也是它们的乘积：
6 ＝ 1 ＋ 2 ＋ 3 ＝ 1×2×3。

毕达哥拉斯学派将6这样的数称作**完美数**[1]（perfect
number），意思是这个数是其所有真因数之和。对于
一个数，我们把严格小于这个数本身的因数叫作它的
真因数。这种完美性着实罕见。前5个完美数是6，
28，496，8128和33 550 336。对于这些偶的完美数我
们已经了解了很多，然而直至今日，依然没有人能回
答古代人提出的基本问题，即是否有无穷多个这类特
殊的数。另外，没有人找到过一个奇的完美数，也没
有证明其不存在。任何奇完美数必然极其地大，并且

1　又称完全数或完备数。

由于奇完美性，这个数必须满足一长串特殊的性质。但是，所有这些限制条件还不足以排除这样一个数存在的可能——可以想象，这些特殊性质会引导我们去搜寻还未曾现身的第一个奇完美数，它可能只是在等着被发现。

28　　欧几里得早就发现，偶完美数与一列非常特殊的素数有紧密的联系。它们被称为**梅森素数**（Mersenne prime），是以17世纪的法国教士马兰·梅森（Marin Mersenne，1588—1648）命名的。

梅森数（Mersenne number）是形如2^p-1的数，这里的p是一个素数。举个例子，如果你取前四个素数2，3，5和7，那么可以看出前四个梅森数是3，7，31和127。读者朋友可以很快验证它们都是素数。如果p不是素数，比方说$p=ab$，那么$m=2^p-1$当然也不是素数，因为可以验证在这种情况下m含有因数2^a-1。倘若p为素数，则对应的梅森数常常是素数，至少在我们看来是这样的。

早在公元前300年，欧几里得就阐释过：一旦你有一个梅森素数，那么就存在一个与之对应的完美数，即$p=2^{p-1}(2^p-1)$。读者朋友可以迅速验证，前四个梅森素数确实给出上面所说的前四个完美数。例如，用第三个素数5作为种子，我们得到完美数

$p = 2^4(2^5 - 1) = 16 \times 31 = 496$，即前述列表里第三个完美数。$P$ 的因数是直到 2^{p-1} 的 2 的各次幂，以及这些数乘上素数 $2^p - 1$。现在剩下要做的就只是一项练习了：将所谓的几何数列（将在第 5 章中解释）求和，以便检查 P 的真因数之和确实是 P。

在 18 世纪，伟大的瑞士数学家莱昂哈德·欧拉（Leonhard Euler，1707—1783）进一步证明了上述论断的逆命题，即每一个偶完美数都属于这一类型。这样，欧几里得和欧拉共同建立了一个梅森素数和偶完美数之间的一一对应关系。可是，下一个问题出现了：所有的梅森数都是素数吗？很遗憾，并非如此。失败仅咫尺之遥，因为第五个梅森数等于 $2^{11} - 1 = 2047 = 23 \times 89$。的确，我们甚至不知道梅森素数的数列是否会终结——也许最终，在某个点之后所有的梅森数都是合数。

尽管如此，梅森数依然是素数的候选，因为可以证明，一个梅森数 m 的任何真因数——假如存在的话——拥有 $2kp + 1$ 这样的特定形式。比如，当 $p = 11$，借助这个结论，我们只需检验被形如 $22k + 1$ 的素数除的情况。这两个素因数 23 和 89，分别对应于值 $k = 1$ 和 $k = 4$。这个关于梅森数因数的事实还带来一个意外之喜，它提供了第二种方法，使我们看出一定存在无穷

29

多素数。因为它表明，2^p-1的最小素因数大于p，因而p不可能是最大的素数。由于这适用于任意素数p，我们可以推断不存在最大的素数，于是素数数列可以永远延续下去。

因为我们没有办法随心所欲地构造素数，所以在任一时刻，都存在着一个最大的已知素数。如今，这项桂冠总是落在一个梅森素数头上，这要归功于国际合作的互联网梅森素数大搜索项目（Great Internet Mersenne Prime Search，GIMPS）。这是一个始于1996年的志愿合作项目，它使用上千台并行工作的个人计算机，集成了一整套为此目的定制的算法来检验梅森数的素性。当前的世界之最是在2008年8月宣布的，它是2^p-1，$p=43\ 112\ 609$。另外2009年4月又发现了一个新的p为$42\ 643\ 801$的梅森素数。这些数有大约1300万位，用普通的十进制记法需要上千页纸才能写下来[1]。

不那么完美的数

传统上人们对数的认识往往集中在单个数上，

---

1 2018 年 12 月 21 日，已知的最大素数已更新为 $2^{82\ 589\ 933}-1$。有兴趣的读者可以参阅 GIMPS 项目官方网站 https://www.mersenne.org/。

这些数被认为有特殊的甚至是奇妙的性质，就比如说完美数。不过，220和284是一对拥有类似特征的数。它们是第一对**相亲数**[1]（amicable pair），意思是每个数的真因数之和等于另一个——这是推广到数对的一种完美性。法国著名的业余数学家皮埃尔·德·费马（Pierre de Fermat，1601—1665）找到了其他的相亲数，如17 296和18 416，而欧拉更是发现了好几十对。出人意料的是，他们都漏掉了一对小的数，即1184和1210，这是由16岁的尼可罗·帕格尼尼（Nicolò Paganini）在1866年发现的。当然，我们还可以走得比数对更远一些，去寻找完美的三元数组、四元数组等。更长的循环比较罕见，但仍会出现。

我们可以从任何数出发，找到它的真因数之和，接着继续重复这一过程，从而得到所谓的**真因数和数列**（aliquot sequence）。结果通常是令人失望的，因为我们一般会得到一条迅速抵达1的链，然后这个过程就终止了。举例说，即便是从一个看起来很有希望的数开始，比如12，链条还是很短：

$$12 \rightarrow (1+2+3+4+6) = 16 \rightarrow (1+2+4+8) = 15$$
$$\rightarrow (1+3+5) = 9 \rightarrow (1+3) = 4 \rightarrow (1+2) = 3 \rightarrow 1。$$

1　又称亲和数、友爱数、友好数。

困难在于，一旦你碰上一个素数，就结束了。完美数当然是例外，它们都会给我们一个循环，而相亲数则给我们一个双循环：220→284→220···。

能产生超过两个元素的循环的数叫作**多亲数**（sociable number），相关研究直到20世纪才开始，因为那之前它们从没有被人发现过。直至今天，还没有生成三元环的多亲数被找到，虽然现在已经知道了120个四元环数链。最早的一些例子是由 P. 普莱（P. Poulet）在1918年找到的。第一个是一个五元环数链：

$$12\ 496→14\ 288→15\ 472$$
$$→14\ 536→14\ 264→12\ 496。$$

普莱的第二个例子令人惊叹，时至今日还没发现其他能与之比肩的数链：从14 316开始，我们得到一个长度为28的循环。所有已知的其他数的循环长度均小于10。到今天，关于相亲数和多亲数，还没有像欧几里得和欧拉关于完美数那样漂亮的定理。不过，由于现代强大的计算能力，这类问题经历了一次由数值实验推动的复兴，人们也得出了一些新的结论。

根据一个数的真因数之和是小于、等于还是大于这个数本身，我们可以将所有数划分为三类：**亏数**（deficient number）、**完美数**（perfect number）和**盈数**（abundant number）。比如，就像我们已经看到的，12

是一个盈数，18和24也是，因为它们的真因数之和分别为21和36。

在整数中进行初步的搜索，你可能由此猜测盈数也就是6的倍数而已。当然，任何大于6的形如$6n$的数都是盈的，因为$6n$的因数一定包含1，2，3以及n，$2n$，$3n$，这些加起来大于原来的数$6n$。但是，这一观察也可以被推广到不仅限于6的倍数，因为我们可以将同样的推理应用于任何完美数k。nk的因数将含有1，以及完美数k的所有因数乘上n所得出的数，于是nk的所有真因数加起来至少会得$1+nk$。所以，任何完美数的倍数都是盈的。例如，28是完美的，因而$2 \times 28 = 56$，$3 \times 28 = 84$等都是盈的。

因此我们看到，完美数的倍数是盈数。同样的道理，盈数的倍数也一样。发现了这一点之后，你或许仍然会猜测，所有的盈数只是完美数的倍数。然而，你不用看太远，就会找到这个猜想的第一个例外。70是盈的，但它的因数没有一个是完美的。70是第一个所谓的**奇异数**（weird number），不过不是因为上述原因（这个名字的来源下面会解释）。

有了这些发现，你可能还会认为，因为似乎不存在奇完美数，所以很可能也不存在奇盈数。换句话说，进一步的猜想可能变成了所有奇数都是亏的。倘   32

若计算前几百个奇数的真因数和，似乎可以确证这一理论，但是这个说法最终还是被发现是错的。检验一下945，它的真因数和为975。现在，闸门被打开了，因为一个盈数的任意倍数都是盈的，所以945的奇数倍立刻给我们提供了无穷多奇盈数。

比起不假思索地逐个检验奇数，要是我们再精明一点的话，可能会更快地发现这个反例。要想一个数有很大的真因数和，它需要很多因数，其中还要包含大因数，而这些大因数又是由小因数配对在一起产生的。于是我们可以通过将小素数乘起来构造具有大真因数和的数。如果我们只关心奇数，那么我们应该看由前几个素数——3，5，7等——构成的乘积。这个粗略的准则会使你很快检验到$3^3 \times 5 \times 7 = 945$，于是你也就在奇数中找到了盈性。

有时我们会发现，具有某些性质的数里，最小的也有很大的值，这种情况并不少见。尤其是当想找的数需要有某种因数结构，而这种结构是由你想要的性质决定的。于是那个最小的数可能极其大。不过如果我们在求解过程中利用给定的性质的话，它并不一定很难找到。这种数谜的一个例子是找到一个数，它既是一个立方数的5倍，又是一个五次方数的3倍。答案是

$$7\ 119\ 140\ 625 = 5 \times 1125^3 = 3 \times 75^5 。$$

并不难看出，为什么最小的答案都有数十亿这么大的值。任何解n都得是3^r5^sm这样的形式，r和s是正幂次，剩下的素因数被归总在整数m里，m不能被3或5整除。如果我们首先关注r的可能取值，可以观察到，由于n是一个立方数的5倍，指数r一定是3的倍数。同时，由于n是一个五次方的3倍，数$r-1$必为5的倍数。同时满足这两个条件的最小r是$r=6$。同样的，指数s一定是5的倍数，而$s-1$必须是3的倍数，最小的可行的s是$s=10$。为了让n越小越好，我们取$m=1$，因此$n=3^6 \times 5^{10}=3(3 \times 5^2)^5=3 \times 75^5$，于是$n$确实是一个五次方的3倍。同时$n=5(3^2 \times 5^3)^3=5 \times 1125^3$，所以$n$也是一个立方数的5倍。

一个更极端的例子是著名的牛群问题（cattle problem），它是由古代最伟大的数学家阿基米德（Archimedes，公元前287—公元前212）提出的。但直到19世纪这个问题才被解决。要满足最初的44行诗中提出的所有限制条件，最小的牛群数量是一个超过200 000位的数！

上面这些讨论给了我们一条警示，那就是只有我们进入非常大的数的领域，数才会展示出它们全部的多样性。出于这个原因，仅仅是不存在少于300位的奇完美数这个事实，并不能说明它们"很可能"不存在。当然，假如真有一个出现了，这个领域内第一流的专家们也会大吃一惊。

让我们再次回到真因数和数列的一般行为这个话题上。我们还可以提出一些简单的问题，却仍然没有人回答得了。真因数和数列可能的情形有哪些？如果这个数列遇上一个素数，那么在这之后它将立即终止于1，其实它也不会以任何其他方式终止。如果这没有终止，这个数列可能是循环的，从而代表了一组多亲数。但是，还有另外一种与之相关的可能性，我们可以通过计算95的真因数和来揭示：

$$95 = 5 \times 19 \rightarrow (1 + 5 + 19) = 25$$
$$= 5 \times 5 \rightarrow (1 + 5) = 6 \rightarrow 6 \rightarrow 6 \rightarrow \cdots。$$

34　　　在这个例子里，虽然95本身不是一个多亲数，但它的真因数和数列最终碰到一个多亲数（更准确地说是完美数6），接着进入了一个循环。

可以设想，还存在一种可能性：一个数的真因数和数列永不遇见一个素数或多亲数。此时，这个数列必然是一个由不同数组成的无穷数列，其中没有一个是素数或多亲数。这可能吗？没人知道。更惊人的是，存在一些小的数，它们的真因数和数列竟然还是未知的（因此它们可能拥有此类无穷真因数和数列）。这些谜一样的数中的第一个是276，它的真因数和数列由以下的数开始：

$$276 \rightarrow 396 \rightarrow 696 \rightarrow 1104 \rightarrow 1872 \rightarrow 3770$$

$$\rightarrow 3790 \rightarrow 3050 \rightarrow 2716 \rightarrow 2772 \rightarrow \cdots。$$

但是没有人确切地知道它最后会变成什么样。

读者朋友可能会想自己探索一下，这样的话，让我来告诉你一个秘密，那就是如何从 n 的素因数分解来计算所谓的**真因数和函数**（aliquot function）$a(n)$：求所有可能的项 $\frac{(p^{k+1}-1)}{(p-1)}$ 的乘积，这里 p 是素数，p^k 是能整除 n 的 p 的最高次素数幂[1]，再减去 n 自己。例如，$276 = 2^2 \times 3 \times 23$，于是

$$a(276) = \frac{2^3 - 1}{2 - 1} \times \frac{3^2 - 1}{3 - 1} \times \frac{23^2 - 1}{23 - 1} - 276$$

$$= 7 \times 4 \times 24 - 276 = 672 - 276 = 396。$$

这与前面列出的 276 的真因数和数列的第二项相等。

对于与真因数和函数具有某种关系的数 n，只需要通过给它们起个名字，我们便可以引入无穷多类的数。就像之前提到的，当 $a(n) = n$ 时 n 是完美的，当 $a(n) > n$ 时 n 是盈的。一个**半完美数**（semiperfect number）n 是

1　素数幂即单一素数的正整数次方。

35 等于自己部分真因数（小于 n）之和的数，因而由定义可以推出，所有半完美数不是完美的就是盈的。比如，18是半完美的，因为 $18 = 3 + 6 + 9$。当一个数是盈数但不是半完美的，它被称作奇异数，最小的奇异数是70。

你可能会认为，这个话题变得过于琐碎了——将任意定义的数的类型冠以名称，这举动确实不能让数字变得有意思，我们应该懂得在什么地方收手。话虽如此，要注意处理这些新问题背后的策略，还是欧几里得和欧拉展示给我们的关于完美数的那一套。回忆一下，欧几里得证明的是如果一个梅森数是素数，那么另一个数就是偶的且是完美的。欧拉则证明了反过程，所有偶完美数都是由这一途径产生的。在公元9世纪，波斯数学家塔比特·伊本·库拉（Thabit ibn Qurra）对于任意数 n 引入了一个三元数组，如果数组里的数都是素数，就可以构造一对相亲数。塔比特的构造方法在18世纪被欧拉进一步推广，但这个加强版公式似乎也只能产生一部分相亲数对，还有很多相亲数不能由这个构造产生。（现在已知差不多1200万对相亲数。）到了现代，克拉维茨（Kravitz）给出了奇异数的一种基于素数的构造方法，并用这个方法成功找到了一个很大的有50多位的奇异数。

本章和前一章是为了通过各种各样的实例，让读者朋友熟悉自然数的因数和因数分解。自然数也叫作**正整数**（positive integer）。这将帮助你为下一章做好准备，你将了解那些思想如何被应用于现代密码学——关于秘密的科学。

04

密码学：素数的秘密生活

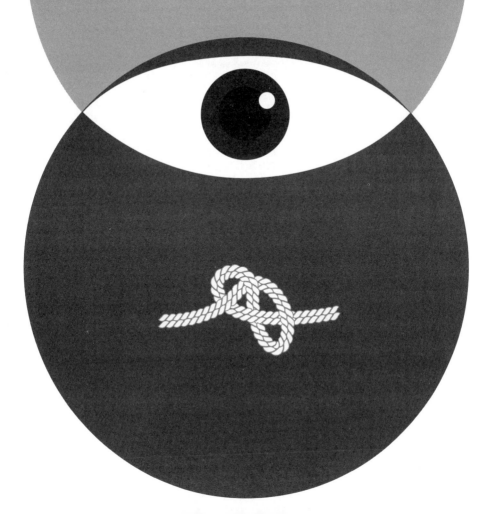

读者朋友现在应该能够体会，从很早开始，自然数的集合就已经被看作谜语和秘密的源泉，产出了很多直到今天都没能解决的问题。对我们中的不少人来说，这已经是继续进行关于数本身严肃研究足够的理由。不过其他人可能会有不同的态度：虽然这些难题可能耐人寻味、充满挑战，但是也可以想象，它们对人类文明的其他方面影响甚微。然而，这样的想法是错误的。

过去的几十年里，人们逐渐意识到，我们时不时会有保密的需求，某些普通信息构成的秘密可以被编码成关于数的秘密。现在，密码学已经得到了全面的应用。我们最为珍贵的秘密，无论是商业的、军事的、个人的、财务的、一般政治性的，还是彻头彻尾丑闻性质的，都可以在互联网上被保护起来——用有关普通自然数的秘密。

36

化身为数的秘密

这一切都是怎么做到的呢？任何信息，无论是一首诗还是一份银行账单，一张武器设计图还是一套计算机程序，都可以用词语来描述。当然，我们可能需要拓展用来表示词语的字母表，使它不仅限于含有普通的字母。我们或许会加上数字符号和标点符号，包括代表词语之间空格的特殊符号。即便如此，我们希望传输的所有信息（包括生成相片和图表的指令）总可以由一张字母表来表达。让我们假设这张表包含的符号不超过1000个。我们可以数一数这些符号，然后用一个独一无二的数来表示每个符号。因为数的成本低廉，取之不尽。为了我们的目的，或许使用位数相同的数会比较方便。比如，每个符号都被一个独一无二的4位个体识别码（personal identification number, PIN）表示。我们可以将这些符号按顺序串连起来，从而得到一个很大很长的数，里面包含故事的全部。我们要是愿意，甚至可以在二进制下做这件事。这样我们可以设计一个方法将信息转译成一长串0和1。于是，我们想要发送的每条信息都可以编码为一个**二进制字符串**（binary string），然后在接收端由具有相应程序的计算机解码，再被编译为我们都可以理解的普通语言。这就是我们的第一层领悟：要传递信息，从理论和实用两方面来说，能从一个人向另一个人发送数字就足够了。

但是将信息变成数并不是关键的思想。明确一点说，将所有信息数字化的具体过程可以被藏起来，不被大众知晓，但这并不能形成有效的保护，免遭窃听。的确，从密码学的观点来看，我们可以将任何信息——所谓的**明文**（plaintext）——与代表它的数等同看待，于是便可以把数看作明文本身。这是因为我们假定，任何人都有办法掌握这两者互相转换的途径。只有当我们用别的数掩盖明文数码的时候，信息才真正具有了保密性。

密码学便是关于密码（cipher，机密的代码）的学问。让我向你介绍一些虚拟角色吧，他们经常出现在密码学所考虑的各类情境中。我们设想爱丽丝（Alice）和鲍勃（Bob）想互相通信，但不想让窃听者伊芙（Eve）听见[1]。我们也许会本能地同情爱丽丝和鲍勃，而将伊芙想象成坏人。但是这可能与真相相反，伊芙或许代表了正义的警方，努力保护着我们免受鲍勃和爱丽丝的邪恶计划的伤害。

38

1　"窃听者"的英语单词为 eavesdropper，因此虚拟的窃听者常用名字 Eve 来代表。

无论参与者的道德立场如何，爱丽丝和鲍勃都可以运用一个古老的方法，将伊芙排除在对话内容之外，哪怕伊芙截取了他们之间传递的信息。方法就是用**密钥**（cipher key）来加密数据，而这个密钥只有爱丽丝和鲍勃自己知道。他们可以预定在一个安全的环境会面，交换一个秘密数字（比方说57），然后各自回家。当时机到来时，爱丽丝想要发送一条信息给鲍勃。这里为了叙述方便，我们假设信息可以用一个1~9之间的数字来表示。在那个重大的日子，爱丽丝想将信息"8"发给鲍勃。她取出信息，加入秘密数字。也就是说，她通过加上57把真实的数值掩藏了起来，然后将信息8＋57＝65通过一个未经保护的渠道发给鲍勃。鲍勃收到这条信息，减去秘密数字，从而获取爱丽丝的明文65－57＝8。

不过，不怀好意的伊芙很清楚这两个人在干些什么，并且她也确实截获了加密过的信息65。但是她能对它做什么呢？她可能像我们一样，知道爱丽丝发送给鲍勃九种可能的信息1，2，3，…，9中的一个，也知道她通过将信息加上一个数进行了加密，这个**加密数**（enciphering number）一定在65－9＝56到65－1＝64之间。然而，因为她不知道这九个数字中的哪一个被使用了（她被排除在这个秘密之外），她没法进一步搞清楚爱丽丝给鲍勃发送的明文信息。九种信息中的每一种都有相同的可能性。她知道的全部就是爱丽丝给鲍勃发送了一条信息，但是不知道信息的内容。

看起来爱丽丝和鲍勃对伊芙已经防得滴水不漏，他们似乎可以使用这个奇妙的数57来掩藏所有想说的内容，从而不受限制地通信。但是，实际并非如此。他们最好换一换这个数，实际上每次都使用一个新的密码会更好，不然这套系统就会开始泄露线索给伊芙。比如说，在未来某一周爱丽丝想向鲍勃传送一条相同的信息8。每件事都会与之前一样，再一次伊芙从电波中截获了神秘的数65，但这次会让她读出一些东西。伊芙会知道，无论这条信息是什么，这和爱丽丝第一周发给鲍勃的是一样的——而这类事情正是爱丽丝和鲍勃所不希望伊芙知道的。

当然，对于爱丽丝和鲍勃来说，这看起来也不是什么大问题。当他们第一次见面"互换密钥"时，爱丽丝可以不只是约定一个密码，而是提供给鲍勃一张长长的有顺序的列表，里面有上千个密码。他们可以依次使用这些密码，从而避免了在公开通信中出现有意义重复的可能性。

我们确实也是这样操作的。这种密码系统在业内被称为**一次性密码本**（one-time pad）。发送者和接收者从密码本中找到一个一次性的数，用以掩藏他们的明文。当信息被发送和解密后，密码本中的那一页会被发送者和接收者一起撕掉。一次性密码本代表了一种彻底安全的系统，因为在公共领域传输的不安全文本不含有任何关于明文内容的信息。为了解码，拦截者需要拿到密码本才能获得加密/解密的钥匙。

密钥和密钥交换

一次性密码本似乎完全解决了安全通信的问题。从某种角度上说确实如此。但是，参与者必须交换一份密钥，才能使用一次性密码本。类似的密码都有这样的问题。在实践中，交换密钥很麻烦。对于高层通信，比如在白宫和克里姆林宫之间，钱不是问题，所以必要的信息交流会在最高安全级别下开展。另外，在日常生活中，各类人和机构都需要以保密的方式互相沟通。参与者负担不起安全交换密钥所需的时间和精力，即使通过受信任的第三方来安排，加密可能依然价格不菲。

所有使用了几千年的密码——直到 20 世纪 70 年代——都有一个共同的特点：它们都是**对称密码**

（symmetric cipher），就是说加密和解密的钥匙在本质上是一样的。无论是尤利乌斯·恺撒（Julius Caesar）的简单的字母位移式密码，还是第二次世界大战中的复杂的英格玛密码（Enigma Cipher），它们都摆脱不掉共同的弱点，即一旦对手知悉你是如何编码信息的，他们就能与你一样顺利地解码。为了使用对称密码，通信双方需要一种安全的密钥交换方式。

一直以来，我们默认加密代码有不可避免的原则——要运用一套密码，双方需要用某种方式交换相应的密钥，并对敌人保密。的确，有人可能把它当作了数学常识。

这种假设恰恰会令一个数学家心生疑惑。本质上，我们面对的是一个数学问题，因而人们会预期这样一条"原理"有着坚实的基础，甚至表达成某种形式的数学定理。然而，并没有这种定理。之所以没有，是因为这条原理根本就是不对的。下面这个思想实验可以证明。

从爱丽丝那里传送一条机密信息给鲍勃，这本身并不一定需要交换一份密钥，因为他们可以按下面的程序来操作。爱丽丝写好她要给鲍勃的明文信息，然后将它放进一个盒子里，再挂上她自己的锁，只有爱丽丝有锁的钥匙。她接着将盒子寄给了鲍勃。当然，

41

鲍勃没法打开它，不过他可以给盒子加上第二把锁，而只有他一个人有这把锁的钥匙。接下来，盒子被寄还给爱丽丝，她会打开自己的锁，再次把盒子寄给鲍勃。这次，鲍勃便可以打开盒子，读到爱丽丝的信息。寄送过程中，我们知道伊芙即使想从中作梗，也没办法看到内容，因此信息是安全的。这样，一条机密信息便可以通过不安全的渠道安全地传送，却不需要爱丽丝和鲍勃交换密钥。这个假想的情境说明，在密信的传递过程中，没有定律规定密钥必须转手。在真实系统中，爱丽丝和鲍勃的"锁"可能是他们各自对信息的编码，而不是一个分隔潜在窃听者和明文的实体设备。爱丽丝和鲍勃可以利用这个初始的交换来建立一套普通的对称密码，接下来这套密码便可以掩藏未来的所有通信。

其实在真实世界中，安全的通信渠道经常是这样建立起来的。不过，用个人代码代替实体的锁并不是那么容易。解读（即解锁）的过程需要爱丽丝在先，鲍勃在后。不像普通的锁，爱丽丝和鲍勃的编码可能会相互干扰，从而导致这一过程无法进行。但是，1976年，惠特菲尔德·迪菲（Whitfield Diffie）和马丁·赫尔曼（Martin Hellman）首次公开证明了这个方法是有效的。

另一种方法是**不对称密码**（asymmetric cipher）或

者说**公开密钥加密**（public key cryptography）的思想。在这个方法中，每个人发布他们自己的公开密钥，要发送给另一个人的信息都用他的公开密钥来加密。但是，每个人还有一份私人密钥。如果没有私人密钥，使用对应的公开密钥加密的信息就没法解读。如果接着用挂锁比喻的话，爱丽丝提供给鲍勃一个盒子用来装他的明文信息，外加一只开着的锁（她的公开密钥），而只有她自己手里握着钥匙（她的私人密钥）。

看起来，建立一个实用的公开密钥系统需要满足太多条件，因为安全性和易用性这两个要求密不可分，但似乎又互相矛盾。不过，快速、安全的加密方法已经在互联网上广为应用了，即便大家很少意识到它的存在和它为人们提供的保护。让这一切得以实现的，说到底都是数，尤其是素数。

用素数的秘密守护我们的秘密

回忆一下，我们把每条明文信息都看作一个单独的数，我们自然努力想用其他数来掩盖它。最常用的方法是用所谓的RSA（Rivest-Shamir-Adleman）**加密**

过程，这是由它的创始人罗纳德·李维斯特（Ron Rivest）、阿迪·萨莫尔（Adi Shamir）和莱昂纳德·艾德曼（Leonard Adleman）在1978年发表的。在RSA中，每个人的私有密钥由三个数 p，q，d 组成，p 和 q 是（非常大的）素数，而第三个数 d 是爱丽丝保密的**解密数**（deciphering number），我们到下面合适的时候再解释它。爱丽丝公开给大家的是两个秘密素数之积 $n=pq$，以及一个加密数 e（这是一个普通的整数，与第2章中提到的特殊常数 e 没有任何关系）。

为了说明 RSA 如何发挥作用，我们举一个简单的例子。假设爱丽丝的素数是 $p=5$ 和 $q=13$，于是 $n=5\times13=65$。如果爱丽丝把她的加密数设为 $e=11$，那么她的公开密钥就是 $(n,e)=(65,11)$。为了加密信息 m，鲍勃只需要 n 和 e。然而，要想解码鲍勃发送给爱丽丝的经过加密的信息 $E(m)$，就需要有解码数 d。在这个例子中，可以推知 $d=35$，这个我们待会儿就来证明。计算出 d 的数学方法需要知道素数 p 和 q。在这个简单的例子里面，给定 $n=65$，任何人都会很快发现 $p=5$ 而 $q=13$。然而，如果素数 p 和 q 极其地大（通常它们有几百位数字那么长），在实际操作上，至少是在较短的时间（比如说两到三周内），几乎没有任何计算机系统能完成这项任务。总的来说，RSA

43

加密系统是基于一个经验事实，即找到一个很大很大的数 n 的素因数极为困难，困难到在实际操作中无法实现。这个方法真正聪明的地方，在于代表信息的数 m 可以只用公开的数 n 和 e 来加密，但在实际操作中，解密需要知晓 n 的素因数。在这章剩下的部分里，我们就来详细解释这一点。

RSA 是这样起作用的：鲍勃通过网络发送的不是 m 本身，而是 m^e 除以 n 所得的**余数**（remainder）。然后爱丽丝拿到这个余数 r，计算 r^d 除以 n 得到的余数，就能重新得到 m。这背后的数学保证了爱丽丝得到的结果正是原始的信息 m，爱丽丝的计算机可以进一步将它解码为普通明文。当然，对于任何真实生活中的"爱丽丝"和"鲍勃"，这一过程都是在幕后无缝衔接地完成的。

这么看来伊芙所缺的唯一重要的东西是解密数 d。倘若伊芙知道 d，那她也能像爱丽丝一样完美地解码信息。事实上，存在着一个特殊的方程，d 恰好是它的一个解。从计算的角度来讲，借助公元前 300 年的《几何原本》[1]（*Books of Euclid*）中发表的欧几里得算法，求解这个方程是很容易的，这并不困难。麻烦

1　一般称为 *The Elements of Euclid*，共有 13 卷。

的地方在于，除非你知道 p 和 q 中至少一个，否则不可能准确地找到那个要解的方程。这便是挡在伊芙道路上的障碍。

我们可以再进一步解释，以上涉及的数如何在这个系统中各司其职。首先，很明显鲍勃一开始就面临着一个大问题，m 很大，n 更是可怕（在200位数字这个量级上）。即便 e 的值不那样夸张，m^e 也是极其大的。计算出它之后，我们还得将 m^e 除以 n 来得到余数 r，这代表了被加密的文本。这些计算太过繁杂，以至于看起来也许并不可行。我们需要意识到，即使现代计算机异常强大，它们还是有能力极限。当计算涉及很高次的幂，就可能会超过任何计算机处理能力的极限。我们不能假设电脑可以在短时间内完成任何我们交给它们的计算任务。

鲍勃有根救命稻草——他完全可以不做很长的除法就找到要求的余数 r。实际上，余数仅仅取决于余数。这里我们举一个例子来说明：7^{39} 的最后两位是多少？（换句话说，当这个数被100除后余多少？）为了回答这个问题，我们可以从计算7的前几次幂开始：$7^1 = 7$，$7^2 = 49$，$7^3 = 343$，$7^4 = 2401$，$7^5 = 16\ 807$，……。不过很快我们就发现，离 7^{39} 还远着的时候，这些数已经变得相当大，我们都处理不过来了。另外，

44

随着我们算出一个又一个幂次，一个关键的规律出现了。当计算连续的幂次时，结果的最后两位数字仅依赖于前一个数的最后两位。这是因为我们做乘法时，百位及以上的数字并不会影响到结果在个位和十位上的数字。

同时，因为 7^4 末尾两位是 01，所以接下来四个幂的末尾依次是 07，49，43，接着又是 01。因此，随着我们挨个计算幂次，末尾两位的数字只会一遍又一遍地重复这个长度为 4 的循环。回到我们手上的问题，由于 $39 = 4 \times 9 + 3$，我们会经历这个循环 9 次，然后还需要三步来计算 7^{39} 的最后两位数，因此结果一定是 43。

这样的技巧是相当普适的。比方说，为了找到某个幂次 a^b 除以 n 所得的余数，我们只需要取 a 除以 n 所得的余数 r，并追踪 r 的各次幂除以 n 之后的余数。余数 r 一定是大于或等于 0、小于或等于 $n-1$ 之间的一个数。在我们只关心 r 的时候，数学家们说我们是在求**模**（modulo）n。我们舍弃了所有 n 的整数倍，因为它们除以 n 余 0，所以不会对最终的余数 r 有任何贡献。

你可能还是在怀疑，我是不是通过选择特殊的例子操纵了证据，这个例子里一个很小的幂次就给出了余数 1——这里 7^4 比 100 的某个整数倍大 1。然而，

45

你怀疑的情况只在部分程度上成立。事实上，如果我们取任意两个数 a 和 n，它们的最大公因数为 1，我们说这些数是**互素**（coprime）的，那么总存在一个指数 t，使得幂 a^t 等于 1 模 n——也就是说被 n 除时余 1。从这个角度说，连续次幂的余数会构成周期为 t 的循环。但是，预测 t 的值很难。不过人们知道 t 总等于一个特殊的数或是它的某个因数。这个数传统上被写 $\varphi(n)$，代表**欧拉 φ 函数**（Euler phi function）的值。

那么什么是 $\varphi(n)$？它被定义为小于 n 的与 n 互素的数的个数。例如，设 $n=15$，那么我们关心的数集为 $\{1, 2, 4, 7, 8, 11, 13, 14\}$，这里我们列出了所有直到 15 但与 15 没有共同的因数的数（除了不可避免的因数 1）。因为这个集合有 8 个元素，所以可以看出 $\varphi(15)=8$。幸运的是，有一个更简洁的方法可以找到 $\varphi(n)$，不需要总是明确地列出所有小于 n 并与之互素的整数，再数它们的个数。跟大部分有类似特性的函数一样，这个值可以用 n 的素因数分解来表达。对，我们只需要知道 n 的素因数，因为用 n 乘以所有可能的分数 $(1-\frac{1}{p})$ 就可以得到 $\varphi(n)$，这里 p 遍历 n 的所有素因数。比如，15 的素因数为 3 和 5，因此这里答案是

46
$$\varphi(15)=15\times(1-\frac{1}{3})(1-\frac{1}{5})=15\times\frac{2}{3}\times\frac{4}{5}=8。$$

这跟我们直接从定义得到的结果是一样的。使用这个方法，你可以自己验证 $\varphi(100)=40$。因此，可以推出 7^{40} 同余于 1 模 100。当然，就像我们已经看到的，余 1 的 7 的最小幂次不是 40，而是它的因数 4。

以上这些都是为了表明，鲍勃确实可以求出发送给爱丽丝的数 m^e 模 n，同时不需要鲍勃的计算机做出太多努力。不过，在实际操作中涉及的数依然大到可怕，因此我们有必要进一步说明如何处理它们。计算 m^e 所涉及的高次幂可以分阶段进行，这个过程叫作**快速求幂**（fast exponentiation）。简而言之，这一方法运用连续求平方以及幂的相乘来得出 m^e 模 n。我们可以用二进制形式的 e 引导算法，从而在相对少的步数里快速找到想要的余数。

欧几里得教爱丽丝找到她的解密数

解密数是接收者的魔杖，能让信息重见天日。挑选数 d 的标准是使乘积 de 除以 $\varphi(n)$ 余 1。因为 $n=pq$ 是两个不同的素数的积，所以函数值 $\varphi(n)=pq(1-\dfrac{1}{p})(1-\dfrac{1}{q})=(p-1)(q-1)$。其实，在小于 $\varphi(n)$ 的范围内，具有想要的性质的数 d 有且只有一个。

为了找到d，爱丽丝的电脑可以利用一个代数工具——欧几里得算法，这一工具已经有2300多岁了。稍后我们就来介绍它。如果伊芙的计算机知道去解哪个方程，那它当然也能做到同样的事情。然而，因为 47 p和q是爱丽丝私有的，$(p-1)(q-1)$也是，因此伊芙并不知道从哪里着手。

加密数（公开的）e需要满足一个温和的限制条件，才能保证d的存在。爱丽丝必须确保e与$\varphi(n)$没有公因数。这很容易做到，爱丽丝可以检验用不同的素数除$\varphi(n)$的结果，从而保证既不泄露p和q的值也让e满足限制条件。实际应用中，e的值常常使用第四个所谓的**费马素数**（Fermat prime），即$e=65\ 537=2^{16}+1$。这个值$2^{2^4}+1$，具有一个尤其稀有的性质，即可以用直尺和圆规作出一个有e条边的正多边形。不过，它在密码学中的用处在于它是一个很大的（恰好比某个2的幂大1的）素数，这非常适合运用之前提到的快速求幂过程。

回到欧几里得算法。这个算法是通过推广以下的观察结果得到的，即对于两个数$a>b$，可以通过连续的相减来找到**最大公因数**（highest common factor）。最大公因数也叫作**最大公约数**（greatest common divisor）。我们注意到$r=a-b$有一项性质：a，b，r中任意两者的公因数也是第三个数的因数。例如，如果c

是 a 和 b 的公因数，于是 $a=ca_1$ 并且 $b=cb_1$，我们看到 $r=a-b=ca_1-cb_1=c(a_1-b_1)$，这就得出了 r 包含 c 的一个因数分解。于是，a 和 b 的最大公因数等于 b 和 r 的最大公因数。因为这两个数都小于 a，我们现在面对的是跟之前一样的问题，不过是相对于两个更小的数。重复应用这个方法，最终会得到一对数，它们的最大公因数可以一眼看出。（实际上，最后手中的两个数会变成相等的，因为如果不是这样，我们可以继续多做一步。这对数共同的值就是我们找的那个数。）

比如，要找 $a=558$ 和 $b=396$ 的最大公因数，第一次减法后我们得到 $r=558-396=162$，因此新数对是 396 和 162。由于 $396-162=234$，所以我们的第三对数是 234 和 162。随着我们继续下去，完整的数对依次是：

$$(558，396) \rightarrow (396，162) \rightarrow (234，162)$$
$$\rightarrow (162，72) \rightarrow (90，72) \rightarrow (72，18) \rightarrow (54，18)$$
$$\rightarrow (36，18) \rightarrow (18，18)。$$

因此 558 和 396 的最大公因数是 18。

还可以根据待考察的数对各自的素因数分解来写出它们的最大公因数。在这个例子里，$558=2\times3^2\times31$，而 $396=2^2\times3^2\times11$；取两个分解中各个素数的共同次幂，我们得最大公因数为 $2^2\times3^2=18$。然而，对于大数而言，使用欧几里得算法需要的工作量少得多，因为一

48

般执行减法运算比寻找素因数分解更简单。

欧几里得算法的另一项优点是总可以倒着做，这样便可以将最大公因数用原始的两个数来表示。为了更好地看清楚这是怎么做到的，我们在刚才这个例子里将计算压缩。在依次相减的过程中，同样的数重复出现了好几次，我们可以把它们表达在一个方程里。这样我们就得到以下几个等式：

$$558＝396＋162；$$

$$396＝2×162＋72；$$

$$162＝2×72＋18；$$

$$72＝4×18。$$

从第二行开始到最后一行，我们可以用各个等式逐个消去中间余数。在这个例子中，先利用倒数第二个等式，然后是它上面的那个，我们得到：

$$18＝162－2×72＝162－2×(396－2×162)$$
$$＝5×162－2×396。$$

最后我们再用第一个等式，把第一个中间余数162也消去：

$$5×162－2×396＝5×(558－396)－2×396$$
$$＝5×558－7×396＝18。$$

无论是对于实践还是理论，可以倒过来执行这一程序都是很重要的。特别是在解密里，为了找出爱

49

丽丝的解密数 d，我们想要 d 满足 de 除以 $\varphi(n)$ 余 1 的条件。为了简洁，我们用一个单独的符号 k 来代表 $\varphi(n)$。现在就可以看出我们坚持要 e 和 k 互素的原因了。因为如果它们的最大公因数是 1，当我们对 e 和 k 执行欧几里得算法时，最终出现的余数自然是 1。倒过来执行这一算法，我们就能最终把 1 表示成 e 和 k 的组合。特别地，我们会找到整数 c 和 d，它们满足 $ck+de=1$，或者换句话说 $de=1-ck$。因此 de 除以 k 会余 1。

这个相对简单的过程将给出爱丽丝的解密数 d：直接从方程里得出的 d 的值可能不在 1 到 k 的范围内；倘若不在，通过加上或减去合适的 k 的倍数，我们最终可以找到那个 d，在给定范围内，它是唯一一具有 de 除以 k 余 1 这个神奇性质的数。（我们可以轻松证明 d 的唯一性，不过这里还是不要离题太远了。）这便是如何计算解密数 d 的方法。我们可以回到前面的例子来说明，这里 $p=5$，$q=13$，于是 $n=pq=5\times13=65$。我们有 $\varphi(n)=(p-1)(q-1)=4\times12=48$。爱丽丝设定 $e=11$，由于 11 与 48 互素，这在游戏规则所允许的范围内。应用欧几里得算法于 $\varphi(n)=k=48$ 和 11，可得：

$$48=4\times11+4;$$

$$11=2\times4+3;$$

$$4=1\times3+1。$$

50   这显示 k 和 e 的最大公因数确实是 1。将算法反转，我们得到：

$$1=4-3=4-(11-2\times4)=3\times4-11$$
$$=3(48-4\times11)-11=3\times48-13\times11。$$

为了满足 $11d$ 除以 48 余 1 的条件，我们解出 d 的初步值 -13。为了得到一个在要求范围内的正的 d 的值，我们在这个数的基础上加上 48，于是 $d=48-13=35$。

d 能帮助爱丽丝解密信息，其原因可以归结为**模算术**（modular arithmetic）的特性，以及当 de 除以 $k=\varphi(n)$ 时余 1 这一事实。爱丽丝计算 $(m^e)^d=m^{de}$ 模 n。现在 de 具有 $1+kr$ 的形式，这里 r 是某个整数。正如之前解释的那样，m^k 除以 n 余 1，这通常被称为**欧拉定理**（Euler's Theorem），而这对于 $(m^k)^r=m^{kr}$ 也是对的。因此，$m^{1+kr}=m\times m^{kr}$，它除以 n 余 m。（详细的验证需要一点代数运算，不过结果的确是这样的。）通过这个方法，爱丽丝得到了鲍勃的信息——m。

顺便指出，我们在证明素因数分解唯一性的时候缺少了一环，欧几里得算法恰好提供了这缺失的环节。因为它使得我们能够验证欧几里得性质，即如果素数 p 是乘积 ab 的一个因数，比方说 $ab=pc$，那么 p 是 a 和 b 之中至少一个的因数。如果 p 不是 a 的一个因数，那么由于p是素数，a和p的最大公因数是1。应用欧几里得算法于a和p这对数，并将其反转，我们可以找到整数r和s，使得$ra+sp=1$。这已经足够证明p是b的一个因数了。由于$ab=pc$，我们有：

$$b=b\times 1=b(ra+sp)=r(ab)+psb$$
$$=r(pc)+psb=p(rc+sb)。$$

这便是想要找的b的分解，它显示p正是一个因数。

总而言之，RSA加密背后的关于数的理论保证了系统的可靠性。当然，要保证系统的完整，还需要遵守很多这里没有解释的协议。可能出现的问题包括身份验证（authentication）（假如伊芙伪装成鲍勃联系爱丽丝怎么办？）、不可抵赖性（non-repudiation）（假如鲍勃装作伊芙发送了信息给爱丽丝怎么办？）以及身份欺诈（identity fraud）（假如爱丽丝滥用鲍勃发给她的保密的身份信息，试图在网上假扮他怎么办？）。另外，当可预测的或者重复的信息大量出现，这个系统的其他弱点也可能会暴露。不过，这些困难在任何公开密钥加密系统中都可能出现。它们是可以被克服的，并且总体来说与背后的数学技术没有太大关系，而那些数学技术才是保证加密的高质量和稳定性的因素。

51

这一章展示了素数以及整除性和余数理论的一项主要应用。我们不仅在广义的原理上，还在细节层面对此进行了解释，这都要感谢欧几里得的古代数学和欧拉在18世纪的贡献。

我们这本书的第一部分会在第5章告一段落，该章里我们将要介绍一些特殊类型的整数，它们与某些自然呈现的分组现象有关。

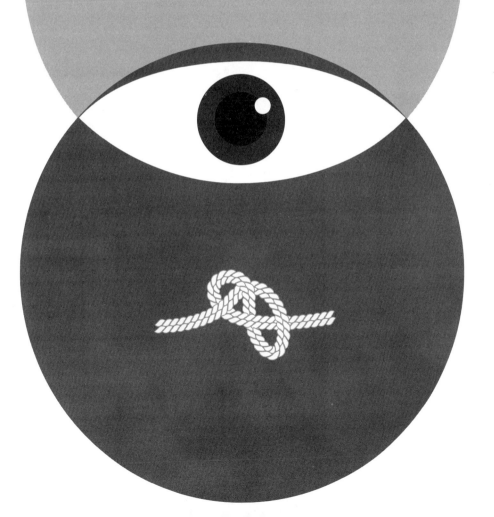

05

计数的数

从计数问题中自然产生的数很重要，因此它们已
经被研究得很深入了。这里我将介绍二项式系数，以
及卡特兰、斐波那契和斯特林所发现的数。这些数被
用于枚举某些自然形成的集合。不过，还是让我们从
一些非常基本的数列开始吧。

三角形数、算术数列和几何数列

因为它们在二项式系数里还会出现，让我们花点
时间复习一下三角形数。这一数列的第 n 项，记为 t_n，
定义为前 n 个正整数的和。它的值依赖于 n，可以用下
面这个技巧来计算。我们将刚刚提到的和的形式写作
t_n，接着以倒序再写一遍：

$$t_n = 1+2+3+\cdots+(n-2)+(n-1)+n;$$
$$t_n = n+(n-1)+(n-2)+\cdots+3+2+1。$$

将这两个版本的 t_n 相加，结果显而易见是 $2t_n$。但
我们这么做是为了将 1 和 n、2 和 $n-1$、3 和 $n-2$ 配成
对。每一对的和都相等，为 $n+1$，且一共有 n 个这样

53 的数对。于是可以推得 $2t_n = n(n+1)$。换句话说，第 n 个三角形数是 $\frac{1}{2}n(n+1)$。例如，从 1 到 1000 所有整数之和为 $500 \times 1001 = 500\ 500$。

事实上，用这个方法我们可以得到对形如 a，$a+b$，$a+2b$，$a+3b$，$\cdots$ 的算术数列的前 n 项和的一般规则。我们首先处理比例上的变化。将 t_n 的表达式乘以 b，我们得到 $b+2b+3b\cdots+nb=\frac{b}{2}n(n+1)$。然后计算它的前 $n-1$ 项的和——只需在刚刚得到的公式中用 $n-1$ 代替 n，即 $\frac{b}{2}n(n-1)$。现在，再给每一项加上 a，包括作为首项的额外的 a，就得到了最一般的算术数列。这意味着我们需要将刚才的和再加上 na。于是，算术数列前 n 项的一般求和公式为：

$$a+(a+b)+(a+2b)+\cdots+[a+(n-1)b]$$
$$=na+\frac{b}{2}n(n-1)。$$

例如，取 $a=1$ 和 $b=2$，则前 n 个奇数之和为 $n+(n-1)=n+n^2-n=n^2$，即 n 的平方。

如果把加法操作替换为乘法，算术数列就变成了**几何数列**[1]（geometric series）。算术数列中，相邻两项相差一个**公差**（common difference），即我们的 b。换句话说，从一项到下一项，我们要加上 b。几何数列

---

1 即等比数列。

中，我们还是取一个任意数 a 为首项，但是通过乘一个固定的数——称为**公比**（common ratio），得到下一项。这个比值记为 r。也就是说，典型的几何数列具有 a，ar，ar^2，$\cdots$ 的形式，其第 n 项为 ar^{n-1}。就像算术数列一样，几何数列的前 n 项和也有一个公式[1]：

$$a+ar+ar^2+\cdots+ar^{n-1}=\frac{a(r^n-1)}{r-1}。$$

要想看出这一公式的正确性，最快的方法是 54 将等式两边同乘 $(r-1)$ 并将括号展开。等式左端我们有：

$$(ar+ar^2+ar^3+\cdots+ar^n)-(a+ar+ar^2+\cdots+ar^{n-1})。$$

这一表达式可以**裂项相消**（telescope），即一个括号中，几乎每一项都可以与另一括号中的一项互相消去，仅剩下 $ar^n-a=a(r^n-1)$。由此可见我们的求和公式是正确的。举个例子，设 $a=1$，$r=2$，我们得到 2 的各次幂之和：

$$1+2+4+\cdots+2^{n-1}=2^n-1。$$

第 3 章中欧几里得通过梅森素数导出了偶完全数，这里的公式恰好可以让你验证他的方法。

1　该公式中 $r \neq 1$。

阶乘、排列和二项式系数

我们已经看到，第 n 个三角形数来自对 1 到 n 之间所有的数求和。这个过程中，倘若将加法换成乘法，我们就得到了所谓的阶乘。这一概念已经在第 2 章中出现过。

阶乘常常现身于计数和概率问题中，比如打扑克时抽到特定牌的概率。因而它有单独的记号：n 的阶乘记为 $n! = n \times (n-1) \times \cdots \times 2 \times 1$。随着 n 的增长，三角形数的大小增长得相当快，增长率差不多能达到 n^2 的一半，然而阶乘变大还要快得多——很快就能增大到百万量级。比如 $10! = 3\ 628\ 800$。阶乘由感叹号来代表，恰恰提醒着我们那令人惊叹的增长速度！

具体来说，$n!$ 表示了排列 n 个物体有多少种不同的方法，如将 n 个球排成一串。这是因为第一个位置你有 n 种选择；确定第一个球之后，第二个位置剩下 $n-1$ 种选择；第三个位置有 $n-2$ 种选择，以此类推。如果我们仅限于选择 r 个球做排列，并将不同方法的数目记为 $P(n,r)$，我们说从 n 个球中一次取出 r 个球一共有 $n \times (n-1) \times (n-2) \times \cdots \times (n-r+1)$ 种排列。这也可以方便地用两个阶乘的比值来表示：$P(n,r) = \dfrac{n!}{(n-r)!}$。例如：你从 52 张扑克牌中抽取 5 张牌，一共存在

$P(52，5)=52×51×50×49×48$ 种可能的结果。当然，打牌时所谓的手牌与抽到的顺序无关，只要是这些牌就行了。这5张牌有 $5!=120$ 种不同的排列方式。因此，一套扑克5张手牌真正不同的组合有 $\dfrac{P(52，5)}{120}=2\,598\,960$ 种，大约有250万之多。

　　在关于计数的问题——或称为枚举问题中，最特殊的一类数便是**二项式系数**（binomial coefficient）。之所以叫这个名字，是因为它们是将二项式 $(1+x)n$ 展开后 x 的各阶幂次前的系数。二项式系数 $C(n，r)$ 代表了我们从 n 个元素中挑选出 r 个元素一共有多少种不同的方法。例如，$C(4，2)=6$，因为从4个元素中取一对有6种方法（不在乎这两者的次序）。再具体些，假设我们有4位儿童A，B，C和D，那么有6种方法从中选出1对：AB，AC，AD，BC，BD和CD。

　　二项式系数可以用两种不同的方法计算。第一，我们可以推广之前用来计算 $C(52，5)$ 的办法，发现 $C(n，r)=\dfrac{P(n，r)}{r!}$，于是得到以下实用的公式：

$$C(n，r)=\dfrac{n!}{(n-r)!r!}。$$

　　一种值得注意的情形是当 $r=2$ 时，即从 n 个物体中选出一对的方法个数。答案是 $\dfrac{n!}{(n-2)!2!}$。分母中 $(n-2)!$ 项的所有因数都与 $n!$ 中相同的因数消去了，同时 $2!=2$，表达式 $C(n，2)$ 因而简化为 $\dfrac{n(n-1)}{2}$。换句

56

话说，从 n 个物体中选出一对共有 t_{n-1} 种不同方法——第 $n-1$ 个三角形数。比如，我们已知道 $C(4，2)=6$，确实是第3个三角形数。

这个用阶乘计算二项式系数的公式确实提供了一种简便的代数方法，使我们能够证明这些系数的许多特殊性质。然而，如果我们用第二种方法来导出这些整数，这些性质的演化会更清楚。这种方法基于**算术三角形**[1]（arithmetic triangle）（如图2），又称为**帕斯卡三角形**（Pascal's triangle），以纪念17世纪法国数学家和哲学家布莱士·帕斯卡（Blaise Pascal，1623—1662）。算术三角形在过去的1000年里被波斯、印度和中国数学家各自发现。它出现在1303年朱世杰[2]所著《四元玉鉴》的封面上。

这个三角形内部的每个数都是其上方两数之和。它给出了所有二项式系数，可以无限续写下去。比方说，要从7个人中选出5个人共有多少种方法，可以遵循以下步骤：将三角形各行编号，从上向下由0开始。在每行中将元素从左向右编号，依然从0开始。取行编号为7列、编号为5的数（记住从0开始数），答案是21。你注意到每行有对称性：如21也是从7人

57

1　即杨辉三角形。

2　朱世杰，字汉卿，号松庭，元代数学家和教育家。

中挑出2人的方法总数。当从7人中选出5人时，我们也同时挑出了2人，即剩下的那2位。这就解释了上面的现象。这一对称性原则自然适用于每一行。它还体现在公式 $C(n, r) = \dfrac{n!}{(n-r)!r!}$ 中：用 $n-r$ 代替 r，我们还是得到同样的公式，因为分母上仅仅是 r 和 $n-r$ 调换了位置。

图2　算术三角形

　　算术三角形的结构能够给出正确的答案，这一点不难理解。每一行都由上一行所产生。我们可以轻松看出前三行是正确的：例如，第三行中央的2告诉我们从一对人当中选出一位总共有两种方法。顶端的1表明从空集中选出0个元素就只有一种方法。实际上，从任意集合中选出0个元素的方法都是一种，这就是为什么每行都从1开始。我们重点看刚才的例子——共有21＝15＋6种方法从7人中选出5人。这21

种选法自然地分成两类。第一类，有15种方法从前6人中选出4人，我们可以再加上第七位凑成5人组。或者如果我们不选第七位，则要从前6人中一次选出5人，共有6种方法。这个例子告诉我们一行是如何生成下一行的：每个元素都是上面两数之和，按照这一模式从上到下建立起整个三角形。这个规则可用符号表示成以下形式：

$$C(n,\ r)=C(n-1,\ r)+C(n-1,\ r-1)。$$

算术三角形蕴含着丰富的规律。比如：将每行的数分别相加可以得到倍增数列1，2，4，8，16，32，…，即2的各次幂。以1，8，28，56，…这行为例，我们是在将从8个元素中选出0个、1个、2个、3个……元素的方法个数相加，最后得到的是从8个元素中一次选取任意个数的元素共有多少种方法。这一数字为2^8，因为一般一个有n个元素的集合拥有2^n个**子集**（subset）。

上面这一事实也可以直接推出，原因是一个n个元素集合的任意一个子集可以使用长度为n的二进制字符串来识别。方法如下：我们考虑一个集合，比如$\{a_1,\ a_2,\cdots,\ a_n\}$，则一个长度为$n$的二进制字符串定义了它的一个子集，因为字符串中的每个1表示相应的元素a_i存在于我们的子集中。例如，假设$n=4$，字符串0111和0000分别代表 $\{a_2，a_3，a_4\}$ 和空集。由于二进制字符串的每个位置都有两种取值选择，因此共有 2^n 个这样的字符串，一个 n 元素集合便含有 2^n 个子集。

卡特兰数

算术三角形中，从第一行开始，每两行就会有一个数位于正中央：1，2，6，20，70，252，924，…。这些数分别被连续的正整数1，2，3，4，5，6，7，…整除。所得的一列商1，1，2，5，14，42，132，…被称为**卡特兰数**[1]（Catalan number）。用中央二项式系数表示的话，第 n 个卡特兰数可以写成 $\frac{1}{n+1}C(2n，n)$，n 在0，1，2，…中取值。

这种数有种最简单的图形表达，是用 n 段上斜线段和 n 段下斜线段能画出多少组不同的"山脉"（如图3）。

1　尤金·查理·卡特兰（Eugène Charles Catalan），法国和比利时数学家。

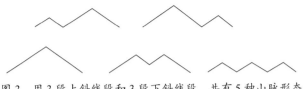

图 3　用 3 段上斜线段和 3 段下斜线段，共有 5 种山脉形态

　　每种不同的山脉构型都对应一组有意义的括号，因此将 n 对括号有意义地排列起来的方法个数，恰好是第 n 个卡特兰数。例如，(())() 和 ((())) 是有意义的括号方法，但 ()(()(不是：有意义是指从左向右数时，左括号的个数从不小于右括号的个数。这对应于山脉始终位于地面上方这一自然条件。比方说，图 3 中第一个和最后一个山脉的构型分别对应于 ()(()) 和 ()()() 这两种括号排列。

　　第 n 个卡特兰数还代表将 $n+2$ 边的正多边形被互不相交的对角线分成三角形的方法个数。沿着这一思路，卡特兰数还有其他解读方法。正如二项式系数，也有公式联系了卡特兰数和更小的卡特兰数，这使对它们的计算变得很简便。

斐波那契数列

恐怕没有第二个数列像**斐波那契数列**（Fibonacci sequence）那样使普罗大众着迷了，它是如下的数列：

1，1，2，3，5，8，13，21，34，55，89，144，233，377，610，…

在起始的两个数之后，每个数都是其之前两数之和。在这一点上，二项式系数与其有相似之处，因为那里每一项也是之前两数之和。但是斐波那契数列的组成方式更简单：

$$f_n = f_{n-1} + f_{n-2}$$

这里 f_n 表示第 n 个斐波那契数，并且我们规定 $f_1 = f_2 = 1$。我们将这种用先行项来定义当前项的公式叫作**递归**（recursion）或**递推关系**（recurrence relation）。

这一数列是从哪里来的呢？它最先是由比萨的莱昂纳多（Leonardo of Pisa）——更有名的称呼是斐波那契——在他著名的**兔子问题**（Rabbit problem）中引入的。一只雌兔出生两个月后达到生育年龄，并在这之后的每个月生下一只雌兔。那么每个月初雌兔的总数由斐波那契数列给出。第一个和第二个月初当然只有一只兔子。第三个月初雌兔生下一只雌兔，因而我们有2只雌兔。到了下个月，它又生下一只，于是共有3只雌兔。

60

再下个月，雌兔总数达到5只，因为雌兔和它的大女儿都能够生育。一般地，在这之后的每个月初，新生雌兔的数量等于两个月前雌兔的总数，因为此刻只有它们处于生育年龄。于是，每月初雌兔总数等于上月雌兔的数量与上上个月雌兔数量之和（斐波那契的雌兔是永生的）。因而斐波那契数列的产生方式完全符合他的雌兔繁殖的方式。

尽管真实世界的兔子并不是以这种异想天开的方式来繁殖的，斐波那契数列依然换着面孔出现在自然界中，包括植物的生长。我们对这一现象的原因已经有了透彻的理解，这与该数列的更微妙的性质有关，即**黄金分割律**（golden ratio）。我们这就来谈谈它。

最简单的数列类型便是我们在本章第一部分介绍的算术和几何数列。虽然斐波那契数列并非它们中的一种，它却与后者有惊人的联系。当计算斐波那契数列邻项之差并将它们也排成一列时，我们得到0，1，1，2，3，5，8，13，…，于是又得到了一组斐波那契数列，只是这次是从0开始的！其中的原因正是这个数列形成的方式：两个相邻斐波那契数之差恰好等于它俩之前的那个数（想要代数地证明这一点，可以将上面的斐波那契递推公式两边同时减去f_{n-1}），所以它不是算术数列。它也不是几何数列，因为相邻两项

61

斐波那契数之比并不是常数。但我们观察邻项之比的时候，它似乎在一个极限值附近稳定下来，而且这个比值很快就趋于稳定了。让我们将每个斐波那契数除以它前面一个数：

$$\frac{34}{21}=1.6190, \quad \frac{55}{34}=1.6176, \quad \frac{89}{55}=1.6182, \quad \frac{144}{80}=1.6180, \quad \cdots。$$

这个逐渐显露的神秘的数，1.6180…，到底是什么呢？这个数 τ 被称为黄金分割比，它也会出现在一些几何问题中，而这些问题看起来跟斐波那契的兔子相差十万八千里。例如，τ 是正五边形的对角线与边长之比（如图4）。任意两条对角线的交点将它们各自分成两段，这两段长度之比也是 $\tau:1$。一对相交的边和一对相交的对角线构成一个菱形（一个"正方的"平行四边形），即如图4中的 $ABCD$。所有对角线的交点又组成了一个小的倒立的五边形。

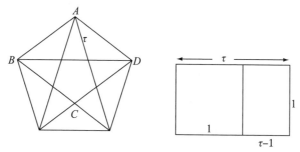

图4 正五边形和黄金长方形

黄金分割比的一个特征是**自相似**（self-similarity）：一些物体包含自身更小的拷贝。这些物体通常含有比值 τ，就像五边形一样。自相似性可以在边长为 τ 和 1 的长方形中观察到。这个长方形有一个独特的性质，如果我们从中切下尽可能大的那个正方形（边长为 1），那么留下的那个小长方形正是原长方形的缩小版拷贝。出于这个原因，图 4 中的图形被称作**黄金长方形**（golden rectangle，如图 4）。τ 的值可以从我们已经给定的性质中推算。我们设原长方形长为 τ，宽为 1。由于大小两个长方形相似，即它们的长宽之比相等，于是得到等式 $\dfrac{\tau}{1}=\dfrac{1}{\tau-1}$。将表达式交叉相乘，则得到方程 $\tau^2-\tau=1$。用标准方法求解这个**二次方程**（quadratic equation）（含有平方项的方程），我们得到一个正的根：

$$\tau=\frac{1+\sqrt{5}}{2}=1.618\,033\,9\cdots。$$

另一种获得 τ 的值的方法是通过它的连分数。连分数能将 τ 和斐波那契数列直接联系起来，我们将在第 7 章中探索这一方法。

不断数下去，斐波那契数列看起来就像一个几何数列，它的公比是黄金分割比。正是由于这一性质和它简单的构成规则，斐波那契数列无处不在。

斯特林数和贝尔数

像二项式系数一样，**斯特林数**[1]（Stirling number）经常在计数问题中出现。它依赖于两个变量，n 和 r。斯特林数 $S(n, r)$ 是将一个有 n 个元素的集合分割成 r 个子块的方法的个数，每一块都非空，且无关于块的次序和块内部元素的顺序。（严格地说，这些称为第二类斯特林数。第一类斯特林数与此相关，但代表了非常不同的东西，即将 n 个物体排列成 r 个环的方法总数。）例如，含有元素 a，b，c 的集合只能以一种方式分成三块：$\{a\}$，$\{b\}$，$\{c\}$；或是以三种方式分成两块，分别是 $\{a, b\}$，$\{c\}$ 和 $\{a\}$，$\{b, c\}$ 和 $\{a, c\}$，$\{b\}$；或是以唯一一种方式分成一块：$\{a, b, c\}$。因此 $S(3, 1)=1$，$S(3, 2)=3$ 以及 $S(3, 3)=1$。由于将一个 n 元素集合分割为一块或是 n 块都只有一种方式，因此 $S(n, 1)=1=S(n, n)$。如果我们仿照帕斯卡三角形，也将斯特林数放置在一个三角形中，将得到如图 5 所示的阵列。现在我们来解释这个三角形是如何产生的。

63

---

1 詹姆斯·斯特林（James Stirling），苏格兰数学家。埃里克·坦普尔·贝尔（Eric Temple Bell），英国数学家、科幻小说家。

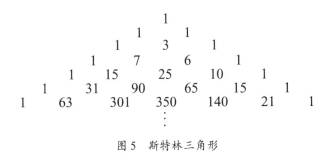

图 5　斯特林三角形

　　这些数也满足了一个递推关系，即每个数都联系到阵列中之前的数。就像二项式系数一样，每个斯特林数都可以由它上方的两个数生成，但这次不再是简单的加和。另外，我们看到二项式系数生成的算术三角形具有行对称性，这在斯特林三角形中不再成立。如$S(5，2)=15$，然而$S(5，4)=10$。不过递推规则依然简单。比如，90这一项等于$15+3\times25$。这其实揭示了一般情形：要找到三角形中的某个数，取其上方的两个数，将第二个数乘以当前未知数所在的（自身行内的）列数，再加上第一个数。（不同于算术三角形，这次列数从1开始计。）用类似的方法，$S(5，4)=10=6+4\times1$。以上计算规则中只有加粗的部分跟算术三角形的情形不同，但这足以使对斯特林数的研究难度大大超过二项式系数。举个例子，我们推导出了一个简单的、基于阶乘的显式公式，可以计算所有二项式

64

系数。类似地，第 n 个斐波那契数也有一个基于黄金分割比的幂次的通项公式[1]，但是对于斯特林数，还没有这类公式为人所掌握。

这个递推关系并不难解释。我们的推理类似于二项式系数的递归，给出的递推式也与那里的形式一致，只是相差了一个乘数。为了将一个 n 元素集合分成 r 个非空子块，我们可以采取两种不同的方法。我们可以取集合的前 $n-1$ 个元素，并将其分成 $r-1$ 个非空块，共有 $S(n-1, r-1)$ 种方法，最后一个元素将构成第 r 个块。或者，我们可以将集合的前 $n-1$ 个元素分成 r 个非空块，这有 $S(n-1, r)$ 种方法，接下来再决定将最后一个元素放进 r 个块的哪一个，这就需要用 r 乘以目前的方法数。因此有

$$S(n, r) = S(n-1, r-1) + rS(n-1, r),$$
$$(n=2, 3, \cdots)$$

用这个递归公式，我们就可以基于上一行计算每一行斯特林三角形的值。如，设 $n=7$ 和 $r=5$，我们得到：

$$S(7, 5) = S(6, 4) + 5S(6, 5) = 65 + 5 \times 15$$
$$= 65 + 75 = 140。$$

可以用定义直接计算 $S(n, 2)$ 和 $S(n, n-1)$。将一

1　如果可以将数列 $\{a_n\}$ 的第 n 项用一个含参数 n 的式子表示出来，则称该式为该数列的通项公式。

个 n 元素集合分割成两个子集，这一过程可以由一个长度为 n 的二进制字符串来描述，其中1表示相应位置的元素在第一个子集中，而0则表示该元素属于第二个子集（类似于我们证明 n 元素集合的子集个数是 2^n）。于是，有 2^n 个这样的有序子集对。但是因为分割与块的次序无关，我们将这个数目除以2，便可得到将 n 元素集合分成两个子集的方法个数，即 2^{n-1}。最后，还需要从中减掉1，去除掉其中一个子集为空的情况。因此，$S(n, 2) = 2^{n-1} - 1$。对照图5，你可以检查看看，这个公式给出了右上到左下方向第二对角线上的数，即1，3，7，15，31，63，…。

另一种极限情况是将一个 n 元素集合分成 $n-1$ 块，这等价于选唯一一个含有两个元素的子块。选择的方法个数是 $C(n, 2) = \dfrac{1}{2}n(n-1)$——第 $n-1$ 个三角形数（见图5从左上往右下的第二个对角线）。

算术三角形中任意一行的和给出了对应2的幂次——一个集合的子集数量。类似地，斯特林三角形的第 n 行的和给出的是将 n 个物体分成任意个数子块的方法总数，这被称作第 n 个**贝尔数**（Bell number）。

分拆数

如果待分割集合中的 n 个物体是一模一样、无法区分开的，将整个集合分拆为子块的方法数就变得小得多了。这称为第 n 个**分拆数**[1]（partition number）。每一个特定的分拆对应将 n 写成一些不考虑次序的正整数的和。例如，$1+1+1+1+1$ 是 5 的一个分拆，还有 6 种其他分拆。因为我们还可以将 5 表示成 $1+1+1+2$，$1+2+2$，$1+1+3$，$2+3$，$1+4$，或直接就是 5。因此第 5 个分拆数为 7（对比第 5 个贝尔数，后者可由斯特林三角形计算，即 $1+15+25+10+1=52$）。没有简单的精确公式可以计算第 n 个分拆数，但有一个复杂的公式。该公式基于印度天才数学家斯里尼瓦瑟·拉马努金（Srinivasa Ramanujan，1887—1920）给出的一个优美近似。

分拆具有一种简单的对称性，那就是将 n 分拆为 m 个数的方案数等于将 n 分拆后所得数中最大值恰为 m 的方法个数。要想看到这一结论的正确性，一种方法是通过分拆的**费勒斯图像**（Ferrar's graph）——或称**杨表**[2]（Young diagram）。这个图表并不神秘，无非是将分

66

1　又称拆分数或分割数。

2　又称杨氏矩阵。

拆表示成元素逐行减少的点阵。

在图6的例子中，我们把17拆分为5＋4＋4＋2＋1＋1，注意到其从左向右各列也以降序排布。如果我们绕着左上到右下的对角线翻转整个点阵，我们就得到图示的第二个费勒斯图像，这个图像可以阐释为分拆17＝6＋4＋3＋3＋1。对第二个图像做同样的翻转，又会回到第一个图像。我们称这两种分拆互为**共轭**（dual）。这一对称性表明两种类型的分拆方案数是相等的：一种是m为结果中最大的数的分拆（即顶端行有m个点），它的共轭是一个有m行的分拆，即拆分为m个数。例如，将17拆分为6个数的方案数，等于将17拆分使得最大数为6的方案数。

图6　共轭分拆，17＝5＋4＋4＋2＋1＋1＝6＋4＋3＋3＋1

数学家们总是会寻找经常在计数问题中出现的这类对称性。这方面的另一个例子是**伯特兰－惠特沃斯选票问题**（Bertrand-Whitworth ballot problem）。假设有两位候选人，经过唱票，获胜一方得到 p 张选票，而失败一方有 q 张票。一个巧妙的几何方法运用所谓的**反射原理**（reflection principle），证明了以下结论：唱票过程给出一种候选人得票情况的排列，从头至尾胜者得票数都领先于败者的排列的个数占所有可能得票排列总数的比例，等于胜者的净胜票数除以总票数 $\dfrac{p-q}{p+q}$。这恰巧等于直到最后一票唱完，胜者净胜票数才增加到 $p-q$ 的可能排列个数占所有可能得票排列总数的比例。两个比例之所以相等，是因为这两种类型的得票排列恰好互为共轭。在一种类型排列的唱票中，将得票次序颠倒过来，即可得到第二种类型排列的唱票，反之亦然。

冰雹数

尽管不是一种计数工具，**冰雹数**（hailstone number）仍然耐人寻味，因为它也是被递推定义的，不过这个数列更像我们在第 3 章中遇到的真因数和数列。以下问题有好几个名字，**考拉兹算法**（Collatz algorithm）、**叙拉古问题**（Syracuse problem），或者

有时就叫 **$3n+1$ 问题**[1]。它基于一个简单的观察，即从任意数 n 开始，经过以下步骤，似乎最终总是得到 1：若 n 是偶数，将其除以 2；若 n 是奇数，用 $3n+1$ 代替它。例如，从 $n=7$ 开始，我们按照这些规则得到以下数列：

$$7 \rightarrow 22 \rightarrow 11 \rightarrow 34 \rightarrow 17 \rightarrow 52 \rightarrow 26 \rightarrow 13 \rightarrow 40$$
$$\rightarrow 20 \rightarrow 10 \rightarrow 5 \rightarrow 16 \rightarrow 8 \rightarrow 4 \rightarrow 2 \rightarrow 1。$$

于是这一猜想对 $n=7$ 成立。实际上该猜想已经被证实对于直到一万亿以上的某个数都是正确的[2]。但是如果你乱动了规则，事情就大不一样了。比如，用 $3n-1$ 代替 $3n+1$ 会导致一个循环：

$$7 \rightarrow 20 \rightarrow 10 \rightarrow 5 \rightarrow 14 \rightarrow 7 \rightarrow \cdots。$$

68　　考拉兹算法产生的数列类似于冰雹，在很长一段时间内它们的取值大起大落，但最终似乎总会降落到地面。在前 1000 个正整数中，有超过 350 个数上升到最大高度 9232，而后则迅速跌落到 1。一旦你遇到 2 的幂次，就会最终得到 1，因为之后这些数不会经历任

1　又名考拉兹猜想、叙拉古猜想、$3n+1$ 猜想、奇偶归一猜想、冰雹猜想、角谷猜想、哈塞猜想、乌拉姆猜想。

2　世界各地的数学爱好者们利用分布式计算，不断地提高这个极限。已知的猜想成立的最大整数似乎已超过 10^{20}（1 亿亿的 100 倍），而仍未找到反例。有兴趣的读者可以参考以下网站：https://boinc.thesonntags.com/collatz/，http://www.ericr.nl/wondrous/。

何爬升，只能一路衰减到底。

所有这些奇妙的特性都可以在基于冰雹数列的图像中被发现，这让人不禁联想起数学和物理中出现的其他混沌现象。在搜索引擎中输入"冰雹数"，你会找到一大堆信息，这些信息看上去奇妙异常，有时候是猜想性质的，但通常不能给出一个确定的结论。

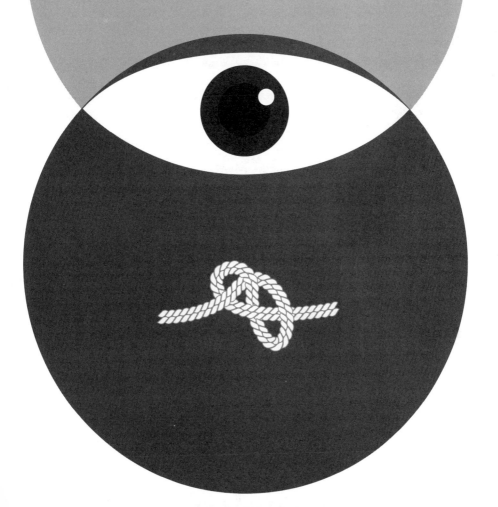

06

数之冰山的水下部分

引言

用于数数的自然数1，2，3，…只是全部数的冰山　69
一角，当然，这也是我们首先发现的部分。一时间我
们或许会相信，冰山除了这个角就没有什么其他东西
了，尤其是如果我们不去看水面以下部分的话。在这
一章的旅程中，我们首先引入负整数。再与正和负的
分数（fraction）结合在一起，我们就得到了名为**有理
数**（rational number）的集合。这个数集常常被看作沿
着**数轴**（number line）分布，其中正数位于0的右边，
而与它们对应的负数则在左边形成镜像。然而，人们
发现数轴上还有其他不能表示为分数的数，其中两个
例子是$\sqrt{2}$和π。**实数**（real number）是数轴上所有数
的统称，它们是所有能被小数展开式所表示的数，如
图7。

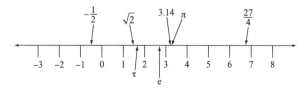

图 7　数轴上在 0 附近的中央部分

不过，人们在19世纪最伟大的成就之一是充分意识到数域其实不是一维的，而是二维的。复数构成的平面才是大部分数学论辩的天然场地。这个结论是数学家和科学家通过解决问题才意识到的——为了能够开展研究，解决现实中的问题，有必要扩展数的边界，尽管很多问题似乎只跟普通的自然数有关。关于这个额外的维度是怎样出现的，我们将在本章的末尾做出解释，并在第8章中进一步探讨这个话题。

加和减

整数指代所有"整的"数组成的集合，包括正的、负的以及0。这个集合通常用字母 Z 来表示，它向两边无穷延伸：

$$\{\cdots,-4,-3,-2,-1,\ 0,\ 1,\ 2,\ 3,\ 4,\cdots\}$$

我们常把整数看作水平数轴上等距的点，它们按以上的次序排列。为了能用整数运算，下面总结了我们需要知道的额外的规则：

（a）加上或减去一个负整数 $-m$：加的时候我们向左移动 m 个位置，减的时候我们向右移动 m 个位置。

（b）乘以负整数$-m$：我们将原整数乘以m，接着再改变符号。

换句话说，加上或者减去负数的方向和正数情况下的相反，而将一个数乘以-1则会使得它的符号反转。比如：$8+(-11)=-3$，$3\times(-8)=-24$，$(-1)\times(-1)=1$。

你无须为最后那个式子困扰。首先，一个负数乘以一个正数得到负数，这是合理的。因为当债务（负的量）产生了利息（一个大于1的正乘数），结果会是更重的债务，也就是说一个值更大的负数。这一点我们都很清楚。一个负数乘以一个负数，应该给出相反的结果，即一个正数，这样才与前面的一致。我们甚至可以给负负得正这个事实一个严格的证明。它基于这样的假设：我们希望扩展的整数系统包含了原来的自然数，并且继续遵守所有代数运算的普通规则。事实上，两个负数的积可以从任何数乘以0等于0推出。（这个结论也不是一个假设，而是代数法则的必然结果。）我们现在有：

$$-1\times(-1+1)=-1\times0=0。$$

将括号拆开，我们看到要想左边等于0，$(-1)\times(-1)$必须与$(-1)\times1$反号，换句话说$(-1)\times(-1)=1$。

分数和有理数

就像减法导致了负数的出现，除法运算同样将我们带到自然数集之外，进入了分数的领域。然而，我们遇到的新的算术具有不同的性质。当相加或相减时，分母（位于下方的数）不同的分数是不相容的。参与运算的分数需要被表示为分母相同的形式，才能求和。乘法相对来说简单一些，因为我们只需要将分子（位于上方的数）和分母分别乘在一起，就能得到答案。除法是乘法的逆运算，因此除以 n 相当于乘以它的倒数 $\frac{1}{n}$。这也适用于一般的分数，要除以分数 $\frac{m}{n}$，我们乘上它的倒数 $\frac{n}{m}$，因为这个步骤反转了乘以 $\frac{m}{n}$ 的效果。

古埃及人偏爱**单位分数**（unit fraction），即那些整数的倒数：$\frac{1}{2}$，$\frac{1}{3}$，$\frac{1}{4}$ 等（虽然他们为 $\frac{2}{3}$ 保留了一个特殊符号）。而像 $\frac{3}{4}$ 这样的分数不被认为是有意义的独立存在的实体。他们将这个量记作两个倒数之和：$\frac{3}{4} = \frac{1}{2} + \frac{1}{4}$。（这里使用的分数的记号当然是现代欧洲式的，其源头是希腊数学。）古埃及人坚信任何分数都可以写成几个不同的单位分数之和。这个结论并不必然，不过这确实总是可以做到的。解释这个结论的过程可以帮助你复习一下处理分数的技巧。

假设有一个分数，比如 $\frac{9}{20}$，如果你想找到它的一

个埃及式分解，只需要从中减去能减去的最大的单位
分数，重复这一过程直至剩下的数自己也是一个单位
分数。这总是可行的，并且涉及的分数的数目不可能
超过原来分数的分子。这是因为在每一步，剩下的分
数的分子总是比之前一个数的分子小——并不必然，
但确实是真的。具体到这个例子里，第一步：

$$\frac{9}{20}-\frac{1}{3}=\frac{27}{60}-\frac{20}{60}=\frac{7}{60}。$$

接着，我们发现小于 $\frac{7}{60}$ 的最大单位分数是 $\frac{1}{9}$。
（要想检验的话，比较交叉相乘的结果：因为
$1\times 60=60<63=7\times 9$，所以 $\frac{1}{9}<\frac{7}{60}$。）再次相减，我
们看到

$$\frac{9}{20}-\frac{1}{3}-\frac{1}{9}=\frac{7}{60}-\frac{1}{9}=\frac{21}{180}-\frac{20}{180}=\frac{1}{180}。$$

因此，我们找到了原分数的埃及分解：

$$\frac{9}{20}=\frac{1}{3}+\frac{1}{9}+\frac{1}{180}。$$

虽然这个减去最大单位分数的贪心法总是可行的，
但它不一定给出最短的分解，因为即便在这个例子里，
我们也能看出 $\frac{9}{20}=\frac{1}{4}+\frac{1}{5}$。不过，$\frac{9}{20}$ 的这个双分数分解
可以用**艾赫米姆莎草纸**（Akhmim papyrus）上所记载
的方法找到。艾赫米姆莎草纸是在尼罗河（Nile）上

73

的城市艾赫米姆找到的一张希腊羊皮纸，它的年代可以追溯到公元500—公元800年。使用现代记号，这个技巧可以表达为以下的代数恒等式。这个等式很好验证：

$$\frac{m}{pq}=\frac{m}{p(p+q)}+\frac{m}{q(p+q)}。$$

将这个等式应用于 $m=9$，$p=4$，$q=5$，我们立即得到

$$\frac{9}{20}=\frac{9}{4\times9}+\frac{9}{5\times9}=\frac{1}{4}+\frac{1}{5}。$$

哪怕是简单的分数加法，你也可能多年没有做过了，因为现在生活中几乎所有运算都是通过十进制格式的小数来完成的。十进制分数在古代中国和中世纪阿拉伯国家就已出现，但直到16世纪下半叶才在欧洲广泛传播，那时人们花了很大精力来改进计算的实用性。然而，为了使用这种十进制形式，我们也付出了一定的代价。在通常的以10为底的算术中，我们利用了任何数都可以写成10的各次幂的倍数之和这一事实。当用十进制表示分数的时候，我们试图将一个数写成 $\frac{1}{10}=0.1$ 的各次幂之和。不幸的是，即便是对于 $\frac{1}{3}$ 这样非常简单的分数，这也没法做到，它的小数展开会无休止地进行下去：$\frac{1}{3}=0.333\cdots$。我们得尊重这一事实，实际使用时需要在一定的数位之后（取决于所

需要的精确度）截断小数展开式。这样我们就用**有限小数**（terminating decimal）来近似精确的分数，以此方式做出妥协。相比于在标准的十进制参照系下开展数的工作所带来的方便，这点不精确显得微不足道。不妨认为，十进制小数展开是最接近于使所有分数都具有一个共同分母的方法。

不过自然有人会问，哪些分数会只有有限位的展开（而哪些没有）？答案是，不太多。通常，一个分数的小数展开会进入一个循环，比方说 $\frac{3}{22} = 0.136\ 363\ 6\cdots$，"36"这部分会永远重复下去。每个分数都会以某种方式产生循环。对于有限小数，比如 $\frac{1}{2} = 0.5$，重复出现的部分仅仅是一串无穷的 0；$\frac{1}{2} = 0.5000\cdots$，于是我们不再提及。在任何情况下，循环部分的长度都不会大于分母的值减 1。这可以通过考虑完整的除法算式来看到：假如分母是 n，那么除法中每一步后的余数是 0，1，$\cdots$，$n-1$ 中的一个。如果在某一步余数为 0，则除法结束，小数展开也就终止了。例如，$\frac{11}{40}$ 严格等于 0.275。否则的话，除法将永远进行下去，某个余数将不可避免地重复。一旦重复出现，我们就会被强制拉进一个循环。因此就出现了一个循环模式，其周期长度不超过 $n-1$。当且仅当分母是若干 2 和 5 的乘积时，小数展开是有限位的，而 2 和 5 正是我们的底数

10的素因数。但若是分母包含任何其他因数，小数便会是无穷的。例如，分母为16，40和50的分数都是有限小数，但像$\frac{1}{14}$和$\frac{1}{15}$这样的分数则是无穷小数，因为它们的分母分别含有因数7和3，这迫使小数展开进入无穷循环。

但是，以上这些恰恰显示了，一个分数的小数展开是否有限并非取决于这个数本身，而是依赖于它和你所取的底数的关系。比方说，假如我们使用**三进制**（ternary）（底数为3），那么0.1就表示$\frac{1}{3}$，因为小数点后的1代表$\frac{1}{3}$，而不是像在十进制展开里那样代表$\frac{1}{10}$。

将一个无穷循环小数反过来转换成一个分数也十分简单，这表明在分数和循环小数之间存在一一对应关系，而我们可以选择一种最适合当前用途的表示方法。下面我们举一个简单的例子：设$a=0.212\ 121\cdots$，因为循环部分的周期为2，因此我们可以通过乘上$10^2=100$将其简化。正如你看到的，我们得到$100a=21.212\ 121\cdots$。这样做是为了让a和$100a$的循环小数部分相等，当两个数相减时，这部分可以互相消去。这使得我们能推断出$99a=21$，于是$a=\frac{21}{99}=\frac{7}{33}$。

这样的技巧常常被用于简化包含无穷重复过程的表达式。比如，考虑下面这个令人生畏的式子：

$$a = \sqrt{2\sqrt{5\sqrt{2\sqrt{5\cdots}}}} \text{。}$$

通过求平方，接着再一次平方，左侧变成 a^4，而右侧的表达式变成：

$$a^4 = 2^2 \times 5 \times \sqrt{2\sqrt{5\sqrt{2\sqrt{5\cdots}}}} \text{。}$$

由于 5 后面跟着的正是 a 的表达式，我们推知 $a^4 = 20a$，于是 $a^3 = 20$，或者 a 是 20 的立方根——如果你更喜欢这样说。在第 7 章中我们会再次用到这个技巧，那里我们将介绍所谓的**连分数**（continued fraction）。

　　分数这一类别是否提供了我们可能需要的所有数了呢？正如之前提到的，所有分数以及它们的负数的总合，形成了被称为有理数的集合，也就是由整的数和它们之间的比值所产生的所有的数。它们对于算术来说是足够的，这意味着，涉及加、减、乘、除四种基本运算的任何结果都不会将你带出有理数的范围。如果我们对此感到满意，那么这个数集就是我们所需的。不过，在下面的小节，我们来解释为什么像上面的 a 那样的数不是有理的。

76

无理数

当特指一个数 a 的时候，无理的（irrational）这个词仅仅表示这个数不是有理数，也就是说它不能被写成一个分数。**无理数**（irrational number）的首次发现是在古希腊。毕达哥拉斯理解了 $\sqrt{2}$ 的无理特性。古希腊人并没有从小数展开的角度来思考问题，他们欣然接受只要是用直尺和圆规作出来的几何图形，其中的长度就代表了真实的量。特别地，**勾股定理**（Pythagoras theorem）告诉我们，一个两条短边长度都为1的直角三角形，其长边长恰好等于 $\sqrt{2}$。

毕达哥拉斯能够证明 $\sqrt{2}$ 不等于任何分数，这显示了无理数的确是存在的。特别是你测定一个正方形的边长后，就没法再用同样的单位精确地测定它的对角线的长度。不然对角线长度就会是边长的分数倍，即 $\sqrt{2}$ 等于这个分数。这两个长度从根本上来说是不相容的，或者用古典文献的话来描述，就是**不可公度的**[1]（incommensurable）。π 也是如此，它大约等于分数 $\frac{22}{7}$，但又不完全一样，并且与你能提出的任何候选分数都不同。（不过"两个1，两个3，两个

1　或称不可通约的。

5"这个好记的比例$\frac{355}{113}$ = 3.141 592 9…相当精确地近似了π的值，直到百万分位。)虽说证明π是无理数非常困难，$\sqrt{2}$的问题却可以用一个简单的反证法轻松解决。首先，我们注意到对于任意数c，c^2的因数中2的最高次幂的指数等于c的因数中2的最高次幂的指数的两倍。于是任何平方数的因数中2的最高次幂的指数必须是一个偶数。例如，24 = $2^3 \times 3$，而576 = 24^2 = $2^6 \times 3^2$。这里，当我们取24的平方的时候，因数中2的最高次幂的指数的确从3变成了6。这个结论总是成立的，并且不仅仅适用于2的幂，也适用于原数的任意素因数的幂。

现在假设$\sqrt{2}$等于分数$\frac{a}{b}$。将这个方程的两边平方，我们推出2 = $\frac{a^2}{b^2}$，于是得到$2b^2 = a^2$。根据之前的假设，方程右侧的因数中2的最高次幂的指数为偶，而左侧的因数中2的最高次幂的指数为奇（由于存在那个额外的2）。这表明该方程是没有意义的，因此最开始将$\sqrt{2}$写成一个分数一定是不可能的。就像毕达哥拉斯一样，我们已经和无理数面对面了。

使用类似的推理，我们能够证明，一般取一个数的平方根（或是立方根甚至是更高次方根）的时候，答案如果不是一个整数，就总是一个无理数。这就解释了当你计算方根的时候，为什么你的计算器上显示的小数从来都没有循环的迹象。

毕达哥拉斯发现要想发展他的数学，他需要一个比分数更大的数域。古希腊人认为，如果可以从一个标准单位长区间出发，仅用一把直尺（并非带刻度的尺子，仅仅是一根直棒）和一只圆规作出一根线段，那么这根线段的长度所代表的数就是"真实的"。人们发现，虽然平方根运算的确引入了无理数，但是数集本身并没有从有理数出去太远。我们称之为**欧几里得数**（Euclidean number）的集合，包括所有那些可以从1出发，通过四则运算以及任意次平方根得到的数。比如，数 $\sqrt{7-\sqrt{\frac{4}{3}}}$ 就是一个这种类型的数。但是立方根也超过了欧几里得工具的范围。这构成了或许是数学里第一个伟大的未解决问题的基础。三个所谓**提洛问题**（Delian problem）中的第一个，就是用尺规构造2的立方根。传说中，提洛岛（Delos）的居民找到德尔菲的祭司（Oracle of Delphi），询问应该如何做才能从雅典驱除瘟疫，而神谕给他们的正是这一任务——问题的表述是将一个正方体祭坛的体积恰好增大一倍。

这个问题在古典时代（classical times）一直无人问津。直到1837年法国数学家皮埃尔·汪策尔（Pierre Wantzel）才将其"盖棺定论"：2的立方根在欧几里

78

得工具所能到达的范围之外。这么晚是因为我们需要一种精确的代数来描述古典工具能达到的极限，这样才能看出2的立方根从根本上讲是一种不同类型的数。实际上，最后这可以归结为证明用平方根和有理数永远不可能造出立方根。这样说的话，这个不可能性听起来似乎更合理一些了。当然，这还不能构成一条证明。

超越数

无理数中还存在着神秘的**超越数**（transcendental number）家族。这些数不能由普通的算术运算或是求方根得出。在给出精确的定义之前，我们先介绍与之互补的集合——**代数数**（algebraic number），其中每个数都是一个拥有整数系数的多项式方程的解。例如，$x^5 - 3x + 1 = 0$ 就是这样的一个方程。超越数被定义为非代数数。

到底有没有这种数呢？答案并不明朗。不过，它们确实是存在的，只是它们的社群十分隐秘，其中每个成员都对自己的会员身份讳莫如深。比如 π 这个数就是超越数的一例，但这不是一目了然的事情。在下

79

一章中，我们将要探索无限集合的性质，那时候我们会解释为什么"大部分"数都是超越的，我们会严密地阐释这个"大部分"的含义。

就目前而言，我介绍一下大概是所有超越数中最著名的一个，数 $e=2.718\,28\cdots$。这个数在高等数学和微积分中经常出现，它是所谓的自然对数的底。自然对数告诉你反比例函数图像下方的面积。当你将两个连续整数的比值 $\frac{n+1}{n}(=1+\frac{1}{n})$ 取 n 次幂，就会得到一列依赖于 n 的数，这个数列的极限值也是 e。用你的计算器求 $(\frac{129}{128})^{128}$——你也可以对它应用"快速求幂"，计算 $\frac{129}{128}$，再平方 7 次，因为 $2^7=128$。

在复利问题中，逐步缩短付款时段，从每年改成每月，再改成每日，等等。我们考虑复利的利率会趋向于什么样的极限值，这时候上面的数列就会出现。为了更好地说明这一点，假设利息以 100% 的年利率计算，一年内分 n 次付款，并计算复利。这意味着你的初始投资会乘以 $(1+\frac{1}{n})$，在一年的时间内总共被乘 n 次，于是你的本金便会被乘以因数 $(1+\frac{1}{n})^n$。利息支付得越频繁，你赚得就越多，因为随着 n 越来越大，你对已获得的利息也越来越早开始收取利息。不过，随着 n 的增大，其等效的年利率（annual percentage rate，APR）并不会无限地增长，而是会趋近于一个值——数学家们称之为上限（upper limit）。在连续复利的情形下，这个极限会乘在你的本金上，它是随着 n 增大时下面这个数的极限值

$$\left(1+\frac{1}{n}\right)^n \to e = 2.718\,28\cdots。$$

80

另一种产生神秘的 e 的方法是将阶乘的倒数相加。这也是一种以很高精度计算 e 的途径，因为这个级数（series[1]）的各项迅速趋近于 0，于是级数本身会很快收敛：

$$e = 1 + \frac{1}{1!} + \frac{1}{2!} + \frac{1}{3!} + \frac{1}{4!} + \cdots。$$

有了这个表达式，我们就能用一种较简单的反证法证明 e 是一个无理数。这里我们概括地介绍一下。假设前述 e 的级数等于一个分数 $\frac{p}{q}$，然后我们在两边同乘以 $q!$。于是左侧变成了一个整数，但是右边则先是一些整数项，后面跟着一个由非整数项组成的无穷数列。通过与一个简单的几何级数做比较，我们可以推出这条"尾巴"加起来小于 1，于是右侧不可能是一个整数，这样我们就得到了反证需要的矛盾。如果要证明 e 不仅仅是无理数，还是超越数，那需要的工

1　此处的 series 作为"级数"的意思，是无穷数列各项之和。注意这与之前 series 的意思不同，那里 series 指数列。

作量就大得多了。

　　e和阶乘的关系也在一个漂亮的公式中体现出来，这个公式是由苏格兰数学家詹姆斯·斯特林（James Stirling，1692—1770）找到的——斯特林数（见第5章）就是以他的名字命名的。他证明了随着n的增大，$n!$的值可以由表达式$\sqrt{2\pi n}(\frac{n}{e})^n$越来越精确地逼近。

　　由于e会以各种不同又很简单的方式出现，所以它渗透了数学的各个分支，并且常常是那些你意料之外的地方。例如，取两幅彻底洗开的扑克牌，翻开每副牌最上面的那张进行比较。重复这个过程，直到用完两副牌。那么，在某一步完美契合的机会有多大呢？也就是说，在某一次翻牌的时候，摸出的两张牌一模一样，无论是梅花7、红桃Q，还是任何其他牌。最后人们发现，做这样的实验，至少出现一次完美契合的实验次数占总次数的比例几乎与$\frac{1}{e}$相等，也就是大约36.8%。我们可以应用所谓的**容斥原理**（inclusion-exclusion principle）来推出这个结果，这是通过将一系列代表修正和反向修正的项相加得来的。在这个例子中，这条原理产生了阶乘倒数的级数，只不过这一次这些项的符号交替变化，这个级数收敛到$\frac{1}{e}$。

实的和虚的

本书的前五章主要都在和正整数打交道。我们强调了整数的因数分解性质,这引导我们去考虑不具有真正分解的数——也就是素数,这个集合在现代密码学中占据了举足轻重的位置。我们还了解了一些具体类型的数,比如和完美数有紧密联系的梅森素数。我们耐心地介绍了一些特殊的整数,对某些自然出现的集合计数的时候,它们扮演重要的角色。在所有这些数当中,大背景都是整数系统,即自然数、它们的负值以及0。

在这一章我们走出了整数的范围,首先是进入有理数的地界(分数,包括正的和负的),接着又走进了无理数。在无理数这个类别中,我们认识了超越数。所有这一切背后的基础是实数系统,实数可以看作所有可能的小数展开式的集合。任何正实数都可以用 $r = n.a_1a_2\cdots$ 的形式来表示,这里 n 是一个非负整数,小数点后面跟着一串无穷多的数字组成的尾巴。如果这条尾巴最终进入一个循环,那么 r 其实是有理数,而我们已经介绍过怎样将这个表达式转换成一个普通的分数。如果没有进入循环,那么 r 是无理的。因此,实数包含了这两种不同的类型——有理数和无理数。

82 　　在我们的数学想象中，我们常常将实数看作对应于数轴上所有的点，从0向外看去，右边是正数，而左边是负数。这给了我们一个对称的图像，负实数构成正实数的镜像。这一对称性在加法和减法运算中得以保留，但不适用于乘法。一旦我们进入乘法的范畴，正负数便不再拥有同等的地位，因为数1被赋予了其他数都没有的性质，它是**乘法单位量**（multiplicative identity）。意思是说对于任意实数r，都有$1 \times r = r \times 1 = r$。乘以1使得任何数原地不动，但是相反地，乘以$-1$会将一个数和它在0的另一边的镜像对调。一旦乘法进入我们的视野，正数和负数在性质上的本质不同便显现了出来。特别是，负数在实数系统中不具有平方根，因为任何实数的平方总是大于或等于0。

　　这一情形恰恰呼唤着我们的**虚数**（imaginary number）登场。在最后一章中我们会重拾这一话题。现在，让我们只做一些介绍性的点评。

　　这些数的出现是因为人们要寻找简单的多项式方程的解。特别是，由于任意实数的平方从不为负，我们找不到方程$x^2 = -1$的解。数学家们并没有被这吓住，而是发明了一个解，记为i，并且赋予了它这样的性质：$i^2 = -1$。这乍看起来似乎很随便，但它其实跟我们之前习以为常的做法并没有太多不同。原因在于，自然数固然很重要，但为了顺利处理有关数的一般问题，我们还是得引入更为广泛的有理数系统，即正、负分数以及0的集合。但是接下来，我们又发现自己没有方程 $x^2 = 2$ 的解，因为我们已经证明，一个有理数的平方不可能恰好为2。为了应付这一状况，我们只能"发明" $\sqrt{2}$。在这里，我们当然也可以采取另外一种态度，声称我们已证明2的平方根就是不存在而已，故事便在此终结。然而，很少有人会止步于此。古希腊人尤其不会喜欢这样一个烂摊子。因为他们能够用尺规构造出代表 $\sqrt{2}$ 的长度，所以在他们的思维方式里，这个数是真实存在的，任何否认这一点的数学系统都是不完善的。

83

我们也可能出于另一个完全不同的原因而同意毕达哥拉斯的看法。我们或许会说，通过小数展开 $\sqrt{2} = 1.141\ 213\cdots$，我们能无限精确地逼近 $\sqrt{2}$，因此 $\sqrt{2}$ 正是被这个完整的无穷展开所代表的数。现代人可能更会被这个说法所打动，于是由此出发坚持认为数的系统需要扩展到有理数以外。

到了 $\sqrt{-1}$ 这里，事情或许又有所不同，因为在我们习惯性地称为"真实的"数集中，似乎并不用担心这个数的缺席。但是随着我们的数学推进了一小点儿，对虚数的需求就变得十分急迫了。当我们对事物数学属性的理解增长到一定程度，一开始对虚数的不情愿就都烟消云散了。

在16世纪，意大利数学家们通过推广二次方程的解法，学会了如何解三次和四次多项式方程，此时这个问题第一次全面浮现出来。后来所说的卡尔达诺法[1]（Cardano method）中，虽然到最后方程的解是正整数，但计算过程常常涉及负数的平方根。从那时起人们逐步发现，使用复数可以让许多数学计算得以开展。复数是形如 $a+bi$ 的数，这里 a 和 b 都是普通的实数。例如，在18世纪，欧拉发现并应用了 $e^{i\pi}=-1$ 这个小小的出人意料的等式。每一个第一次见到它的人都会禁不住惊讶。

在19世纪早期，韦塞尔[2]（Wessel）和阿尔冈[3]（Argand）研究了复数的几何解释——即坐标平面（标准的 xy 坐标）上的点，在这之后"虚的"这一术语被普遍接受为数学用语。将复数 $x+iy$ 和具有坐标 (x,y)

1　吉罗拉莫·卡尔达诺（Girolamo Cardano），意大利学者。卡尔达诺法是求解一般三次方程的方法。

2　卡斯帕尔·韦塞尔（Caspar Wessel），挪威、丹麦数学家。

3　让－罗贝尔·阿尔冈（Jean-Robert Argand），法国业余数学家。

的点对应起来，这使得我们能够通过平面上的点的行为来研究复数的行为。事实证明这是极富启发性的。关于所谓的**复变量**（complex variable）的理论，研究的是依赖于复数——而不仅仅是实数——的函数。经由奥古斯丁·柯西（Augustin Cauchy）的发展，这一理论枝繁叶茂。它现在已经成为数学的一块基石，并且为电信号理论提供了数学基础，而整个X射线衍射领域完全建立在复数的基础上。人们已经证明这些数拥有实实在在的意义。除此之外，这个系统还是完备的，因为每一个多项式在复数系统中都有一组完整的解。我们会在最终章中回到这些话题。不过，在那之前，让我们在下一章中先更近距离地观察一下实数轴的无穷特性。

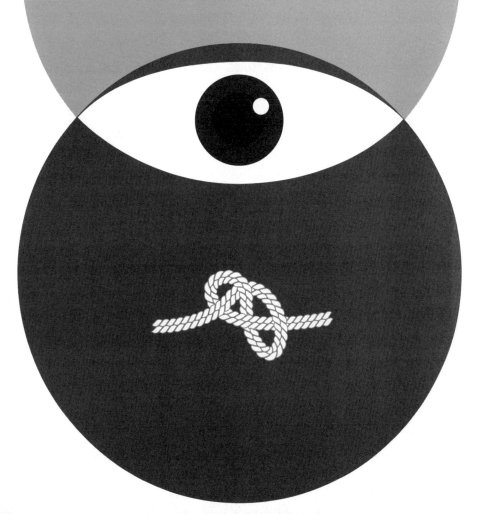

07

向无穷和更远出发!

无穷之中的无穷

伽利略·伽利雷（Galileo Galilei，1564—1642）
是16世纪意大利伟大的博学家，他提醒我们——无限
集合和有限集合的性质有着根本上的不同。正如本书
第一页所暗示的，如果一个有限集合的元素可以和另
一个集合的部分元素配对，那么第一个集合的大小就
小于第二个。然而，与此相反，我们可以用这种方法
将无限集合与自身的子集对应起来（这里子集这个术
语表示原集合内包含的一个集合）。要理解这一点，
我们都不需要超出自然数数列1，2，3，4，…。我们
可以轻易地举出这个集合的任意多个子集，它们都形
成无限集合，从而与全集形成一一对应的关系（如图
8）：奇数1，3，5，7，…；平方数1，4，9，16，…；
不那么明显的素数2，3，5，7，…。并且在每种情况
下，其相应的**补集**（complementary set），即偶数、非
平方数及合数，也都是无穷的。

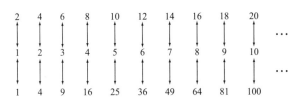

图 8　与自然数配对的偶数和平方数

希尔伯特旅馆

　　大卫·希尔伯特（David Hilbert，1862—1943）是他那个年代最杰出的德国数学家。一家十分奇特的旅馆总是与他的名字联系在一起，它生动地体现了无限集合的奇妙性质。这家旅馆的主要特点是它有无穷多房间，用 1，2，3，…来编号，还夸下海口，希尔伯特旅馆（Hilbert Hotel）总是有空房。

　　一天晚上，这家旅馆却客满了，也就是说每一间房里都住了一位客人。令前台服务员沮丧的是，又一个客人出现了，并要住一间房。幸好经理出手了，他把服务员拉到一边，教他如何处理这种情况，这才避免了尴尬的局面。"让 1 号房的客人搬到 2 号房，"他说，"2 号房的搬到 3 号，以此类推。换句话说，我们通知整个旅馆，要求 n 号房的客人换到 $n+1$ 号房中，这样

1号房就可以空出来给这位客人了!"

因此你看,希尔伯特旅馆的确总是有空间的。但是到底有多大空间呢?

第二天晚上,服务员面临着一个类似但更加考验人的情形。这一次,一艘载着1729名乘客的太空飞船抵达了,所有人都闹着要在已经客满的旅馆中各自住进一间房。不过前台服务员从前一晚吸取了经验,知道怎样推广之前的方法来应付这个额外的旅行团。他让1号房的人去1730号房,2号房的换到1731号房,如此这般。他发出了通知,要求n号房的客人搬进$n+1729$号房间。这就让1~1729号房都空了出来,给新来的人入住。我们的服务员为自己独立处理了昨晚问题的新版本感到骄傲——他这么想也是完全合理的。

然而,最后一天晚上,服务员再次面临同样的情况——一家客满的旅馆,但是这次让他惊恐的不是仅仅出现了几名额外的客人,而是一辆无限大的星际快车,载着无穷多的旅客,每个自然数都对应一位客人。焦头烂额的宾馆服务员告诉司机,这家旅馆已经满员,看不出有什么办法能容纳车上的全部旅客。他或许可以塞下一两个,甚至也可以是任意有限个数,但绝无可能是无穷多的额外客人。这就是不可能!

一场无限大的骚乱眼看就要爆发,就在这关头,

87

经理再一次及时干预。他深晓伽利略关于无限集合的教导，于是告诉巴士司机：完全没问题，在希尔伯特旅馆，任何人都能有房间。他把惊慌失措的前台接待员叫到一边，又给他上了一课。"我们只需要这样做。"他说，"我们让1号房的住客换进2号房，2号房的换到4号房，3号房的去6号房，以此类推。总体而言，n号房的客人应该搬到$2n$号房。这样所有奇数号的房就空了出来，无限星际快车的旅客都能入住。完全没有问题！"

似乎一切都在经理的掌控之中。但是，假设一艘飞船有某种技术，使得实数轴的**连续统**[1]（continuum）上的每一点都对应一位乘客，那么即便是经理也无能为力。每个小数一个人的话，希尔伯特旅馆就会彻底挤爆。在下一小节我们就会知道原因。

康托尔的比较法

当你第一次思考这些问题的时候，它们可能会让你大吃一惊。不过，有一点并不难接受，无限集合的

---

1 通常称实数集（直线上点的集合）为连续统。

性质在某些方面或许与有限集合不太一样，其中一例便是它们与自身的某些子集有同样的大小。在19世纪，格奥尔格·康托尔（Georg Cantor，1845—1918）比我们走得远得多。他发现并非所有无限集合都拥有同样多的元素。这个发现出人意料，不过你一旦注意到它，就不难体会其中的含义。

康托尔要我们考虑以下这个问题。假设我们有一张无限长的数表 L，里面有数 a_1，a_2，…，可以把它们看作以小数形式给出的，那么可以写下一个在 L 中从未出现过的数 a。我们只需要让 a 的小数点后第一位与 a_1 的小数点后第一位不同，小数点后第二位与 a_2 的小数点后第二位不同，小数点后第三位与 a_3 的小数点后第三位不同，以此类推。这样，我们就构造出了数 a，它与列表中任意一个数都不同。这个结论导致了一个直接后果，那便是数表 L 绝对不可能包含所有的数，因为 L 中缺失了数 a。由此可知，全体实数的集合，即所有的小数展开式，不能被写在一个列表里。换句话说，实数集与自然数不能像图 8 里那样建立起一一对应的关系。这条推理链被称为**康托尔对角线论证法**（Cantor's diagonal argument）。为了构造集合 L 外面的数 a，我们想象了 L 的小数列表形式（如图9），并用这个阵列的对角线定义了 a。

　　这里有一些微妙之处。我们或许能把缺失的那个数放在L的开头，这样就能轻易绕过这个困难。这创造出一个更大的列表M，它包含引起麻烦的数a。但是，背后的问题并没有消失。我们可以再一次运用康托尔的构造方法，引入一个崭新的数b，而它不存在于这个新列表M当中。我们当然可以像之前一样，无限次地继续加长现有的列表，然而康托尔的结论依然成立：纵使我们能够不断造出含有之前忽略掉的数的列表，但是永远不可能有那么一张表包含每一个实数。

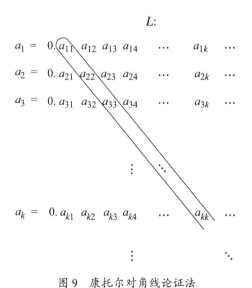

图9　康托尔对角线论证法

因此，全体实数的集合在某种意义上比所有正整   89
数的集合大。虽说两者都是无穷的，但是不像偶数可
以与自然数列表匹配那样，它们没法配对在一起。的
确，假定有一张表包含了区间0~1内所有的数，我们
将康托尔的对角线法应用在这个列表上，那么缺失的
数 a 也将位于这个范围内。因此，类比于之前，我们
同样可以总结出，任何想列出这个区间的全部元素的
尝试都是徒劳的。我们提起这个事实，是因为很快就
要用到它。

其实，很多其他的数集是可以放进一张无穷列表
中的，包括希腊人的欧几里得数。在这一背景下，康
托尔的结果就显得更加出人意料。这里需要一点点创
造力，不过一旦学会几个技巧，就不难证明很多数集
是**可数集合**（countable set）。我们用这个术语来表
示集合可以像自然数一样被逐项列举出来。如若不
然，则将一个无限集合称作**不可数集合**（uncountable
set）。比如，让我们取全体整数的集合 Z，对我们来   90
说，这个集合的自然形态是某种向两个方向无限延伸
的列表。不过，我们可以将它重新排列成一行有起点
的数：0，1，−1，2，−2，3，−3，…。通过将正整数和
各自的负值放在一起，每个整数都会出现在我们造出
的列表里——无一遗漏。更令人惊讶的是，我们也可

以对有理数做同样的处理。从0开始，接着列出所有可以用不超过1的数来表达的有理数（即1和−1），然后是只涉及不超过2的数（即$2, -2, \frac{1}{2}, -\frac{1}{2}$），再下面是那些只用到不大于3的，等等。用这个方法，所有的分数（正的、负的和0）都可以被安置在一个数列中。于是有理数也构成了一个可数集合。欧几里得数也是一样的，如果从有理数出发取任意次的方根，我们考虑结果得到的数组成的集合，它依然是可数的。我们甚至还可以比这个再进一步：所有代数数（在第6章中第一次出现）——就是普通多项式方程的解——形成一个集合，这个集合原则上可以被排列成一个无穷列表。换句话说，我们可以说出一套系统的方法，将这些数全部列出来。（顺着跟有理数同样的思路，可以证明这个结果。）

我们随意地接受任何可能的小数展开的时候，就打开了通往超越数的大门。那些数超出了能从欧氏几何和普通代数方程产生的数的范围。康托尔的证明告诉我们，超越数是存在的，并且有无穷多个。因为假如它们仅仅组成一个有限的集合，那么它们就可以被放在我们的代数数（非超越数）的表单的开头，这样就产生了一张全体实数的列表，而我们已知这是不可能的。令人惊异的是，我们发现了这些奇怪的数是存在的，却还没有指认出其中的任何一个！仅通过互相比较某些无限集合，我们就揭示了这些数的存在。在我们熟悉的代数数和所有小数展开的集合中间，有着巨大的空隙，而超越数正是填充这些空隙的数。用一个天文学的比喻来说，超越数就是数的世界中的暗物质。

91

从有理数到实数，用数学家们的话来说，我们是从一个集合转到了另一个**势**[1]（cardinality）更大的集合。如果两个集合的元素可以一对一地匹配起来，那么它们就等势。用康托尔的方法可以证明，任何集合的势都小于由它的所有子集组成的集合的势。这对于有限集合来说是显然的：在第 5 章我们已经解释了如果一个集合有 n 个元素，那么可以构造出 2^n 个子集。但是，自然数这个无限集合 $\{1，2，3，\cdots\}$ 的所有子集组成的集合 S 到底有多大呢？这个问题不光本身很有趣，我们得到答案的方式也耐人寻味。结论是 S 确实是不可数的。

1　有时也称底数。

罗素悖论

假设 S 是可数的，那么自然数的子集可以按某种顺序列举出来：A_1，A_2，…。现在，任意一个数 n 可能是 A_n 的元素，也可能不是。让我们考虑由所有不属于集合 A_n 的数 n 所组成的集合 A。现在，A 是自然数的一个子集（有可能是空集），于是它应该也在某个时候出现在了之前说的列表里，比方说 $A = A_j$。现在出现了一个无法回答的问题：j 是 A_j 的元素吗？如果答案是"是"，那么由 A 定义方式，我们可以推出 j 不是 A 的元素。但是 $A = A_j$，这自相矛盾。另一种可能的答案是"不是"，j 并非 A_j 的元素，在这种情况下，通过定义我们再一次推断 j 是 $A = A_j$ 的一个元素，于是我们又遇到了矛盾。因为矛盾不可避免，我们的原始假设——自然数的子集能被可数地列举，必为假。的确，这个方法成功证明了任何可数无限集合的子集所组成的集合是不可数的。

这种自指式风格的证明是由伯特兰·罗素（Bertrand Russell，1872—1970）引入的。当时的背景稍有不同，他是为了导出**罗素悖论**（Russell's paradox）。罗素将这个方法应用于"所有不属于自己的集合组成的集合"，并问出了以下令人尴尬的问

92

题：这个集合是否是自身的一个元素？最后，"是"会推出"否"，而"否"会得出"是"，这迫使罗素得出结论，这样的集合不可能存在。

19世纪90年代，康托尔自己就从"所有集合组成的集合"这个思想中发现了一个隐含的矛盾。的确，罗素承认他的悖论受到康托尔工作的启发。无论如何，我们从所有这些讨论中总结出的经验是：不能简单地想象数学集合可以随意引入，对于如何描述集合需要设置一些限制条件。从那以后，集合论学家和逻辑学家一直在为这些悖论造成的后果绞尽脑汁。这些困难最令人满意的解决方案，是现在已经成为标准的**ZFC集合论**（包含选择公理的策梅罗-弗兰克尔集合理论[1]）。

显微镜下的数轴

不同类型的数交织在一起，将整个数轴联结成了一个连续体。当我们观察这些类型的数的分布时，就得到不同的无穷数集。看待这些集合的大小可以有

---

1 恩斯特·策梅罗（Ernst Friedrich Ferdinand Zermelo），德国数学家。亚伯拉罕·弗兰克尔（Abraham Fraenkel），以色列数学家。

不同的方式。有理数只是一个可数集，但是它密集地填充在数轴上，其分布的方式与整数大不相同。给定任意两个不同的数 a 和 b，总存在一个有理数在它们之间。这两个数的平均值 $c = \dfrac{a+b}{2}$，当然是一个在它俩之间的数，不过它可能是无理的。但如果 c 是无理数，我们可以用一个有理数 d 来近似它。我们可以用有限小数，也就是让 d 和 c 直到小数点后很多位拥有相同的数字。如果取 $\sqrt{2} = 1.414\cdots$ 作例子，我们知道 $\sqrt{2}$ 和 1.414 相差不到 0.001，而每多取一位，就可以保证得到的有理数能更精确地逼近 $\sqrt{2}$（平均来说，10 倍于之前的精度）。只要前面这些一致的数位足够多，那么这两个数的差别就会很小，于是 c 和 d 都会位于 a 和 b 之间。小数点后需要的位数取决于一开始的 a 和 b 相差多大，但我们总是能够找到满足条件的有理数 d（如图 10）。正是出于这个原因，我们说有理数集在数轴上是稠密的（dense）。当然，我们还可以用同样的论证，说明从 a 到 d 的区间也会被另一个有理数分开。这样，我们就能得出结论，对于任意两个数，无论它们的差别有多小，中间一定存在无穷多个有理数。特别强调，不存在一个叫作最小正分数的东西，因为给定任意正数，在它和 0 之间总存在一个有理数。

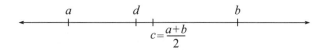

图 10　数轴上任意给定的不同位置都被有理数分隔开

无理数也不甘示弱，它们也构成了一个稠密的集合。在解释这一点之前，让我先指出一旦我们找到了一个无理数，比方说毕达哥拉斯数 $\sqrt{2}$，闸门就打开了，我们立即可以找出无穷多个。当我们让一个有理数加上一个无理数时，结果总是无理数。例如，$\sqrt{2}+7$ 是无理数。类似地，如果我们将一个无理数乘上一个有理数（非0），结果会得到另一个无理数。这两个说法都可以用简单的反证法证明。这样，我们可以找到想要多小就有多小的无理数：$t=\dfrac{\sqrt{2}}{n}$ 对于任何自然数 n 都是无理的，当我们取越来越大的 n 时，t 就会无限接近0。因此我们看到，就像有理数一样，不存在最小的正无理数。所以，也不存在最小的正数这样的东西。

回到给定的数 a 和 b。再一次，令 c 为它们的平均值。如果 c 是无理数，我们就得到了要求的数（无理数）。如果 c 是有理数，设 $d=c+t$，这里 t 是上一段我们说到的无理数。根据之前的结论，d 也是无理数。如果我们让 t 里面的 n 足够大，总可以保证 d 足够接近

94

145

两个给定数 a 和 b 的平均值 c，从而也位于它们之间。这样，我们看到无理数同样组成了一个**稠密集**（dense set）。就像有理数，我们也可以推知数轴上任意两个数之间有无穷多无理数。

因此，有理数集和它的补集——无理数集，在一方面是类似的（它们在数轴上都是稠密的），在另一方面却又不同（前者是可数的，后者则不是）。

康托尔三分集

现在，对于有理数和无理数如何织就整个实数轴，我们已经有了更清晰的认识。有理数组成了一个可数集合，但同时也稠密地填充在数轴上。与之相反，**康托尔三分集**（Cantor's middle third set）是单位区间的一个不可数子集，却是稀疏分布的。它是如下文的构造的产物。

我们从单位区间 I 开始，也就是从 0～1 的所有实数，包括 0 和 1。构造康托尔集的第一步是删掉这个区间中间的 $\frac{1}{3}$[1]，也就是 $\frac{1}{3}$ 和 $\frac{2}{3}$ 之间的所有数。剩下的集合

---

1 删掉的是开集，即（$\frac{1}{3}$，$\frac{2}{3}$）。

包括两个区间：$0 \sim \frac{1}{3}$，以及 $\frac{2}{3} \sim 1$。第二步，我们将这两个区间的中间 $\frac{1}{3}$ 分别去掉。第三步，我们移除剩余区间各自的中间 $\frac{1}{3}$，以此类推。在这个过程中，I 内部一直没有被移走的点组成了康托尔三分集——C（如图11）。

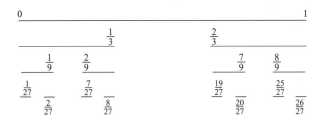

图11　康托尔三分集第一到四层的形成过程

在这个过程中，当我们从一步前进到下一步的时候，根据定义，剩余小区间的总长度会变成前一个阶段的 $\frac{2}{3}$。由此可知，在第 n 步，剩余区间总长为 $(\frac{2}{3})^n$。随着 n 增大，这个表达式趋向于0。由于康托尔集 C 是由所有步骤结束后剩下的点组成，可推出 C 的"长度"，或者叫测度，一定为0。

我们可能会怀疑，在我们倒洗澡水的时候把宝宝也一起倒了出去，或许 C 里面根本不剩下什么了。三分点集是空的吗？答案是掷地有声的：不！有无穷多的数留在了 C 里面。要看到这一点，最好的办法是我们将区间中的数转换成以3为底的"小数"来表示，即三进制，因为整个构造过程就是基于 $\frac{1}{3}$ 的倍数。在三进制小数中，数 $\frac{1}{3}$ 和 $\frac{2}{3}$ 被分别赋予符号 0.1 和 0.2。去掉单位区间的中间 $\frac{1}{3}$ 的时候，我们扔掉了所有的三进制小数以 0.1 打头的数。实际上，在整个过程中，我们恰好去除了所有那些三进制展开中出现过 1 的数[1]。C 里面正是那些完全由数字 0 和 2 组成三进制展开式的数。（比如，$\frac{3}{4}$ 从这个无穷的剔除过程中幸存了下来，因为在三进制下，它具有循环展开式 0.202 020 20…。）

接下来我们将会有一个令人惊喜的发现。取 C 中任意数 c 的三进制形式，将每个 2 都替换成 1，我们就得到了单位区间中某个数的二进制展开式。这在 C 和 I 的所有数（写成二进制形式）之间建立了一一对应关系。由此可知，C 的势与 I 相等。由于后者是一个不可数集（由康托尔对角线论证可得），因此康托尔三分集不仅是无穷的，还是不可数的。

于是我们就有了一个集合 C，从某个意义上讲它的大小可以忽略（测度为 0），但是用另一种方式估计，C 又是巨大的，因为它与 I——因而与整段实数轴——等势。

另外，与稠密集相去甚远，C 是**处处不稠密**（now-

1　在三进制中，0.1 可用 0.0222… 表示。

here dense）的。回忆一下，当我们说一个像有理数这样的集合是稠密的，我们指的是当我们取一个数 a 时，在 a 附近的一个小区间里总能找到有理数，不管这个区间有多小，我们都能做得到。我们说 a 的任意**邻域**（neighbourhood）都包含有理数集的元素。康托尔集拥有完全相反的性质——不属于 C 的数在数轴上可能从来不会遇上 C 里的数，前提条件是它们将视野限制于所在位置附近足够狭窄的区域。想要看清这一点，取任一不在 C 中的数 a，于是 a 的三进制展开式中至少有一个1：$a = 0.\cdots1\cdots$，比如说第 n 位上的是1。a 附近有一个足够小的区间，其中的任意数 b 的三进制展开式有不止前 n 位与 a 的相同，那么所有这些数都不属于怪异的集合 C，因为它们的三进制展开式也都包含至少一个1。

康托尔集的任何数 a 也并不会感到太孤独，因为当 a 观察数轴上任何包含它自己的区间 J，不论多么小，a 总能在身边的邻居中找到同在 C 里的元素（也有不在 C 中的数）。我们可以让给定区间 J 里的一个数 b 同时属于 C，只需规定 b 的三进制展开式拥有与 a 足够多相同的位数，但又不包含1。实际上，J 包含有不可数个 C 的成员。

总结一下，康托尔三分集 C 拥有可能有的最大数

97

量的元素，当C的成员左右看去的时候，它们的兄弟姐妹在周围到处可见。然而，对于不属于C的数，C就像不存在一样。在它们的邻域内，看不到一个C中元素的身影，而集合C本身的测度也为0。对它们来说，C几乎什么也不是。

丢番图方程

数轴上的某些重要的集合可以用方程的语言来描述。组成可数集的有理数，是简单的线性方程的解：分数$\dfrac{b}{a}$（$a \neq 0$）是方程$ax - b = 0$（a和b是整数）的解。像$\sqrt{2}$一样不能由这种方式产生的数称作无理数，并组成了一个不可数集，它们不像有理数那样能跟自然数配起对来。无理数中又有超越数，即便我们允许以上这类方程中出现x的高次项，也永远得不到超越数。人们已经知道，π是一个超越数，但$\sqrt{2}$不是，因为它是方程$x^2 - 1 = 0$的解。这种方法通过不同类型方程的解来定义数的种类。

不过，当我们往反方向走时，产生了一条富有趣味的研究路线。我们要求不仅方程的系数是整数，并且解也得是整数。这里举一个经典的例子。

98

一个装着蜘蛛和甲虫的盒子里有46条腿，问两种生物各有多少只？ 这个小小的谜题可以用试错法轻松解决，但是仔细观察下面两点，我们可以学到些东西。第一，它可以被一个方程来表示：$6b+8s=46$。第二，我们只对这个方程的某些种类的解感兴趣，即甲虫（b）和蜘蛛（s）的数量都是整数的解。一般来说，当我们只限定于搜寻特殊类型的解时，相应的方程组就被称作**丢番图方程**（Diophantine equation）。通常情况下我们要找的是整数或是有理数解。

要求解本例中这样的线性丢番图方程，有一个简单的方法。首先，将方程除以系数的最大公因数。在这个例子中，系数是6和8，因此它们的最大公因数是2。消去这个公因数2之后，我们得到一个等价的方程——也就是说一个有同样解的方程：$3b+4s=23$。如果做完这次除法之后，右侧不再是整数，那就表明该方程没有整数解，我们可以就此罢手。下一步骤是取系数当中的一个（通常用最小的那个，因为这样最简单），并将方程用它的倍数来表达。这里最小的系数是3，我们的方程可以写成 $3b+3s+s=(3×7)+2$。整理后我们得到 $s=(3×7)-3b-3s+2$。这样做的目的在于揭示出 s 有 $3t+2$ 这样的形式，这里 t 是某个整数。将 $s=3t+2$ 代入我们的方程，整理出 b 的表达式。我们得到

$$3b+4(3t+2)=23 \rightarrow 3b=15-12t \rightarrow b=5-4t。$$

现在，我们有了丢番图方程完备的整数解：$b=5-4t$，$s=3t+2$。t选择任意一个整数值都给出一组解，而所有整数解都具有这样的形式。

当然，我们的原始问题还有附加的限制条件，即 b 和 s 两者都大于等于0，因为不存在负数个蜘蛛或者甲虫。因此，只有两种可行的 t 值：$t=0$ 或 $t=1$。这给了我们两组可能的解，5只甲虫和2只蜘蛛，或者1只甲虫和5只蜘蛛。假如我们对原题咬文嚼字，认为两种生物都必须有不止一只[1]，那么我们便得到传统的答案：5只甲虫和2只蜘蛛。

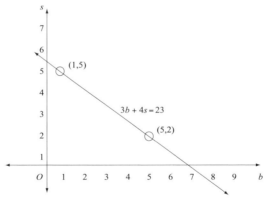

图12　线性方程图像直线上的栅格点

1　在英文原题中，"蜘蛛"和"甲虫"都使用了复数形式的名词，即它们各自不止一只。

这种类型的问题称作线性问题，因为它所涉及方程的图像由排成一条直线的无穷多个点组成。丢番图问题则是要找到这条直线上的**栅格点**（lattice points），也就是那些两个坐标值都是整数的点（如图12）。或者，如果我们只允许正数解，则只能是在第一象限里面的栅格点。

然而，一旦我们允许方程中出现平方和更高次方，对应的问题的性质会变得更加多样化和有趣。在这种类型中的一个经典问题上我们已经获得了完整的解，那就是找出所有的**勾股数**[1]（Pythagorean triple）：满足 $a^2+b^2=c^2$ 的正整数 a，b，c。当然，得名勾股数是因为你可以用这三个正数作为边长画出一个直角三角形。典型的例子是（3，4，5）三角形。给定任意勾股数，我们只需要将它们乘上任一正整数，就能得到更多的勾股数，因为勾股方程依然成立。例如，我们可以将刚才的例子翻倍，得到（6，8，10）这组数。不过，这给出的是一个相似三角形，它和原来那个有一模一样的比例关系，因为改变的只是整体尺寸而不是形状。给定第一个三角形，我们只需用原来单位的一半来测量边长，就可以使三角形的尺寸数值变为之

100

---

1 勾股数或称商高数或毕氏数。

前的两倍，也就得到了第二组勾股数。但是，也有本质上不一样的勾股数，比如（5，12，13）和（65，72，97）。

所以，要描述所有的勾股数，只需要描述最大公因数为1的所有三元素组（a，b，c）就行了，因为一切其他的勾股数都仅仅是这些的放大版。方案如下：取任意一对互质的正整数m和n，其中一个为偶数。假设m表示两者中大的那个数，构造三元数$a=2mn$，$b=m^2-n^2$及$c=m^2+n^2$，那么这三个数a，b，c就给出一组勾股数（这里用代数可以轻松验证），并且这三个数没有公因数（也不难检验）。上面的三个例子就可以这样得到。在第一个例子里取$m=2$和$n=1$，第二个里取$m=3$和$n=2$，而最后一种情况我们有$m=9$，$n=4$。要检验反过来的命题需要更多努力。任何勾股数都可以用这种方法来生成，只需取合适的m和n的值。另外，这样的表示法还是唯一的，于是两对不同的（m，n）不可能产生同样的勾股数（a，b，c）。

相应的立方和更高次的方程却没有解：对于任何指数$n \geq 3$，没有正整数组x，y和z满足$x^n+y^n=z^n$。这就是著名的**费马大定理**（Fermat's last theorem）。未来它可能被称作怀尔斯定理，因为它是由安德鲁·怀尔斯爵士[1]（Sir Andrew Wiles）在20世纪90年代最终证明的。即便是在立方的情况下，这也是一个非常困难的问题，这是由欧拉首先解决的。不过，可以相对简单地证明两个四次方数之和不可能是一个平方数（因此当然不可能是一个四次方），并且这就足以将原来的问题简化为指数 n 是一个素数 p 的情况（意思是如果我们对所有素指数的情况解决了这个问题，便可以立即得到一般的结论）。确实，在19世纪的时候，指数 n 为所谓的**正则素数**（regular prime）的情形得到了证明。然而，要实现问题的完全解决，还得等到怀尔斯解答了一个叫作谷山-志村猜想[2]（Shimura-Taniyama Conjecture）的深刻问题之后。

不过，被研究最多的丢番图方程是**佩尔方程**（Pell equation）$x^2 - ny^2 = 1$，这里 n 是一个正整数，但不是平方数。人们在很早以前就已经认识到了它的重要性。早至公元前400年，希腊和印度似乎就有人研究过它了，因为这个方程的解给出了 $\sqrt{n}$ 的很好的有理数近似，即 $\frac{x}{y}$。例如：当 $n = 2$ 时，方程有一组解，即数对 $x = 577$ 和 $y = 408$，并且 $(\frac{x}{y})^2 = 2.000\ 006$。这个方程与一个希腊人称为**辗转相减**（anthyphairesis）的

---

1 安德鲁·怀尔斯爵士（Sir Andrew Wiles），英国数学家，居于美国。

2 谷山丰和志村五郎，均为日本数学家。

几何过程有关。在这个过程里，我们从两条线段出发，反复地从长的线段中截去短的那段，有点类似于欧几里得算法，不过是应用在有连续取值的长度上。实际上，第3章中提到的阿基米德牛群问题恰好也会导出一个佩尔方程。

公元150年前后，丢番图（Diophantus）自己研究了佩尔方程的一些版本。不过，是伟大的印度数学家婆罗摩笈多（Brahmagupta）解出了这个方程，他的方法又被婆什迦罗二世（Bhaskara II）所改进，后者揭示了如何从已有的种子解出发创造新的解。在欧洲，是费马敦促数学家们注意佩尔方程，而完整的理论则要归功于著名的法国数学家约瑟夫–路易·拉格朗日（Joseph-Louis Lagrange，1736—1813）（英语名称"佩尔"是历史上的一个偶然事件）。一般的解法基于$\sqrt{n}$的连分数展开。

斐波那契和连分数

回忆一下斐波那契发现的数列：1，1，2，3，5，8，13，21，…，我们在第5章中进行了介绍。从这个数列中取一对相邻的数，将它们的比写成1加上一个

分数。现在，如果我们"埃及化"这个分数，也就是反复地让分数部分的分子分母同除以分子，就会出现一个引人注目的规律。比方说

$$\frac{13}{8}=1+\frac{5}{8}=1+\frac{1}{1+\frac{3}{5}}=1+\frac{1}{1+\frac{1}{1+\frac{2}{3}}}=1+\frac{1}{1+\frac{1}{1+\frac{1}{1+\frac{1}{1+\frac{1}{1}}}}},$$

我们得到了一个仅含有 1 的多层分数，并且随着计算持续进行，选出的这对相邻数之前的每对斐波那契数的比值会依次出现。这样的现象每次都会发生：正是由于这些数的定义，每个斐波那契数都比下一个的两倍要小，因而相除之后会得到商 1，余数则是前一个斐波那契数。你也许想起来，相邻斐波那契数的比值趋近于黄金分割比——τ，这说明 τ 是仅由 1 构成的连分数的极限值。

正如第 5 章所介绍的，如果一个值产生于一个无穷多次重复的过程，那么它也许能用一个基于此过程的方程来表示。假设我们将 1 组成的无穷分数塔的值设为 a，我们看到 a 满足 $a=1+\dfrac{1}{a}$ 这一关系，因为位于分数第一层分号下方的，正是另一整个 a。从这里，可以看出 a 满足二次方程 $a^2=a+1$，它的正根是 $\tau=\dfrac{1+\sqrt{5}}{2}$。

从这个过程中产生的连分数本身就有重要意义。

103　当用有理数来近似任意一个无理数y的时候，我们会自然地使用y的小数表示。这非常适用于一般的计算，但是在数学上，依附于一个特定的底数却不太自然。本质问题在于，我们能多好地用分母相对较小的分数来逼近y。有没有一种办法，能找到一系列的分数，既能高精度地逼近y，同时又保持较小的分母，在这两个矛盾的要求中取得最佳平衡？答案就在于一个数的连分数表达形式，并通过越来越多层的截断实现这一目的。

由于我们在表达式中使用的多层分号，连分数看起来十分别扭。但是，我们可以轻易避开书写所有这些分号的不便——因为每个分子都是1，为了指明我们所说的是哪个连分数，只需要记录相除后的那些商。比如，分数$\dfrac{25}{91}$的表达式可以如下推演：

$$\frac{25}{91}=0+\frac{1}{3+\dfrac{16}{25}}=0+\frac{1}{3+\dfrac{1}{1+\dfrac{9}{16}}}=\cdots\circ$$

最终产生的连分数可以用列表[0，3，1，1，1，3，2]来代表。正如我们已经看到的，黄金分割比的连分数表达为[1，1，1，1，…]。用一个类似于循环小数的记号，我们写作 $\tau = [\bar{1}]$。在 $\dfrac{25}{91}$ 的连分数中，第一个商 3 是从 $91 = 3 \times 25 + 16$ 得来的，这也是对 $(91, 25)$ 应用欧几里得算法得到的第一行等式。事实上，正是由于这个原因，作用于两个数的欧几里得算法中的每一行都对应于连分数中的一行。特别是，从一个**既约分数**[1]（reduced fraction）（分子分母互质）出发，在计算对应的连分数的过程中出现的每一个分数，都适用于同样的规律。

黄金分割比所提供的这个特殊例子打开了一条新的思路，即我们也许能表示其他的无理数，当然不是用有限的连分数（它们自己显然是有理数），而是用无穷连分数。但是，怎样才能产生一个数 a 的连分数呢？为了看清这个过程，读者朋友需要容许我玩一个小小的代数上的把戏，下面就是做法。

104

计算一个数 a 的连分数 $a = [a_0, a_1, a_2 \cdots]$ 有两步。数 a_0 是 a 的整数部分，用 $a_0 = \lfloor a \rfloor$ [2] 表示。（例如，$\pi = 3.1415926\cdots$ 的整数部分由 $\lfloor \pi \rfloor = 3$ 给出。）一般来说，$a_n = \lfloor r_n \rfloor$，即 r_n 的整数部分，这里余数项 r_n 是由 $r_0 = a$，$r_n = \dfrac{1}{r_{n-1} - a_{n-1}}$ 递归定义的。将这个方法应用于

1　又称最简分数。

2　该符号表示向下取整。

$a_n = \sqrt{2}$ ，并且使用分母有理化的代数技巧（有些读者对此可能已经很熟悉了），考虑到 $\lfloor \sqrt{2} \rfloor = 1$ ，我们得到

$$a = r_0 = \sqrt{2} = 1 + (\sqrt{2} - 1), \quad 于是\ a_0 = 1;$$

$$r_1 = \frac{1}{r_0 - a_0} = \frac{1}{\sqrt{2} - 1} = \frac{\sqrt{2} + 1}{(\sqrt{2} - 1)(\sqrt{2} + 1)} = \sqrt{2} + 1, \quad a_1 = \lfloor r_1 \rfloor = 2。$$

接下来我们得到

$$r_2 = \frac{1}{r_1 - a_1} = \frac{1}{\sqrt{2} + 1 - 2} = \frac{1}{\sqrt{2} - 1} = \frac{\sqrt{2} + 1}{(\sqrt{2} - 1)(\sqrt{2} + 1)} = \sqrt{2} + 1,$$

因此 $r_1 = r_2 = \cdots = \sqrt{2} + 1$ ， $a_1 = a_2 = \cdots = 2$ ，所以 $\sqrt{2} = [1, \overline{2}]$ 。

事实上，拥有循环的连分数表达式的数包括有理数（即有限的连分数表达式），以及二次方程的解。比如说 τ ，上面我们已经看到了 τ 是方程 $x^2 = x + 1$ 的一个解；还有 $\sqrt{2} = [1, \overline{2}]$ ，它满足 $x^2 = 2$ 。其他一些例子包含的循环则更令人难以捉摸，如 $\sqrt{3} = [1, \overline{1, 2}]$ ， $\sqrt{7} = [2, \overline{1, 1, 1, 4}]$ ， $\sqrt{17} = [4, \overline{8}]$ 和 $\sqrt{28} = [5, \overline{3, 2, 3, 10}]$ 。不过，无理数平方根的连分数展开式有着非常特殊且引人注目的一面。这些展开式以整数 r 打头，接着它们的循环部分是一串回文数列（palindromic sequence）（数列中的数反着读与正着读一样），再后面跟着 $2r$ 。在前面所有的例子中都能观察到这一点：比方说 $\sqrt{28}$ ，我们看到 $r = 5$ ，展开式的回文部分为 3 ， 2 ， 3 ，后面跟着 $2r = 10$ 。对

于 $\sqrt{2}$ 和 $\sqrt{17}$，回文部分是空的，但规律依然存在，只不过是以一种简单的形式出现。可以证明，一个数的连分数表达式是唯一的——两个不同的连分数有不同的值。

在用有理数对无理数的逼近中，连分数的重要性在于所谓的**收敛子**[1]（convergent），即原始数的有理数近似，它们是通过截取某一层以前的连分数表达式，再求出相应的有理数来得到的。它们代表了对原始数的最优近似，也就是说任何更好的近似的分母都将比收敛子的分母大。黄金分割比的收敛子是斐波那契比值。由于 τ 的连分数表达式中每一项都是1，这些比值收敛的速度被尽可能地延缓了。出于这个原因，没有比 τ 更难用有理数逼近的数了，而斐波那契比值是你能取得的最佳结果。

如果一个连分数的某个收敛子的分母为 q，那么这个近似值总是在距离真实数值 $\dfrac{1}{\sqrt{5}q^2}$ 的范围之内，并且连分数的收敛子轮流低估和高估被逼近的值。然而，在有理数逼近这个问题上，像 τ 和 $\sqrt{2}$ 这样的欧几里得数总是最难的。有一些特殊的超越数，它们的性质似乎与有理数的世界离得不能再远了，但依然可

---

1 又称渐进分数。

以被很好地逼近，它们的收敛子以极快的速度接近目标。

上一节末尾我们提到了佩尔方程$x^2-ny^2=1$，它与这里的联系在于，如果要找方程的解(x, y)，使x取最小的可能正值，那么这样的解存在，并且可以在$\sqrt{n}$的连分数的收敛子中找到。例如，当$n=7$时，$\sqrt{7}$的收敛子数列的前几项为$\frac{2}{1}$, $\frac{3}{1}$, $\frac{5}{2}$, $\frac{8}{3}$。正是$x=8$，$y=3$提供了佩尔方程$x^2-7y^2=1$的最小的解，也就是所谓的**基本解**（fundamental solution）。不过，有时候基本解并不会很早就在展开式中现身：比如，$x^2-29y^2=1$的最小正解为$x=9801$和$y=1820$。当然，一旦这个基本解(x, y)被确定，其他所有的解都可以通过以下途径得到：求连续的次方$(x+y\sqrt{n})^k(k=1,2,3\cdots)$，得到展开括号后的表达式，再分别提取有理和无理部分的系数。用这个方法，佩尔方程的完整解集就可以通过$\sqrt{n}$的连分数表达式求得。

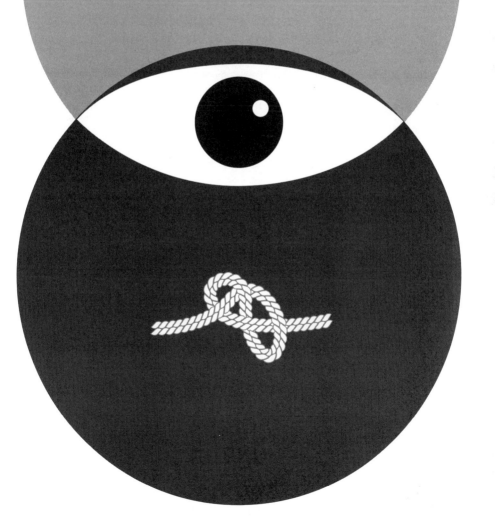

08

并非我们熟知的数

实数和复数

　　构造复数的过程比构造实数容易得多，实施起来
也顺利得多。创造实数的第一个步骤是发展出有理
数，这时候我们得解释到底什么是分数。一个分数，
譬如说 $\frac{2}{3}$，其实仅是一对整数，但是我们用这个既熟
悉又怪异的方式来表达。分数的思想不难理解，但是
相应的算术操作需要一些努力才能掌握。在这个过程
中，你的老师顺便提了一下，像 $\frac{2}{3}$, $\frac{4}{6}$, $\frac{6}{9}$ 这些分数都
是"相等的"——虽然它们是不同的数对，但在切馅
饼时，它们代表了相同大小的分块。这接受起来并不
难，不过它使得我们注意到一个事实，即一个有理数
实际上是无穷多等价的分数的集合，其中每个元素都
能用一对整数来表示。这听起来很吓人，或许我们不
乐意朝这方面想太多，因为想象一下要操作整数对
的无限集合，就让人感到不舒服。我们有一根救命稻
草，那就是任何分数都有唯一一个简化形式，也就是
当分子和分母互质的时候。从一开始的分数中消去所
有公因数，你就能得到这个最简形式。一旦你熟悉了

分数的性质和使用它们的规则，就应该不会出错了。

不过仔细观察一下，你会发现当自己做加法的时候，你已经隐含地在摆弄整数对的无限集合了。

然而，当我们进一步努力想要弄清楚实数到底是什么的时候，事情变得更糟了。让我们从毕达哥拉斯的问题说起。他发现没有一个分数等于 $\sqrt{2}$，因此我们可以引入一个新的符号 r，并使其拥有 $r^2=2$ 的性质。这样从有理数和这个新的数 r 出发，我们就得到了一个新的数域（field）。这之所以可行，原因在于所有形如 $a+br$ 的数——其中 a 和 b 是有理数——都遵循代数的一般规则。我们甚至可以做除法，因为这种数的倒数也保留了同样的形式。通过叫作分母有理化的炫酷代数小技巧，我们就能看出这一点。

新的数 r 和 $-r$ 组成了方程 $x^2=2$ 的两个解，那么 $x^2=3$ 呢？我们似乎需要再增加一个新的数，才能求解这个方程，因为很容易验证没有形如 $a+br$ 的数会平方得 3。［这里一个简单的反证法就够了：假设 $(a+br)^2=3$，这使你推出 $\sqrt{2}$ 和 $\sqrt{3}$ 中至少有一个是有理数的错误结论。］

我们会很想把这些关于特定方程的烦恼都丢在一边，直接声称我们已经知道实数是什么了——它们是所有可能的小数展开式组成的集合，包括正的和负的。这我们已经很熟悉了，在实际应用中大家也知道如何运用它们，因此我们觉得自己的位置是坚实的——至少在我们开始问一些很基本的问题之前。数的主要特点在于你可以加、减、乘和除。但是，举例来说，你怎样才能将两个无限不循环小数相乘呢？我们指望小数的长度有限，然后你就可以"从最右端开始"，但对于无限小数来说没有这样的东西。其实这是可以做到的，不过从理论和实际操作上讲它都很复杂。如果你解释如何加和乘都非常困难的话，这个数的系统似乎就不够令人满意。

109

还有其他的小陷阱。当你将 $\frac{1}{3}$ 乘以 3 时，答案为 1。当你将 0.333… 乘以 3，答案当然是 0.999…。两个不同的小数展开式确实能表示同一个数：1.000… ＝0.999…。事实上，任何一个有限小数都是这样的，比如 0.375＝0.374 999…。正因为我们看到两个不同的小数展开可以等于一样的数，所以，我们声称小数和实数是同一个东西严格来说是不太对的。另外，如果我们换一个进制底数，那么拥有不唯一小数展开的数会跟之前不一样，这又增加了额外的复杂性。倘若我们用小数来定义实数，我们就使得这一构造依赖于一个随意做出的选择（十进制）。假如我们用二进制来进行同样的构造，得到的"实数"集还会是相同的吗？我们的"相同或不同"是什么意义上的呢？

你也许会觉得上面所提出的基本问题耐人寻味，或者你会对我们的自省感到不耐烦。毕竟，之前所有的航程都是一帆风顺的，我们似乎是在自找麻烦。但有一点是无法忽视的。数学家们认为，任何时候我们引入新的数学对象，重点是要从已知对象出发再构造它们，就像分数可以被看作一对普通整数。这样，我们能够仔细地定义新推广的系统所遵循的规则，从而了解自己所处的位置。倘若我们完全忽视基础，日后它便会出来找麻烦。例如，微积分学脱胎于对运动的研究，它发展得极快，并且获得了光辉的成就，比如预测行星的轨道。然而，像对待有限事物一样处理无限事物，有时候能赋予我们惊人的洞察力，有时候却完全没有意义。将数学系统建立在坚实的基础上，我们就能学会如何分辨真假。在实践中，数学家们经常沉迷于"形式化"（formal）的操作，这是为了能看清远方的海面上是否会浮现出崭新的定理。要是结果值得注意，我们就可以通过回溯基本概念和引用已经恰当地建立起来的结果，来严格地证明它。

这就是为什么尤利乌斯·戴德金（Julius Dedekind）要不辞辛苦、形式化地构造实数系。现在，我们将他的思想称为实数轴的**戴德金分割**（Dedekind cut）。
不过，对于无理数存在性导致的两难问题，第一个
成功提出解决方案的数学家是尼多斯的欧多克索斯
（Eudoxus of Cnidus，他活跃于公元前380年）。借助
于他所著的《比例论》（*Theory of Proportions*），阿基
米德使用所谓的穷竭法（Method of Exhaustion）严格
地推导出了弯曲形状的面积和体积，而这比微积分的
发明早了大约1900年。

数的最后一块拼图——虚数单位

i的平方为−1，这个新符号的引入是一个巨大的
成功，因为它一次性地解决了很多问题，不仅是为
方程提供了一个解，同时使得所有多项式方程都可
解，还帮忙解决了不少其他方面的问题。对于任意负
数——$-r$，我们显然有两个平方根。$\pm i\sqrt{r}$ 这两个数
的平方都是$-r$，这一方面是由于$i^2 = -1$这项性质，
另一方面是因为我们假设，就像普通的算术一样，乘
法可交换，这意味着对于任意两个数z和w，$zw = wz$。
如果我们坚持要求复数$a+bi$的系统应该包含实数（对
应于$b=0$的情况）的性质，并且所有正常的代数规则

也都还适用，我们不会遇到任何困难，反而会发现很多惊喜。复数的集合——表示为C——是一个"域"。域除了一系列其他性质以外，还保证了除法是能进行的。但是，要看出这是怎么实现的，我们最好离开实数轴这条单向轨道，去看看二维世界的样子。

111　　复数的算术可以在**复平面**（complex plane）内清楚地表示。我们将复数$a+bi$看作坐标平面内的点(a, b)。当我们将两个复数$z=(a, b)$和$w=(c, d)$相加时，我们只是将它们的第一和第二个元素分别相加，这里$z+w=(a+c, b+d)$。如果我们使用符号i，那么举个例子，我们就有$(2+i)+(1+3i)=3+4i$。

这对应于平面上的**向量**（vector）和，也就是有向线段（向量）首尾相加在一起（如图13）。在这个例子里，我们从坐标为$(0, 0)$的**原点**（origin）开始到点$(2, 1)$结束，画下第一个箭头。要加上$(1, 3)$代表的数，我们从点$(2, 1)$开始再画一个箭头，表示在水平方向（即实轴的方向）向右移动1个单位，以及在竖直方向（即虚轴的方向）向上移动3个单位，最终到达坐标为$(3, 4)$的点。用同样的方法，我们可以通过实部和虚部分别相减来定义复数的减法。例如，$(11+7i)-(2+5i)=9+2i$。这可以看作从向量$(11, 7)$开始，减去向量$(2, 5)$，在点$(9, 2)$结束。

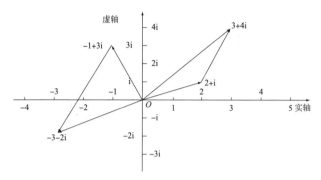

图 13　复数的相加即有向线段的相加

　　乘法就是另外一回事了。形式上说很容易：我们 112
通过把括号拆开，将两个复数相乘，记住 $i^2 = -1$。假
设**乘法分配律**（Distributive Law）仍然成立，这让我
们能用通常的方法打开括号，那么乘法如下：

$$(a+bi)(c+di)=a(c+di)+bi(c+di)$$
$$=ac+adi+bci+bdi^2$$
$$=(ac-bd)+(ad+bc)i。$$

　　除法可以用**复共轭**（complex conjugate）的方法
来计算。一般地，$z=a+bi$ 的共轭是 $a-bi$，记作 $\bar{z}$。
换句话说，$\bar{z}$ 是 z 相对于实轴的镜像。乘法运算 $z\bar{z}$ 给
出 a^2+b^2，这是一个实数，因为我们发现虚部为 0。这
等于从原点到 z 的距离（记作 $|z|$）的平方。用符号写
出来就是 $z\bar{z}=|z|^2$。现在，我们就可以操作复数除法
了，只需要分子分母同乘除数的共轭，这样便能使除

数变成一个纯实数。这可以类比于分母有理化——从分号下面消去平方根的标准技巧，当时我们用它计算了 $\sqrt{2}$ 的连分数。例如，

$$\frac{15+16i}{2+3i} = \frac{(15+16i)(2-3i)}{(2+3i)(2-3i)} = \frac{30-45i+32i-48i^2}{2^2-6i+6i-3^2i^2}$$

$$= \frac{(30+48)-(45-32)i}{2^2+3^2} = \frac{78-13i}{13} = 6-i。$$

我们可以用一般化的复数，而不是具体的数值，来将复数相除的结果表示成普适的形式。它由两个数的实部和虚部构成，就像我们在复数乘法中做的一样。不过，只要理解了这一技巧，我们就不一定非要推出并记住最后的公式了。

我们如果把坐标系从普通的直角坐标转换成**极坐标**（polar coordinate），就会发现乘法有了一种几何解释。在这个系统中，一个点 z 依然由一个有序数对所确定，我们将其写作 (r, θ)。数 r 是从原点 O，在这里叫作**极点**（pole），到我们的点 z 的距离。因此 r 是一个非负的量，所有具有相同 r 值的点形成一个圆心在极点、半径为 r 的圆。我们用第二个坐标 θ 来表示 z 在这个圆上的位置，θ 是从实轴到 Oz 这条线逆时针方向走过的角度。数 r 称为 z 的**模**，而角度 θ 称作 z 的**辐角**（argument），如图14。

113

172

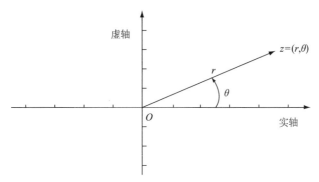

图 14　一个复数在极坐标下的位置

假设现在我们有两个复数，z 和 w，它们的极坐标分别为 (r_1, θ_1) 和 (r_2, θ_2)。我们发现，它们的积 zw 的极坐标有一个简单美妙的形式。组合的规则甚至可以用日常语言清晰地表述出来：积 zw 的模即 z 和 w 的模的乘积，而 zw 的辐角为 z 和 w 的辐角之和。用符号表示，zw 的极坐标为 $(r_1 r_2, \theta_1 + \theta_2)$。实数的乘法包含在这个更一般的规则里：比如，一个正实数 r 拥有极坐标 $(r, 0)$。如果我们乘上另一个数 $(s, 0)$，结果是意料之中的 $(rs, 0)$，对应于实数 rs。

这个表示方式能够更充分地体现复数乘法的特点。复数单位 i 的极坐标是 $(1, 90°)$。通常，在这些情况下，我们并不用度数来度量角，而是用自然的数学单位**弧度**（radian）：一个圆有 2π 弧度，因而转动一弧度相当于沿着中心在原点的单位圆的周长移动

114

一个单位。1弧度大约是57.3°。假设我们现在取任意复数$z=(r, \theta)$，乘以i=(1，90°)，我们发现$zi=(r, \theta+90°)$。也就是说，乘以i相当于绕着复平面的中心旋转一个直角。再换个说法，直角，这个最基本的几何思想，可以用一个数来表示。

的确，若是将复平面的一个给定区域内的所有点加上或乘以一个复数z，这一效果可以用几何方法来表示。想象平面内任意一个你喜欢的区域，如果给区域内的每一点都加上z，我们就只是将每个点都往同一个方向移动相同的距离，这个方向和距离是由z代表的箭头——或者我们经常说的向量——来决定的。也就是说，我们将这个区域**平移**（translate）到平面上的另一个位置，而它的形状、大小和姿态都保持不变，这里姿态不变是指该区域没有经过任何旋转或反射。但是，将你的区域中每个点都乘以$z=(r, \theta)$则有两个效果，一个由r引起，另一个由θ造成。区域内每个点的模都增大r倍，因此该区域的所有尺寸也都增大了r倍（因而它的面积乘了因数r^2）。当然，如果$r<1$，那么我们最好把这个"扩张"描述成收缩，因为新的区域会比原来的小。不过，区域将保持它的形状——例如，一个三角形会被映射为一个相似的三角形，它的各个角和以前一样大。θ的作用就像我们上面

已经解释过的，是将区域沿逆时针方向绕极点转过角度
θ。那么，将你的区域中所有点都乘上z的总效果是扩展
区域，并绕极点旋转。新的区域将和之前的有同样的形
状，但取决于r的大小，会有不同的尺寸，同时将会有
一个不同的姿态，这是由旋转角θ决定的。

其他结果

复数的极坐标版本尤其适合进行幂和方根运算，
因为要求$z=(r，\theta)$的n次方。我们只需要求模的同样
次方，并将θ自己相加n次，从而得到$z^n=(r^n，n\theta)$。同
样的公式也适用于分数幂和负幂次，除法也可以用极
坐标来理解。与实数一样，除以一个复数z意味着乘
上它的倒数$w=\dfrac{1}{z}$，但w是什么数呢？给定$z=(r，\theta)$，
w具有性质$zw=(1，0)$，即相乘为1的那个数。这显示
我们必须取$w=(\dfrac{1}{r}，-\theta)$，因为这样我们才得到要求的
$w=(r，\theta)(\dfrac{1}{r}，-\theta)=(r\dfrac{1}{r}，\theta-\theta)=(1，0)$。在直角坐标形
式中，我们需要使用复共轭。极坐标里则给出了另一
种方法。

复数有极多的应用，甚至是在很基础的层次上。
直角坐标和极坐标的相互转换将三角函数引入了进

来，这种应用方式有很多优点。例如，推导重要的三角恒等式是一道标准的学生习题，而在用了极坐标后，这些等式是十分自然的结论。取任意单位模（即 $r=1$）的复数，用直角坐标和极坐标分别计算它的某次幂，令这两种形式的答案相等，这就给出了一个三角方程。

由基本的三角学可知，极坐标为 $(1, \theta)$ 的点的直角坐标是 $(\cos\theta, \sin\theta)$。如果我们现在将两个这样的复数 $z=\cos\theta+i\sin\theta$ 和 $w=\cos\varphi+i\sin\varphi$ 在直角坐标中相乘，可得：

116 $$zw=(\cos\theta\cos\varphi-\sin\theta\sin\varphi)+i(\cos\theta\sin\varphi+\sin\theta\cos\varphi)。$$

同样的乘法在极坐标中给出：

$$zw=(1, \theta)(1, \varphi)=(1, \theta+\varphi)=\cos(\theta+\varphi)+\sin(\theta+\varphi)。$$

对比该乘积的两个版本的实部和虚部，就可以轻松得到三角学中标准的和角公式：

$$\cos(\theta+\varphi)=\cos\theta\cos\varphi-\sin\theta\sin\varphi,$$

$$\sin(\theta+\varphi)=\cos\theta\sin\varphi+\sin\theta\cos\varphi。$$

或者，极坐标形式的复乘法可以由这些三角公式推导出。实际上，我们在这里未经证明就给出了极坐标形式下的乘法，它通常是将三角公式应用于直角坐标形式来推导出的。

现在，随着复数的使用，指数函数——或者说幂函数与看起来无关的三角函数之间的联系浮现了出来，更多的结果可以因此轻松得到。假如我们没有跨入由 −1 的平方根所提供的传送门，我们也许可以窥见这一联系，但却不能理解它。分别取指数函数中被称为偶的和奇的部分，就产生了所谓的**双曲函数**（hyperbolic function）。对于每个三角恒等式，除了符号上可能不同，都相应存在一个等价的由双曲函数表达的形式。在任何具体例子中，这都可以轻松验证。问题是为什么会发生这一现象？一类函数的行为为何会如此紧密地反映在另一类中，而后者来自完全不同的定义、具有完全不同的性质？解开这一谜团的关键在于公式 $e^{i\theta}=\cos\theta+i\sin\theta$，它表明指数函数和三角函数其实是紧密相连的，但这只能通过使用虚单位 i 做到。一旦发现了这一点（它令人惊讶，一点也不明显），用这个公式提供的两种可互换的表示方式计算，再令实部和虚部分别相等，我们就可以清楚地看到之前描述的那些结果都是顺理成章的。但要是没有这个公式，所有这些依然是个谜。

117

复数和矩阵

乘以 i 代表绕复平面的中心转动一个直角。让我们来仔细研究一下这个事实所导致的一些结果。若 $z = x + iy$，展开括号和对乘法重新排序，可得 $i(x + iy) = -y + ix$，因此点 (x, y) 经过这个旋转变成了 $(-y, x)$，如图 15。这样，乘以 i 可以看作在平面上对点操作。这一操作有一个特殊性质，即对于任意两点 z 和 w，以及任意实数 a，我们有 $i(z + w) = iz + iw$ 和 $i(aw) = a(iw)$。

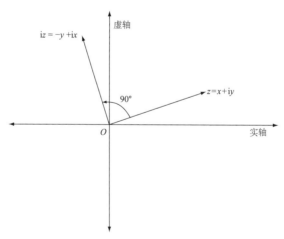

图 15　乘以 i 将一个复数旋转一个直角

另外，如果我们将一个实数 a 乘上一个复数 $(x+\mathrm{i}y)$，我们得 $a(x+\mathrm{i}y)=ax+\mathrm{i}(ay)$。用复平面上的点来说，我们将 (x,y) 移动到了 (ax,ay)，或者用另一种方法写就是 $a(x,y)=(ax,ay)$。

118

具有这两条性质的一类运算称为**线性的**（linear），它们在数学的所有领域都极其重要。这里，我只希望提醒你注意一个事实，那就是这样一个运算 L 的效果完全由它在两个点 $(1,0)$ 和 $(0,1)$ 上的行为决定。因为让我们假设 $L(1,0)=(a,b)$ 和 $L(0,1)=(c,d)$，那么对于任何点 (x,y)，我们有 $(x,y)=x(1,0)+y(0,1)$，于是应用线性运算的性质，我们得到：

$$L(x,y)=L(x(1,0)+y(0,1))=xL(1,0)+yL(0,1)$$
$$=x(a,b)+y(c,d)=(ax,bx)+(cy,dy)$$
$$=(ax+cy,\ bx+dy)。$$

这些信息可以总结在所谓的**矩阵方程**（matrix equation）中：

$$(x,\ y)\begin{pmatrix} a & b \\ c & d \end{pmatrix}=(ax+cy,\ bx+dy)。$$

这里我们举了矩阵相乘的一个例子，它展示了这样的运算在一般情况下如何进行。**矩阵**（matrix）是由数组成的矩形阵列，它代表了另一种二维的数的对象。矩阵渗透了高等数学的几乎所有领域，同时包括纯数学和应用数学。它们代表了代数学中的一个重要部分。矩阵已经被证明有用到什么程度呢？现代数学的很大一部分便是努力要将自己用矩阵的语言表达出来。两个有相同行数和列数的矩阵可以逐项相加。比如，要找到两个矩阵之和的第二行第三列的元素，我们只需要将两个矩阵中相应位置的元素相加。不过，乘法赋予了矩阵一个新的重要特点，前面这个例子已经体现出了矩阵乘法的规则——积矩阵中的每个元素都是第一个矩阵的某行与第二个矩阵中的某列进行**点乘**（dot product）得到的。这是说，第一个矩阵的某行元素与第二个矩阵的某列元素分别相乘后再相加。

矩阵遵循代数里通常的法则，除了乘法交换律（commutativity of multiplication）。也就是说，对于两个矩阵*A*和*B*，一般来说*AB*=*BA*是不对的。然而，矩阵乘法是**可结合的**（associative），这意味着书写任意长度的矩阵连乘时，不需要括号也不会引起歧义。

平面上的线性变换（linear transformation）通常是指绕着原点的旋转、相对于通过原点的直线的反射、相对原点的扩大或收缩，以及所谓的**剪切**（shear），或者说**搓**（slanting）。剪切是指让点平行于一根固定的轴移动，移动的长度与每个点到固定轴的距离成正比，就类似于一本书的各页可以依次滑动那样。对于任意一连串这样的变换，其效果都可以通过将所有对应的矩阵乘在一起来体现，这会给我们一个单独的矩阵，它包含了所有这些变换依次执行之后的最终效果。就像我们已经看到的那样，得到矩阵的各行正是两个点 $(1, 0)$ 和 $(0, 1)$ 经过变换后得到的像。这两个点称为**基向量**（basis vector）。

现在，对于代表绕原点逆时针旋转直角的矩阵 J，我们自然地认为它应该模仿乘以虚单位 i 时我们观察到的数的行为。因为点 $(1, 0)$ 被转到了点 $(0, 1)$，类似地点 $(0, 1)$ 移动到了 $(-1, 0)$，所以这两个新向量组成了矩阵 J 的行。将 J 平方可得一个矩阵，它的几何效果是把点绕原点转过 $2 \times 90° = 180°$。下面我们就通过乘法来计算这个矩阵。例如，要找出 J^2 右下角的元素，我们取第二行和第二列的点乘，即 $(-1) \times 1 + 0 \times 0 = -1 + 0 = -1$。完整的计算如下：

$$J^2 = \begin{pmatrix} 0 & 1 \\ -1 & 0 \end{pmatrix} \begin{pmatrix} 0 & 1 \\ -1 & 0 \end{pmatrix} = \begin{pmatrix} -1 & 0 \\ 0 & -1 \end{pmatrix} = -I \text{。}$$

矩阵 I 的行是 $(1\ 0)$ 和 $(0\ 1)$，它是**单位矩阵**（identity matrix）。这么称呼是因为它就像数 1 一样，当乘另一个矩阵 A 时结果还是 A。矩阵 $-I$ 代表了绕原点半周，它的行为类似于 -1，同时 $(-I)^2 = I$。所有这些性质的最终结果是，对于实数 a 和 b，矩阵 $aI+bJ$ 在加法和乘法的意义上很好地模仿了复数 $a+bi$ 的行为，因此它给出了复数域的一个矩阵表示。对应于典型的复数 $a+bi$ 的矩阵是

$$\begin{pmatrix} a & b \\ -b & a \end{pmatrix}。$$

代表复数的矩阵是满足乘法交换律的。当然就像之前提到的，这并不能推广到所有矩阵的乘积。另一个矩阵会出问题的地方是并非所有矩阵都能"逆转"。对于大部分方阵 **A**（一个行数和列数相等的矩阵），我们可能找到一个唯一的**逆矩阵**（inverse matrix）**B**，使得 **AB=BA=I**。但是，逆矩阵存在与否，取决于一个单独的数。这个数与相应的方阵联系在一起，叫作它的**行列式**（determinant）。笼统地说，从矩阵的每行各取一个数，使它们占据不同的列，将它们相乘并赋予不同的符号，再将所有可能的这样的乘积相加，就得到了行列式。对于前文介绍的典型的 2×2 矩阵，行列式即为数 $\triangle = ad-bc$。行列式用处很多，它具有优良的性质。例如，$\triangle$ 代表了对应的变换的面积缩放因子：一个面积为 a 的形状经过一个行列式为 $\triangle$ 的矩阵所对应的变换，会变为面积为 $\triangle a$ 的形状（倘若 $\triangle$ 为负，这个形状还会经过一次反

射，将原始的朝向颠倒过来）。另外，两个方阵乘积
的行列式，是这些矩阵行列式的乘积。在 $\triangle=0$ 时，
方阵 A 没有逆矩阵。除此情况之外，A 有逆矩阵 B。行
列式为 0 在几何上对应于一个 **退化的**（degenerate）变
换，这时变换后得到的图形面积为 0，比如说一条线
段，甚至是一个单独的点。

　　对于一个复数 $z=a+b\mathrm{i}$ 的矩阵，我们注意到
$\triangle=a^2+b^2$，它永远不为 0，除了 $z=0$ 的时候。当然，
以前 0 从来没有倒数，这在更广阔的复数的世界里也
仍然适用。不过，这也确认了每个非零的复数都有一
个倒数。

　　到这里，我们已经站在了一个广阔世界的边缘，
前方是线性代数、表示论[1] 以及它们在多元微积分里的
应用。我们就不再往远处走了。但是，读者应该知道
矩阵其实不仅仅适用于三维，还适用于 n 维空间，通
常这是通过 $n\times n$ 大小的矩阵实现的。虽然这些阵列变
得更大更复杂了，但是矩阵自己依然是一个二维的数
值对象。

121

1　数学中抽象代数的一支。

复平面以外的数

在两个重要的意义上，所有复数组成的域 **C** 是完备的。假设有一个复数的无穷数列，它的各项往越来越小的圆圈里聚集，圆圈的半径趋向于 0，我们称这个数列是收敛的。任何复数的收敛数列都趋近于一个极限复数。这对实数来说也是真的，但不适用于有理数——对于任何无理数，其相继的小数近似都代表了一个有理数的数列，这个数列趋近于一个有理数范围之外的极限。另外，**C** 在代数意义上是完备的（或者说是封闭的），意思是可以证明，任何多项式方程 $p(z) = a + bz + cz^2 + \cdots + z^n = 0$ 都有 n 个（复数）解：$z_1, z_2, \cdots, z_n$，这使得 $p(z)$ 自己可以彻底地因式分解为 $p(z) = (z-z_1)(z-z_2)\cdots(z-z_n)$。

复数在这里和其他问题上获得了出人意料的成功，这在很大程度上消除了将数系进一步拓展到复平面以外的需求。事实上，要想构造一个范围更大的数字系统，从而在包含 **C** 的同时又保留代数中所有的常规法则，这是不可能实现的。并且，只有两个推广的系统能做到保留一些代数结构，即**四元数**（quaternion）和**八元数**（octonion）。虽然它们的使用不如复数来得广泛，但是四元数在某些领域中得到了应用，比如三维计算机图形学。八元数可以看作一对四元数，它们不仅缺乏乘法的可交换性，甚至连乘法的可结合性质也丢失了。

一个四元数是形如 $z = a + b\mathrm{i} + c\mathrm{j} + d\mathrm{k}$ 的数，第一部分 $a + b\mathrm{i}$ 是一个普通的复数，同时两个**四元数单位**（quaternion unit）j 和 k 满足 $\mathrm{j}^2 = \mathrm{k}^2 = -1$。为了进行四元数的乘法，我们需要知道虚单位量如何相乘，这由以下规则决定：ij=k，jk=i，ki=j。反过来的积拥有相反的符号，比如 ji=−k。其实，所有这些积都可以通过一个额外的方程：ijk=−1 来推出。于是，四元数构成了一个增广了的代数系统，这个系统满足除乘法交换律以外的所有代数法则，失去交换律的原因在于上面提到的反向相乘时符号的变化。这个系统的相容性也可以通过 2×2 的矩阵表达来显示，不过这次我们不仅有实的元素，同时还允许出现复元素。数 1 再一次对应于单位矩阵 I，但是单位量 i，j 和 k 则对应于矩阵：

$$\mathrm{i} = \begin{pmatrix} \mathrm{i} & 0 \\ 0 & -\mathrm{i} \end{pmatrix}, \ \mathrm{j} = \begin{pmatrix} 0 & 1 \\ -1 & 0 \end{pmatrix}, \ \mathrm{k} = \begin{pmatrix} 0 & \mathrm{i} \\ \mathrm{i} & 0 \end{pmatrix}。$$

而典型的四元数 z 有矩阵形式：

$$z = \begin{pmatrix} a + b\mathrm{i} & c + d\mathrm{i} \\ -c + d\mathrm{i} & a - b\mathrm{i} \end{pmatrix}。$$

然而，这种将四元数表示为矩阵的方法不是唯一的。其实，复数的矩阵表达也有其他等价的形式。甚至，表示四元数还可以不用复数，只不过这要以使用更大的矩阵为代价：四元数可以表示为某些只含有实数的 4×4 矩阵。

有时我们需要进行一些运算，其结果却不能被现有的数系所容纳。对这类计算的需求催生了新类型的数和对旧系统的推广。每个文明都是从自然数开始的，涉及数的片段的计算产生了分数，涉及债务的计算引出了负数，以及正如毕达哥拉斯发现的，涉及长度的计算产生了无理数。并非所有关于数的事务都能用整数以及它们的比值来处理，虽然这一发现已经十分久远，但这个事实依然深刻又微妙。随着科学变得越来越复杂，所需要的数的系统也必须成熟起来，才能处理这些进展。科学家们一般不会异想天开地主动创造新的数系，相反，在一开始，这些新数常常是被不情愿地、犹豫不决地引进来，用以应付科研中遇到的难题。例如，虽然在19世纪就被引入，但矩阵直到20世纪初才在量子力学中取得了不容置疑的地位。当时的科学家们遇到了一个形如 $q=AB-BA$ 却又不为 0 的量。在其他可交换的数系中，q 当然会是 0，因此这里需要的是一种他们以前从没遇到过的数值对象：它们是矩阵。

现在，看起来似乎数学和物理的世界已经拥有足够多种类的数了。虽然还存在本书没有提到的数的类型，但是自20世纪上半叶以来，我们还不需要对数学和科学中常用的数进行大的改造。

本书中我们对数学进行了一次"热气球观光之 124
旅"，伴随着以上的观察结果，我们也到该说再见的时候了。我们从地面出发，渐渐升到了空中，我希望从这个高度上，丰富多彩又神秘莫测的数的世界能够吸引读者朋友的注目。

名词对照

AKS 素性测试	AKS primality test
RSA 加密过程	RSA enciphering process
ZFC 集合论	ZFC set theory

A

埃拉托斯特尼筛法	Sieve of Eratosthenes
艾赫米姆莎草纸	Ahkmim papyrus

B

八元数	octonian
半完美数	semiperfect number
贝尔数	Bell number
冰雹数	hailstone number
伯特兰－惠特沃斯选票问题	Bertrand-Whitworth ballot problem
伯特兰－切比雪夫定理	Bertrand's postulate
补集	complem entary set
不对称密码	asymmetric cipher
不可公度的	incommensurable

不可数集合	uncountable set

C

超越数	transcendental number
乘法单位量	multiplicative identity
乘法分配律	Distributive Law
稠密集	dense set
处处不稠密	nowhere dense
搓	slanting

D

代数数	algebraic number
戴德金分割	Dedekind cut
单位分数	unit fraction
单位矩阵	identity matrix
底数，基数	base number
递推关系	recurrence relation
递归	recursion
点乘	dot product
丢番图方程	Diophantine equation
对称密码	symmetric cipher
对数	logarithm
多亲数	sociable number
多项式	polynomial

共轭	dual
勾股定理	Pythagoras theorem
勾股数	Pythagorean triple

H

行列式	determinant
合数	composite number
弧度	radian
互素	coprime
黄金分割律	golden ratio
黄金长方形	golden rectangle

J

基本解	fundamental solution
基向量	basis vector
极点	pole
极坐标	polar coordinate
几何数列	geometric series
既约分数	reduced fraction
加密数	enciphering number
剪切	shear
阶乘	factorials
解密数	deciphering number
矩阵	matrix
矩阵方程	matrix equation

密码	cipher
密码学	cryptography
密钥	cipher key
明文	plaintext

N

| 逆矩阵 | inverse matrix |
| 牛群问题 | Cattle problem |

O

欧几里得数	Euclidean number
欧几里得算法	Euclidean algorithm
欧几里得性质	Euclidean property
欧拉 φ 函数	Euler phi function
欧拉定理	Euler's Theorem

P

帕斯卡三角形	Pascal's triangle
佩尔方程	Pell equation
平方数	square number
平移	transtate

Q

| 奇异数 | weird number |

R

| 容斥原理 | inclusion-exclusion principle |

S

三角形数	triangular number
三进制	ternary
栅格点	lattice points
十进制，以十为底	base ten
实数	real number
势	cardinality
收敛子	convergent
数轴	number line
双曲函数	hyperbolic function
斯特林数	Stirling number
四元数	quaternion
四元数单位	quaternion unit
素数	prime number
素数，素的	prime
素数大搜索项目	GIMPS
素因数分解	prime factorization
算法	algorithm
算术三角形	arithmetic triangle
算术数列	arithmetic sequence

T

提洛问题	Delian problem
兔子问题	Rabbit problem
退化的	degenerate

W

完美数	perfect number
威尔逊定理	Wilson's theorem
位值进位法	positional value
无理数	irrational number
无平方因数的数	square-free number

X

线性的	linear
相亲数	amicable pair
向量	vector
虚数	imaginary number
斜拉古问题	Syracuse problem

Y

杨表	Young diagram
一次性密码本	one-time pad
因数，因子，约数	factor / divisor
因数分解	factorization
印度－阿拉伯数字系统	Hindu-Arabic number system
盈数	abundant number
有理数	rational number
有限小数	terminating decimal
余数	remainder
原点	origin

Z

辗转相减	anthyphairesis
真因数	proper factor
真因数和函数	aliquot function
真因数和数列	aliquot sequence
正则素数	regular prime
正整数	positive integer
中央二项式系数	central binomial coefficient
子集	subset
自然对数	natural logarithm
自然数	natural number
自相似	self-similarity
最大公因数	highest common factor
最大公约数	greatest common divisor

Peter M. Higgins

NUMBERS

A Very Short Introduction

Contents

Preface

The purpose of this little book is to explain, in language that will be familiar to everyone, what are the various kinds of numbers that arise and how they behave. Numbers allow comparisons between all manner of things, and anyone with no understanding of numbers would be lost in the modern world where things numerical are there to greet us at every turn. We should realize however that, despite their familiarity, numbers have no physical existence but rather are abstractions that we elicit from the world we find ourselves in. To develop a clear picture of how they operate, it is sometimes better to consider them in their own right, without reference to anything else.

This *Short Introduction* is not a refresher course in arithmetic, nor will that much be said on the history of the number system. Rather its purpose is to explain numbers themselves and the kinds of behaviour they exhibit. A glance at the list of chapters reveals that the first part of the book deals mainly with ordinary counting numbers, while in the second half we go beyond that. By exploring natural problems that arise in commerce and science, the need to freely perform calculations eventually has taken us, by stages, into the arena of the complex numbers, which is the principal underlying framework for most number matters. This may sound a little daunting but rest assured, the hard work has already been done for you.

The modern number system did not come to us gift-wrapped but rather has developed over many centuries. There were long periods of confusion, which had two root causes. The first was the lack of an efficient way to represent the numbers we need that would allow us to manipulate them. The second, which was related to the first, was philosophical agonizing over the interpretations of various number types and whether or not they are meaningful. Nowadays we are much more sure of ourselves when it comes to what we do and don't need to worry about when dealing with numbers, making it possible to give a complete picture of the number world in a single short account like this one. That is not to say that all mystery has vanished – far from it, as you will discover as you read on.

Peter M. Higgins
Colchester, England, 2011

List of illustrations

Chapter 1
How not to think about numbers

We are all used to seeing numbers written down, and to drawing some meaning from them. However, a numeral such as 6 and the number that it represents are not one and the same thing. In Roman numerals, for example, we would write the number six as VI, but we realize that this stands for the same number that is written as 6 in modern notation. Both symbolize collections of the kind corresponding to six tally marks: I I I I I I. We shall first spend a little time considering the different ways that we represent and think about numbers.

We sometimes solve number problems almost without realizing it. For example, suppose you are conducting a meeting and you want to ensure that everyone there has a copy of the agenda. You can deal with this by labelling each copy of the handout in turn with the initials of each of those present. As long as you do not run out of copies before completing this process, you will know that you have a sufficient number to go around. You have then solved this problem without resorting to arithmetic and without explicit counting. There are numbers at work for us here all the same and they allow precise comparison of one collection with another, even though the members that make up the collections could have entirely different characters, as is the case here, where one set is a collection of people, while the other consists of pieces of paper.

What numbers allow us to do is to compare the relative size of one set with another.

In the previous scenario you need not bother to count how many people were present as you did not have to know – your problem was to determine whether or not the number of copies of the agenda was at least as great as the number of people, and the value of these numbers was not required. You will, however, need to take a count of the number present when you order lunch for fifteen and certainly, when it comes to totting up the bill for that meal, someone will make use of arithmetic to work out the exact cost, even if the sums are all done on a calculator.

Our modern number system allows us to express numbers in an efficient and uniform manner, which makes it easy to compare one number with another and to perform the arithmetical operations that arise through counting. In the day-to-day world, we employ base ten for all our arithmetic, that is to say we count by tens, and we do that for the accidental reason that we have ten digits on our hands. What makes our number system so effective, however, is not our particular choice of base but rather the use of *positional value* in number representation, where the value of a numeral depends on its place in the number string. For example, 1984 is short for 4 ones plus 8 lots of ten plus 9 hundreds plus 1 thousand.

It is important to understand what we mean when we write numbers in particular ways. In this chapter, we will think about what numbers represent, discover different approaches to counting, meet a very important set of numbers (the primes), and introduce some simple number tricks for finding them.

How counting was sorted out

It is worth taking a few moments to appreciate that there are two distinct stages to the process of building a counting system based on, for instance, tens. Two basic tasks that we impose on children are remembering how to recite the alphabet and learning how to count. These processes are superficially similar but yet have fundamental differences. Our language is based on a 26-letter alphabet and, roughly speaking, each letter corresponds to a sound that we use to speak words. In any case, it is certainly true that the English language has developed so that it can be written using a set of 26 symbols. However, we cannot compile dictionaries unless we assign an order to our alphabet. There is no particularly natural order available and the one that we have settled on and all sing in school, $a, b, c, d, \ldots$ seems very arbitrary indeed. To be sure, the more frequently used letters generally occur in the first half of the alphabet, but this is only a rough guide rather than a rule, with the common letters s and t, for example, sounding off late in the roll call. By contrast, the counting numbers, or *natural numbers* as they are called, $1, 2, 3, \ldots$ come to us in that order: for example, the symbol 3 is meant to stand for the number that follows 2 and so has to be listed as its successor. We can, up to a point, make up a fresh name for each successive number. Sooner or later, however, we have to give up and start grouping numbers in batches in order to handle the unending sequence. Grouping by tens represented the first stage of developing a sound number system, and this approach has been near universal throughout history and across the globe.

There was, however, much variation in detail. The Roman system favours gathering by fives as much as tens, with special symbols, V and L, for five and for fifty respectively. The Ancient Greek system was squarely based on grouping by tens. They would use specific letters to stand for numbers, sometimes dashed to tell the reader that the symbol should be read as a number rather than as a letter in some ordinary word. For example, π stood for 80 and γ for 3, so they might write $\pi\gamma$ to denote 83. This may look equally as efficient, and indeed much the same as our notation, but it is not. The Greeks still missed the point of the positional system as the value of each of their symbols was fixed. In particular, $\gamma\pi$ could still only represent the same number, 3 + 80, whereas if we switch the order of the digits in 83 we have the different number 38.

In the Hindu-Arabic system, the second stage of number representation was attained. Here the big idea is to make the value of a symbol dependent upon where it occurs in the string. This allows us to express any number with just a fixed family of symbols. We have settled on the set of ten numerals 0, 1, 2, $\cdots$, 9, so the normal number system is described as *base ten*, but we could build our number system up from a larger or a smaller collection of basic symbols. We can even manage with as few as two numerals, 0 and 1 say, which is what is known as the *binary* system, so often used in computing. It is not the choice of base size, however, that was revolutionary but the idea of using position to convey extra information about the identity of your numbers.

For example, when we write a number like 1905, the value of each digit depends on its place in the number string. Here there are 5 units, 9 lots of one hundred (which is 10 × 10), and one lot of one thousand (which is 10 × 10 × 10). The use of the zero symbol is important as a placeholder. In the case of 1905, no contribution comes from the 10's place, but we cannot ignore that and just write 195 instead, as that represents an entirely different number. Indeed, each string of digits represents a different number and it is for that reason that huge numbers may be represented by short strings. For instance, we can assign a unique number to every human being on Earth using strings no longer than ten digits and in this way give a personal identifier to every individual belonging to this huge set.

Societies of the past sometimes used different bases for their writing of numbers but that is much less significant than the fact that nearly all of them lacked a true positional system with full use of a zero symbol as a placeholder. In view of how very ancient is the civilization of Babylon, it is remarkable that they among the peoples of the ancient world came closest to a positional system.

They did not, however, fully embrace the use of the not-so-natural number 0 and eschewed using the empty register in the final position the way we do to distinguish, for example, 830 from 83.

The conceptual hurdle that had to be cleared was the realization that zero was indeed a number. Admittedly, zero is not a positive number but it is a number all the same and until we incorporate it into our number system in a fully consistent manner, we remain handicapped. This crucial final step was taken in India in about the 6th century AD. Our number system is called Hindu-Arabic as it was communicated from India to Europe via Arabia.

Living with and without decimals

Of course, we have now extended the base ten positional idea into fractional parts giving the familiar decimal number system. When we write 3.14, for instance, the 1 after the decimal point stands for one lot of $\frac{1}{10}$, a tenth part, and the 4 similarly stands for $\frac{4}{100}$. This two-decimal-place form of a number is very familiar to us as we deal in decimal currency where the smallest unit is not one dollar, or pound, or euro, as the case may be, but the 'penny' or 'cent', which is one-hundreth part of the main currency unit. Decimal arithmetic is the natural extension of the base ten system and in practice it represents the best way to carry out ordinary sums. Despite all its advantages, the decimal approach had a slow and hesitant genesis. It remained within the province of a mathematical elite until the latter part of the 16th century, when it finally found its way into commercial arithmetic and general usage. Even after that time, grouping based on numbers other than powers of ten persisted. Britain did not adopt decimal currency until 1971. And part of the English-speaking world still resolutely sticks with yards, feet, and inches. In defence of Imperial Units, they are convenient in size, being very much attuned to the human scale of things. Our hands are six to eight inches long and we are five to six feet tall, so we surround ourselves with objects of similar size, which are then readily measured in units of feet and inches. However, ten inches to the foot could have worked just as well and would have been more easily dealt with by our base ten calculators.

Adopting a particular base for a number system is a little like placing a particular grid scale on a map. It is not intrinsic to the object but is rather akin to a system of coordinates imposed on top as an instrument of control. Our choice of base is arbitrary in character and the exclusive use of base ten saddles us all with a blinkered view of the set of counting numbers: $1, 2, 3, 4, \cdots$. Only by lifting the veil can we see numbers face to face for what they truly are. When we mention a particular number, let us say for example forty-nine, all of us have a mental picture of the two numerals 49. This is somewhat unfair to the number in question as we are immediately typecasting forty-nine as $(4 \times 10) + 9$. Since $49 = (4 \times 12) + 1$, it may just as easily be thought of that way and, indeed, in base twelve, forty-nine would therefore be written as 41, with the numeral 4 now standing for 4 lots of 12. However, what gives the number forty-nine its character is that it equals the product 7×7, known as the *square* of 7. This facet of its personality is highlighted in base seven, as then the number forty-nine is represented as 100, the 1 now standing for one lot of 7×7.

We would be equally entitled to use another base, such as twelve, for our number system: the Mayans used twenty and the Babylonians base sixty. In one way, the number 60 is a good choice for a counting base as 60 has many divisors, being the smallest number divisible by all the numbers from 1 through to 6. A relatively large number such as 60 has the disadvantage, however, that to use it as a base would require us to introduce 60 separate symbols to stand for each of the numbers from zero up to fifty-nine.

One number is a *factor* of another if the first number divides into the second a whole number of times. For example, 6 is a factor of

$42 = 6 \times 7$ but 8 is not a factor of 28 as 8 into 28 goes 3 times with a remainder of 4. The property of having many factors is a handy one to have for the base of your number system, which is why twelve may have been a better choice than ten for our number base as 12 has 1, 2, 3, 4, 6, and 12 as its list of factors while 10 is divisible only by 1, 2, 5, and 10.

The effectiveness and sheer familiarity of our number system embues us with a false confidence and with some inhibitions. We feel happier with a single whole number than with an arithmetical expression. For example, most people would rather talk about 5969 than 47×127, although the two expressions represent the same thing. Only after 'working out the answer', 5969, do we feel that we 'have' the number and can look it in the eye. There is, however, an element of delusion in this as we have only written the number as a sum of powers of ten. The general shape of the number and other properties can be inferred more from the alternative form where the number is broken down into a product of factors. To be sure, this standard form, 5969, does allow direct comparison with other numbers that are expressed in the same way but it does not reveal the full nature of the number. In Chapter 4, you will see one reason why the factorized form of a number can be much more precious than its base ten representation, which can keep vital factors hidden.

One advantage that the ancients did have over us is that they were not mentally trapped within a decimal-style mindset. When it came to number patterns, it was natural for them to think in terms of special geometric properties that a particular number may or may not enjoy. For example, numbers such as 10 and 15 are *triangular*, something that is visible to us through the triangle of pins in ten-pin bowling and the triangular rack of fifteen red balls in snooker. But this is not something that comes to mind from the base ten displays of these numbers alone. The freedom the ancients enjoyed by default we can recapture by casting aside our base ten prejudices and telling ourselves that we are free to think of numbers in quite different ways.

Having emancipated ourselves in this way, we might choose to focus on factorizations of a number, that is to say the way the number can be written as a product of smaller numbers multiplied together. Factorizations reveal something of the number's inner structure. If we suspend the habit of thinking of numbers simply as servants of science and commerce, and take a little time to study them in their own right without reference to anything else, much is revealed that otherwise would remain hidden. The natures of individual numbers can manifest themselves in ordered patterns in nature, more subtle than mere triangles and squares, like the spiral head of a sunflower, which represents a so-called Fibonacci number, a number type that will be introduced in Chapter 5.

A glance at the prime number sequence

One of the glories of numbers is so self-evident that it may easily be overlooked – every one of them is unique. Each number has its own structure, its own character if you like, and the personality of individual numbers is important because when a particular number arises, its nature has consequences for the structure of the collection to which that number applies. There are also relationships between numbers that reveal themselves when we carry out the fundamental number operations of addition and multiplication. Clearly any counting number greater than 1 can be expressed as the sum of smaller numbers. However, when we start multiplying numbers together, we soon notice that there are some numbers that never turn up as the answer to our sums. These numbers are the *primes* and they represent the building blocks of multiplication.

A *prime number* is a number like 7 or 23 or 103, which has exactly two factors, those necessarily being 1 and the number itself. (The word *divisor* is also used as an alternative word for factor.) We do not count 1 as a prime as it has only one factor. The first prime then is 2, which is the only even prime and the following trio of odd numbers 3, 5, and 7 are all prime. Numbers greater than 1 that are not prime are called *composite* as they are composed of smaller numbers. The number $4 = 2 \times 2 = 2^2$ is the first composite number; 9 is the first odd composite number, and $9 = 3^2$ is also a square. With the number $6 = 2 \times 3$, we have the first truly composite number in that it is composed of two different factors that are greater than 1 but smaller than the number itself, while $8 = 2^3$ is the first proper *cube*, which is the word that means that the number is equal to some number raised to the power 3.

After the single-digit numbers, we have our chosen number base $10 = 2 \times 5$, which is special nonetheless being *triangular* in that $10 = 1 + 2 + 3 + 4$ (remember ten-pin bowling). We then have a pair of *twin primes* in 11 and 13, which are two consecutive odd numbers that are both prime, separated by the number 12, which in contrast has many factors for its size. Indeed, 12 is the first so-called *abundant number*, as the the sum of its *proper factors*, those less than the number itself, exceeds the number in question: $1 + 2 + 3 + 4 + 6 = 16$. The number $14 = 2 \times 7$ may look undistinguished but, as the paradoxical quip goes, being the *first* undistinguished number makes it distinguished after all. In $15 = 3 \times 5$, we have another triangular number and it is the first odd number that is the product of two proper factors. Of course, $16 = 2^4$ is not only a square but the first fourth power (after 1), making it very special indeed. The pair 17 and 19 are another pair of twin primes, and I leave the reader to make their own observations about the peculiar nature of the numbers 18, 20, and so on. For each you can make a claim to fame.

Returning to the primes, the first twenty of them are:

2, 3, 5, 7, 11, 13, 17, 19, 23, 29, 31, 37, 41, 43, 47, 53, 59, 61, 67, 71.

Clearly, near the very beginning of the number sequence, primes are commonplace as there is little opportunity for small numbers to have factorizations. After that, the primes become rarer. For example, there is only one triple of consecutive odd primes: the trio 3, 5, 7 is unique, as every third odd number is a multiple of 3, and so this can never happen again. The thinning process of prime occurrence is, however, quite leisurely and surprisingly erratic. For example, the thirties have only two primes, those being 31 and 37, yet immediately after 100 there are two 'consecutive' pairs of twin primes in 101, 103 and 107, 109.

The primes have been a source of fascination for thousands of years because they never run out (a claim that we shall justify in the next chapter) yet they arise among the natural numbers in a somewhat haphazard fashion. This mysterious and unpredictable facet of their nature is exploited in modern cryptography to safeguard confidential communication on the Internet, which is the subject of Chapter 4.

Checking for primality: prime divisibility tests

The most simple-minded way of finding all the primes up to a given number such as 100 is to write all the numbers down and cross off the composite numbers as you find them. The standard method based on this idea is called the *Sieve of Eratosthenes* and runs as follows. Begin by circling 2 and then cross off all the multiples of 2 (the other even numbers) in your list. Then return to the beginning, circle the first number you meet that has not been crossed off (which will be 3) and then cross off all its multiples in the remaining list. By repeating this process sufficiently often, the primes will emerge as those numbers that never get crossed out, although some will be circled and some not. For example, Figure 1 shows the workings of the sieve up to 60.

How do you know when you can stop sieving? You need to repeat this process until you circle a number that is greater than the square root of the largest number in your list. For instance, if you do your own sieve for all numbers up to 120, you will need to run

$$②③\ 4\ ⑤\ 6\ ⑦\ 8\ 9\ 10\ 11\ 12\ 13\ 14\ 15$$

$$16\ 17\ 18\ 19\ 20\ 21\ 22\ 23\ 24\ 25\ 26\ 27\ 28\ 29\ 30$$

$$31\ 32\ 33\ 34\ 35\ 36\ 37\ 38\ 39\ 40\ 41\ 42\ 43\ 44\ 45$$

$$46\ 47\ 48\ 49\ 50\ 51\ 52\ 53\ 54\ 55\ 56\ 57\ 58\ 59\ 60$$

1. Prime sieve: the primes up to 60 are the numbers not crossed out

through the sieve for multiples of 2, 3, 5, and 7, and when you circle 11 you can stop, as $11^2 = 121$. At that point, you will have circled as far as the first prime exceeding the square root of your biggest number (120 in this case) with the remaining primes sitting there untouched. All composite numbers will now have been crossed out as each is a multiple of one or more of 2, 3, 5, and 7.

It is not hard to see why the square root of the greatest number n in your list determines the number of passes you need to make. (When explaining properties of arbitrary numbers, mathematicians give names, in the form of symbols, for the subjects of the discussion. For numbers, these names are typically lower-case letters, such as m and n; the product of two numbers $m \times n$ is often abbreviated as mn.) Any listed composite number m will have a prime factor and its *smallest* prime factor must be no more than the square root of n, because the product of two or more numbers that exceed $\sqrt{n}$ is greater than n (and so also greater than m).

Another aspect of the question of primality is whether a particular given number n is prime or composite. To decide that, we can test n for division by each of the primes in turn up to $\sqrt{n}$ and if n passes all these tests it will be prime, and otherwise not. For that reason, it is handy to have some simple ways of testing for divisibility by each of the small primes, 2, 3, 5, 7, ... This need is easily catered for as follows.

It is very easy to test for divisibility by 2 and by 5 as these primes are the prime factors of our number base ten. In view of this, you only need to check the final digit of the number n in question: n is divisible by 2 exactly when its units digit is even (i.e. 0, 2, 4, 6, or 8), and n has 5 as a factor if and only if it ends in 0 or 5. No matter how many digits the number n has, we only need to check the last digit to determine whether we have a multiple of 2 or of 5. For primes that do not divide into 10, we need to do a bit more work but nevertheless there are simple tests for divisibility that are much quicker than resorting to doing the full division sum.

A number is divisible by 3 if and only if the same is true of the sum of its digits. For example, the sum of the digits of $n = 145, 373, 270, 099, 876, 790$ is 87 and $87 = 3 \times 29$ and so n is in this case divisible by 3. Of course, we can apply the test to the number 87 itself and indeed go on taking the sum of digits of the outcome at each stage until the result is obvious. Doing this for the given example produces the following sequence:

$$145, 373, 270, 099, 876, 790 \rightarrow 87 \rightarrow 15 \rightarrow 6 = 2 \times 3.$$

You will see that all the division tests listed here are so quick that you can handle numbers with dozens of digits with relative ease even though these numbers are billions of times greater than the biggest number with which your hand calculator can cope.

The tests given here for the remaining primes up to 20 are chosen because they are all of the same general type. These routines are all simple to apply, although it is less obvious why they work. Although the justifications are not recorded here, the proofs of their validity are not especially difficult.

Let's begin with a test for divisibility of a given number n by 7. Double the final digit of n and subtract that from the number that remains when that final digit is removed. The new number will be a multiple of 7 precisely when the same is true of n. We repeat this process until the outcome is obvious. As a simple example, let us take $n = 3465$: twice 5 is 10 so we take 10 from the 346 to get 336; next we go again, taking twice 6, which is 12 from the 33 to get $21 = 3 \times 7$, and so n is divisible by 7. If you have forgotten your seven times tables, we can go through again: subtracting twice 1 from 2 leaves us with 0, which is divisible by 7, as $\frac{0}{7} = 0$. (It is fine to divide zero by a whole number – it is the reverse, dividing by zero, that has no meaning.) Even a number in the tens of millions can be dealt with easily in this way. In this and subsequent examples, we simply list the output number at each stage of the *algorithm*, which is the name given for a mechanical process such as this one that solves a given type of problem.

$$n = 27,916,924 \rightarrow 2,791,684 \rightarrow 279,160 \rightarrow 27,916 \rightarrow$$
$$2,779 \rightarrow 259 \rightarrow 7$$

and so n is divisible by 7. Each time we run through the loop of instructions, we lose at least one digit, so the number of passes through the loop is about the same as the length of the number with which we begin.

To test whether or not n has a factor of 11, subtract the final digit from the remaining truncated number and repeat. For example, the next number is a multiple of 11 as our method reveals:

$$4,959,746 \rightarrow 495,968 \rightarrow 49,588 \rightarrow 4,950 \rightarrow 495$$
$$\rightarrow 44 = 4 \times 11.$$

To check for divisibility by 13, *add* four times the final digit to the remaining truncated number and precede as with 7 and 11. For instance, the next number turns out to have 13 as one of its prime factors:

$$11,264,331 \rightarrow 1,126,437 \rightarrow 112,671 \rightarrow 11,271$$
$$\rightarrow 1131 \rightarrow 117 \rightarrow 39 = 3 \times 13.$$

For 17 and for 19, we subtract five times the final digit in the case of 17, and add twice the final digit when testing if 19 is a factor, once more applying this step to the truncated number that remains, repeating the process as often as we need. For example, we test $18,905$ for divisibility by 17:

$$18,905 \rightarrow 1,865 \rightarrow 161 \rightarrow 11$$

so it is not a multiple of 17, but for 19, the test gives the opposite conclusion:

$$18,905 \rightarrow 1,900 = 100 \times 19.$$

Armed with this battery of tests, you can readily check the primality of all numbers up to 500 (as $23^2 = 529$ exceeds 500, so 19 is the largest potential prime factor that you need concern yourself with). For example, to settle the matter for 247, we just need to check for divisibility up to the prime 13 (as the square of the next prime, $17^2 = 289$, exceeds 247). Applying the test for 13, however, we learn from $247 \rightarrow (24 + 28) = 52 \rightarrow 13$, that we have a multiple of 13: $(247 = 19 \times 13)$.

The divisibility tests for primes can also be mounted in parallel to furnish divisibility tests for those numbers that are *square-free* products of these primes (numbers not divisible by the square of any prime) such as $42 = 2 \times 3 \times 7$: a number n will be divisible by 42 exactly when n passes the trio of divisibility tests for 2, 3, and 7. However, tests for those numbers that have square factors, such as $9 = 3^2$, do not come automatically, although it is the case that n has 9 as a factor if and only if that is true of the sum of the digits of n.

You might ask, after thousands of years, haven't those clever mathematicians come up with better and more sophisticated methods of testing for primality? The answer is yes. In 2002, a relatively quick way was discovered to test if a given number is prime. The so-called 'AKS primality test' does not, however, provide the factorization of the given number if it happens to be composite. The problem of finding the prime factors of a given number, although in principle solvable by trial, still seems practically intractable for extremely large integers, and for that reason it forms the basis of much ordinary encryption on the Internet, a subject to which we will return in Chapter 4. Before that we shall, in the next two chapters, look a little more closely at primes and factorization.

Chapter 2
The unending sequence of primes

How primes fit into the number jigsaw

How can we be sure that the primes do not become rarer and rarer and eventually peter out altogether? You might think that since there are infinitely many counting numbers and each can be broken down into a product of primes (something explained more carefully in a moment), there must then be infinitely many primes to do the job. Although this conclusion is true, it does not follow from the previous observations, for if we begin with a finite collection of primes, there is no end to the number of different numbers we can produce just using those given prime factors. Indeed, there are infinitely many different powers of any single prime: for example, the powers of the prime 2 are $2, 4, 8, 16, 32, 64, \cdots$. It is conceivable therefore that there are only finitely many primes and *every* number is a product of powers of those primes. What is more, we have no way of producing an unending series of different primes the way we can, for example, produce any number of squares, or multiples of a specific given number. When it comes to primes, we still have to go out hunting for them, so how can we be sure they do not become extinct?

We will all be sure by the end of this chapter, but first I will draw your attention to one simple 'pattern' among the primes worth noting. Every prime number, apart from 2 and 3, lies one side or the other of a multiple of 6. In other words, any prime after these first two has the form $6n \pm 1$ for some number n. (Remember that $6n$ is short for $6 \times n$ and the double symbol $\pm$ means plus or minus.) The reason for this is readily explained. Every number can be written in exactly one of the six forms $6n$, $6n \pm 1$, $6n \pm 2$, or $6n + 3$ as no number is more than three places away from some multiple of six. For example, $17 = (6 \times 3) - 1$, $28 = (6 \times 5) - 2$, $57 = (6 \times 9) + 3$; indeed, the six given forms appear in cyclic order, meaning that if you write down *any* six consecutive numbers, each of the forms will appear exactly once, after which they will reappear again and again, in the same order. It is evident that numbers of the forms $6n$ and $6n \pm 2$ are even, while any number of the form $6n + 3$ is divisible by 3. Therefore, with the obvious exceptions of 2 and 3, only numbers of the form $6n \pm 1$ can be prime. The case where *both* of the numbers $6n \pm 1$ are prime corresponds exactly to the twin primes: for example $(6 \times 18) \pm 1$ gives the pair 107, 109 mentioned in the first chapter. You might be tempted to conjecture that *at least one of* the two numbers $6n \pm 1$ is always prime – this is certainly true for the list of primes up to 100 but the first failure is not far away: $(6 \times 20) - 1 = 119 = 7 \times 19$, while $(6 \times 20) + 1 = 121 = 11^2$, so neither number is prime when we take $n = 20$.

And the principal reason why primes are important is that every number can be written as a product of prime numbers, and that can be done in essentially only one way. To find this special factorization, we just need to factorize the given number in some way and then continue factorizing any composite factors that appear until this can be done no more. For example, we could say that $120 = 2 \times 60$ and continue by breaking the composite factor of 60 down further to give:

$$120 = 2 \times 60 = 2 \times (2 \times 30) = 2 \times 2 \times (2 \times 15) = 2 \times 2 \times 2 \times 3 \times 5.$$

We say that the *prime factorization* of 120 is $2^3 \times 3 \times 5$. We could, however, have came to this by another route. For instance

$$120 = 12 \times 10 = (3 \times 4) \times (2 \times 5) = (3 \times (2 \times 2)) \times (2 \times 5)$$

but rearranging the prime factors from least to greatest still yields the same result as before: $120 = 2^3 \times 3 \times 5$.

At least it did in that example, and this behaviour may be more or less familiar to you, but how can you be sure that this applies to every number? It is clear enough that any number can be broken down into a product of primes but, since there is in general more than one way of tackling this task, how can we be sure that the process will always deliver the same final result? This is an important question, so I will take a few moments to give an outline of the reasoning that allows us to be absolutely sure about this. It is a consequence of another special property of prime numbers that we shall call the *euclidean property*: if a prime number is a factor of a product of two or more numbers, then it is a factor of one of the numbers in that product. For example, 7 is a factor of $8 \times 35 = 280$ (as the product $280 = 7 \times 40$) and we note that 7 is a factor of 35. This property characterizes primes as no composite number can give you the same guarantee: for example, we see that 6 is a factor of $8 \times 15 = 120$ (as $120 = 6 \times 20$) yet 6 is not a factor of either 8 or 15.

The fact that primes always have the above property can be proved using an argument based on what is known as the Euclidean Algorithm, which will be explained in Chapter 4. If we take this on trust for the time being, it is not too difficult to explain why no number could have two different prime factorizations, for suppose there were such a number. There then would be a smallest one that behaved in this way: let us denote it by n and so n has two prime factorizations which, when the prime factors are written in ascending order, are *not* identical. We shall show that this leads to contradiction and so must be false.

If these two factorizations of n had a prime p in common, we could cancel p from both and obtain two different prime

factorizations of the smaller number $\frac{n}{p}$. Since n is the smallest
number with two distinct prime factorizations, this is not possible
and so the sets of primes involved in each factorization of n must
have no prime in common. Now take one prime p that occurs in
one of these factorizations of n. Since this prime p is a factor of n,
it follows that p is a factor of the second factorization, and so, by
the euclidean property, p is a factor of one of the primes, q say, of
the second factorization. *But since q and p are both prime*, this is
only possible if $q = p$, a possibility that we have already discounted
as the two factorizations of n have no common prime. And so we
arrive at a final contradiction, showing that it is impossible for
such a number n to exist. Therefore we conclude that the prime
factorization of every number is unique.

It is worth noting that the uniqueness of prime factorization
would not hold if we included the number 1 among the primes, as
we can adjoin any power of 1 to a factorization and the product
retains the same value. This shows that 1 is fundamentally
different in nature to the primes, and so it is right to frame the
definition of prime number in a way that excludes 1 from the
collection.

Euclid's infinity of primes

Let us return to the question as to how we know that the primes
go on forever and that there is no way past them. If someone
claimed that 101 is the largest prime, you can refute him at once by
showing that 103 has no factors (except for 1 and 103) and so 103
is a larger prime. Your friend might then concede that he made a
slip and that he should have said that it was 103 that is the largest
prime of all. You could then show him up again by demonstrating
that 107 is also prime, but your friend might still persist in his
error by adjusting his position to the largest prime number on
view. He could even retreat a little further and admit that he does
not know the identity of the largest prime but nevertheless
continue to claim that he is certain that there is one.

The best way to settle this question would be to show that, given any conceivable finite collection of primes, we can produce a new prime not in the list. For example, if someone claimed there was a largest odd number out there somewhere, you could refute him by saying that if n is odd, then $n + 2$ is a larger odd number, so there cannot be a largest odd number. This approach, however, is not so easy for the primes – given a finite list of primes, we have no way of using the collection to manufacture a prime that is demonstrably bigger than all of them. Perhaps there is a biggest prime after all? How are we to know that our stubborn friend isn't right?

Euclid of Alexandria (c. 300 BC), the Greek mathematician and father of all things euclidean, did however know. Given a list $p_1, p_2, \cdots, p_k$ where each of the p_i denotes a different prime, he could not find a way of generating a new prime, so he reverted to an argument that is one step more subtle. He showed that there must be one or more new primes *within a certain range of numbers* (but his argument does not allow us to locate exactly where to find a prime within that range).

It goes like this. Let $p_1, p_2, \cdots, p_k$ be the list of the first k primes say, and consider the number n that is one more than the product of all these primes, so that $n = p_1 p_2 \cdots p_k + 1$. Either n is a prime, or is divisible by a prime smaller than itself, which cannot be any of $p_1, p_2, \cdots, p_k$, as if p is any one of these primes, then dividing n by p will leave a remainder of 1. It follows that any prime divisor of n is a new prime that is greater that all the primes $p_1, p_2, \cdots, p_k$ and no more than n itself. In particular, it follows from this that there can be no finite list of primes that contains every prime number, and so the sequence of primes continues on forever and will never be exhausted. Euclid's eternal proof of the infinity of primes is among the most admired in all of mathematics.

Although Euclid's argument does not tell exactly where to find the next prime number, the overall frequency of the primes is now quite well understood. For example, if we take any two numbers, a and b say, with no common factor and consider the sequence $a, a + b, a + 2b, a + 3b, \cdots$, it was shown by the German mathematician Johann Dirichlet (1805–59) that infinitely many members of such a sequence are prime. (Of course, there is no hope if a and b do have a common factor, d say, as then every member in the list is also a multiple of d, and so is not prime.) When $a = 1$ and $b = 2$, we get the sequence of odd numbers which we know, by Euclid's proof, contains infinitely many prime numbers. Indeed, it can be shown through fairly simple adaptations of Euclid's argument that other special cases such as the sequence of numbers of the forms $3 + 4n$, $5 + 6n$, and $5 + 8n$ (as n runs through the successive values $1, 2, 3, \cdots$), each have infinitely many primes. The general result of Dirichlet is, however, very difficult to prove.

Another simply stated result is that there is always at least one prime number greater than any given number n but less than $2n$ (for $n \geq 2$). (As an aid to memory, inequality signs such as this one, which stands for greater than or equal to, always point to the smaller quantity.) This fact, historically known as *Bertrand's Postulate*, can be proved using quite elementary mathematics, although the proof is itself quite tricky. We can verify the postulate for n up to 4000 by making use of the following list of primes. First observe that each number in the list after the initial prime 2 is smaller than twice its predecessor:

$$2, 3, 5, 7, 13, 23, 43, 83, 163, 317, 631, 1259, 2503, 4001.$$

For each n in the range up to 4000, take the largest prime p in the list that is no more than n; the next prime q then lies in the range $n < q < 2n$ and this then ensures that Bertrand's Postulate holds for all n up to 4000. For example, for $n = 100$, $p = 83$, and then $q = 163 < 2 \times 100$. A subtle argument involving the size of the so-called central binomial coefficients (introduced in Chapter 5) then shows that the postulate is also true for n larger than 4000.

However, we do not have to go too far before meeting similar-sounding problems that as yet remain unsolved. For example, no one knows if there is always a prime between any two consecutive squares. Another observation is that there seems to be enough primes to ensure that every even number n greater than 2 is the sum of two of them (*Goldbach's Conjecture*). This has been directly verified for n up to 10^{18}. We might then hope for a proof along the lines above for Bertrand's Postulate, where we show that beyond a certain specified integer N, we may introduce a comparison based on what is known about the distribution of the primes to ensure that there will always be at least one solution in primes p, q to the equation $p + q = 2n$ for any even number $2n \geq N$. This still eludes us, although there are weaker results along these lines – for example, it has been known since 1939 that every sufficiently large odd number is the sum of at most three prime numbers and that every even number is the sum of no more than 300,000 primes. Proof of the full Goldbach Conjecture still seems a long way off.

A simple result that has something of the flavour of the argument type referred to above is that there is a number n less than 4 billion that can be written as the sum of four different cubes in ten distinct ways. It is known that $1729 = 1^3 + 12^3 = 9^3 + 10^3$ is the smallest number that is the sum of *two* cubes in two different ways. However, we do not necessarily have to identify the number n in order to know that it must exist. Sometimes it is possible to know for certain that there are solutions to a problem, without actually finding any of those solutions explicitly.

In this case, we begin by noting that if we take four different numbers no more than a fixed integer m and form the sum of their cubes, the result is less than $4m^3$. However, if $m = 1000$, then an elementary calculation shows that the number of sums of four different cubes is more than 10 times the number $4m^3$, from which it follows that *some* number $n \leq 4m^3 = 4,000,000,000$ must be the sum of four cubes in at least ten different ways. The details involve calculations using binomial coefficients (introduced in Chapter 5) and are not especially difficult.

The global picture of prime distribution is summed up by the observation of the leading 19th-century German mathematician and physicist Karl Friedrich Gauss (1777–1855) that $p(n)$, the number of primes up to the number n, is approximately given by $n/\log n$ and that the approximation becomes more and more accurate as n increases. For example, if we take n to be one million, the ratio of $n/\log n$ suggests that, up to that stage, about one number in every 12.7 should be prime. Gauss's observation, which in detail says something more precise, was not proved until 1896. The logarithm function referred to here is the so-called *natural logarithm*, which is not based on powers of 10, but rather on powers of a special number e, which is approximately equal to 2.718. We shall hear more of this very famous number e in Chapter 6.

The most celebrated undecided question in number theory is the Riemann Hypothesis, which can only be explained in terms of complex numbers, which we have yet to introduce. However, I mention it here as the object of the question can be reformulated using the uniqueness of prime factorization to involve a certain infinite product featuring all the primes. This leads to an interpretation which says that the Hypothesis implies that the overall distribution of the primes is very regular in that, in the long run, primality will apparently occur randomly. Of course, whether or not a particular number is a prime is not a random event but what is meant is that primality, in the realm of the very large, takes on the mantle of randomness, with no additional pattern or structure to emerge. Many a number theorist has a heartfelt wish to see this 150-year-old conjecture settled in their own lifetime.

Since they represent so natural a sequence, it is almost irresistible to search for patterns among the primes. There are, however, no genuinely useful formulas for prime numbers. That is to say, there is no known rule that allows you to generate all prime numbers or even to calculate a sequence that consists entirely of different primes. There are some neat formulas but they are of little practical worth, some of them even require knowledge of the prime sequence to calculate their value so that they are essentially a cheat. Expressions such as $n^2 + n + 41$ are known as *polynomials*, and this one is a particularly rich source of primes. For example, putting n = 1, 7, and 20 in turn yields the primes 43, 107, and 461 respectively. Indeed, the output of this expression is prime for all values of n from $n = 0$ to $n = 39$. At the same time, however, it is clear that this polynomial will let us down when we put $n = 41$, as the result will have 41 as a factor, and indeed it fails for $n = 40$ as

$$40^2 + 40 + 41 = 40(40 + 1) + 41 = 40 \times 41 + 41 = (40 + 1)41 = 41^2.$$

In general, it is quite straightforward to show that no polynomial of this kind can yield a formula for primes, even if we allow powers higher than 2 to enter the expression.

It is possible to devise tests for primality of a number that can be stated in a few words. However, to be of use they would need to be quicker, at least in some cases, than the direct verification procedure described in Chapter 1. A famous result goes by the name of Wilson's Theorem. Its statement involves the use of numbers called *factorials*, which we will meet again in Chapter 5. The number $n!$, read 'n factorial', is just the product of all numbers up to n. For example, $5! = 5 \times 4 \times 3 \times 2 = 120$. Wilson's Theorem is then a very succinct statement: a number p is prime if and only if p is a factor of $1 + (p - 1)!$.

The proof of this result is not very difficult, and indeed in one direction it is nearly obvious: if p were composite, so that $p = ab$ say, then since both a and b are less than p, they each occur as factors of $(p - 1)!$ and so p is a divisor of this factorial as well. It follows that when we divide $1 + (p - 1)!$ by p, we will obtain a remainder of 1. (The case where $a = b$ requires a little more thought.) This is very reminiscent of Euclid's proof for the infinity of primes. It follows that *if* p is a factor of $1 + (p - 1)!$ *then* p must be prime. The converse is a little harder to prove: *if* p is prime *then* p is a factor of $1 + (p - 1)!$. This, however, is the surprising direction of the theorem, although the reader can easily verify particular cases: for example, the prime 5 is indeed a factor of $1 + 4! = 1 + 24 = 25$.

What Wilson's Theorem does is convert the problem of determining whether or not p is prime from a series of division problems (checking division by all primes up to $\sqrt{p}$) into a single division problem. However, the subject of the division, $1 + (p - 1)!$, is huge even for quite small values of p. Despite being a concise statement, Wilson's Theorem is of no real use in identifying particular prime numbers. For example, to check that 13 is prime by Wilson would require us to verify that 13 is a factor of $1 + 12! = 479, 001, 601$. (But by applying the divisibility test for 13 in Chapter 1, the reader can check that Wilson was right!) Compare this to the labour involved in simply checking that 13 is divisible by neither 2 nor 3. Although Wilson's Theorem is not useful in prime verification, it has more than ornamental value and can be used to demonstrate other theoretical results.

As a final observation, we can exploit factorials, which by design have many factors, in order to prove that no *arithmetic* sequence of numbers, that is to say one of the form $a, a + b, a + 2b, a + 3b, \cdots$ can consist *only* of primes as it is possible to show that the gap between successive primes can be arbitrarily large while the common difference between consecutive members of the previous sequence is fixed at b. To see this, consider the sequence of n consecutive integers:

$$(n + 1)! + 2, (n + 1)! + 3, (n + 1)! + 4, \cdots, (n + 1)! + n + 1.$$

Each of these numbers is composite, as the first is divisible by 2 (as each of the terms has 2 as a factor), the second is divisible by 3, the next by 4, and so on up until the final one in the list, which has

$n + 1$ as a factor. We therefore have, for any given n, a sequence of n consecutive numbers, none of which are prime.

Instead of focusing on numbers with the fewest possible factors (the primes), we shall in the next chapter turn to numbers with many factors, although we shall discover that here too there are surprising links to some very special prime numbers.

Chapter 3
Perfect and not so perfect numbers

Perfection in a number

It is often easy to find peculiar properties of small numbers that characterize them – for instance, 3 is the only number that is the sum of all the previous numbers, while 2 is the only even prime (making it the oddest prime of all). The number 6 has a truly unique property in that it is both the sum and product of all of its smaller factors: $6 = 1 + 2 + 3 = 1 \times 2 \times 3$.

The Pythagoreans called a number like 6 *perfect*, meaning that the number is the sum of its proper factors, as we shall call them, which are the divisors strictly smaller than the number itself. This kind of perfection is indeed very rare. The first five perfect numbers are 6, 28, 496, 8128, and 33,550,336. A lot is known about the even perfect numbers but, to this day, no one has been able to answer the basic question of the Ancients as to whether there are infinitely many of these special numbers. What is more, no one has found an odd one, nor proved that there are none. Any odd perfect number must be extremely large and there is a long list of special properties that such a number must possess in consequence of its odd perfection. However, all these restrictions have not as yet legislated such a number out of existence – conceivably, these special properties serve to direct our search for the elusive first odd perfect number, which may yet be awaiting discovery.

The even perfects were known to Euclid to have a tight connection with a very special sequence of primes, known to us as the *Mersenne primes* named after Marin Mersenne (1588–1648), a 17th-century French monk.

A *Mersenne number m* is one of the form $2^p - 1$, where p is itself a prime. If you take, by way of example, the first four primes, 2, 3, 5, and 7, the first four Mersenne numbers are seen to be: 3, 7, 31, and 127, which the reader can quickly verify as prime. If p were not prime, suppose $p = ab$ say, then $m = 2^p - 1$ is certainly not prime either, as it can be verified that in these circumstances the number m has $2^a - 1$ as a factor. However, if p is prime then the corresponding Mersenne number is often a prime, or so it seems.

And Euclid explained, back in 300 BC, that once you have a prime Mersenne number then there is a perfect number that goes with it, that number being $P = 2^{p-1}(2^p - 1)$. The reader can soon verify that the first four Mersenne primes do indeed give the first four perfect numbers listed above: for example, using the third prime 5 as our seed we get the perfect number $P = 2^4(2^5 - 1) = 16 \times 31 = 496$, the third perfect number in the previous list. (The factors of P are the powers of 2 up to 2^{p-1}, together with the same list of numbers multiplied by the prime $2^p - 1$. It is now an exercise in summing what are known as geometric series (explained in Chapter 5) to check that the proper factors of P do indeed sum to P.)

What is more, in the 18th century the great Swiss mathematician Leonhard Euler (1707–83) (pronounced 'Oiler') proved the reverse implication in that every even perfect number is of this type. In this way, Euclid and Euler together established a one-to-one match between the Mersenne primes and the even perfect numbers. However, the next natural question is, are all the Mersenne numbers prime? Sadly not, and failure is close at hand as the fifth Mersenne number equals $2^{11} - 1 = 2,047 = 23 \times 89$. Indeed, we do not even know if the sequence of Mersenne primes runs out or not – perhaps after a certain point all the Mersenne numbers will turn out to be composite.

The Mersenne numbers are natural prime candidates all the same, as it can be shown that any proper divisor, if one exists, of a Mersenne number m has the very special form $2kp + 1$. For example, when $p = 11$, by dent of this result, we need only check for division by primes of the form $22k + 1$. The two prime factors, 23 and 89, correspond to the values $k = 1$ and $k = 4$ respectively. This fact about divisors of Mersenne numbers also provides a bonus in that it affords us a second way of seeing that there must be infinitely many primes, for it shows that the smallest prime divisor of $2^p - 1$ exceeds p, and so p cannot be the largest prime. Since this applies to every prime p, we conclude that there is no largest prime and the prime sequence runs on forever.

Since we have no way of producing primes at will, there is, at any one time, a largest known prime and nowadays the champion is always a Mersenne prime, thanks to the international GIMPS venture (Great Internet Mersenne Prime Search). This is a collaborative project of volunteers, which began in 1996. The project uses thousands of personal computers working in parallel, which test Mersenne numbers for primality using a specially devised cocktail of tailor-made algorithms. The current world champion, announced in August 2008, is $2^p - 1$ where $p = 43, 112, 609$, although a new Mersenne prime was found in April 2009 with $p = 42, 643, 801$. These numbers have about 13 million digits and would take thousands of pages to write down in ordinary base ten notation.

Less than perfect numbers

Traditional number lore often focused on individual numbers thought to have special, if not magical, properties such as those that are perfect. However, a number *pair* with a similar trait is 220 and 284, the first *amicable pair*, meaning that the proper factors of each sums to the other – a kind of perfection extended to a couple. The reknowned amateur French mathematician Pierre de Fermat (1601–65) found other amicable pairs, such as 17,296 and 18,416, while Euler discovered dozens more. Surprisingly, they both missed the small pair of 1184 and 1210, found by 16-year-old Nicolò Paganini in 1866. We can of course try to go beyond pairs and look for perfect triples, quadruples, and so on. Longer cycles are rare but do crop up.

We can begin with any number, find the sum of its proper divisors, and repeat the process, forming what is known as the number's *aliquot sequence*. The result is often a little disappointing in that typically we get a chain that heads to 1 quite rapidly, at which point the process stalls. For example, even beginning with a promising-looking number such as 12, the chain is short:

$$12 \to (1 + 2 + 3 + 4 + 6) = 16 \to (1 + 2 + 4 + 8) = 15 \to (1 + 3 + 5) = 9$$

$$9 \to (1 + 3) = 4 \to (1 + 2) = 3 \to 1.$$

The trouble is, once you hit a prime, you are finished. The perfect numbers are of course exceptions, each giving us a little loop, while an amicable pair leads to a two-cycle: $220 \to 284 \to 220 \to \cdots$. Numbers that lead to cycles longer than two are called *sociable*. They were not studied at all until the 20th century as no one had ever found any. Even today, no number that leads to a three-cycle has been discovered, although there are now 120 known cycles of length four. The first examples were found by P. Poulet in 1918. The first is a five-cycle:

$$12,496 \to 14,288 \to 15,472 \to 14,536 \to 14,264 \to 12,496.$$

Poulet's second example is quite stunning, and to this day no other cycle has been found that comes close to matching it: starting with 14, 316 we obtain a cycle of length 28. All other known cycles have length less than 10. To the present day, there are no theorems on amicable and sociable numbers as beautiful as those of Euclid and Euler on perfect numbers. However, modern computing power

has led to something of an experimental renaissance in this kind
of topic and there is more that can be said.

We can divide all numbers into three types, *deficient, perfect,* and
abundant according to whether the sum of their proper divisors is
less than, is equal to, or exceeds the number itself. For example, as
we have already seen, 12 is an abundant number, as are 18 and 24
as the respective sums of their proper divisors are 21 and 36.

A naive search for abundance among the integers might lead you
to guess that the abundant numbers are simply the multiples of 6.
Certainly, any number greater than 6 of the form $6n$ is abundant,
as the factors of $6n$ must include 1, 2, 3 together with n, $2n$, and
$3n$, which sum to more than the original number $6n$. This
observation can be extended, however, to show that abundance is
not just about sixes as we can argue the same way for any perfect
number k. The factors of nk will include 1 together with all the
factors of the perfect number k, each multiplied by n so that the
sum of all the proper factors of nk will add up to at least $1 + nk$,
and therefore any multiple of a perfect number will be abundant.
For example, 28 is perfect and hence $2 \times 28 = 56, 3 \times 28 = 84$ etc.
are all abundant.

And so we see that multiples of perfect numbers and indeed, by
the same token, multiples of abundant numbers are themselves
abundant. Having made this discovery, you still might guess that
all abundant numbers are simply multiples of perfect numbers.
However, you don't have to look too much further to find the first
exception to this conjecture, for 70 is abundant but none of its
factors are perfect. Indeed, 70 is the first so-called weird number,
but not exactly for this reason (the source of this label is explained
below).

Despite these discoveries, you might still think it likely that, just as
there seem to be no odd perfect numbers, there are no odd
abundant numbers either. In other words, our modified conjecture

might be that all odd numbers are deficient. Calculation of the aliquot sums of the first few hundred odd numbers would seem to confirm this theory, but the claim is eventually debunked upon testing 945, which has 975 as the sum of its proper divisors. Now the floodgates open as any multiple of an abundant number is abundant, and in particular the odd multiples of 945 immediately supply us with infinitely many more odd abundant numbers.

If we act a little more shrewdly, however, we can discover this counter-example more quickly than if we unthinkingly test one odd number after another. For a number to have a large aliquot sum, it needs lots of factors and large factors at that, which themselves come from being paired with small factors. We can therefore *build* numbers with large aliquot sums by multiplying small primes together. If we are focusing on odd numbers only, we should look at those that are products of the first few odd primes, which are $3, 5, 7$, etc. This rule of thumb would soon lead you to test $3^3 \times 5 \times 7 = 945$ and thereby discover the abundance property among the odd numbers also.

It is not that unusual to find that the smallest example of a number with certain properties turns out to be rather large. This is especially true if the specified properties implicitly build a certain factor structure into the required numbers. The smallest example can then turn out to be gigantic, although not necessarily hard to find if we exploit the given properties in our quest for the solution. An example of a number riddle of this kind is to find the smallest number that is five times a cube and three times a fifth power. The answer is

$$7, 119, 140, 625 = 5 \times 1125^3 = 3 \times 75^5.$$

The reason why the smallest solution is in the billions, however, is not hard to see. Any solution n has to have the form $3^r 5^s m$ for some positive powers r and s and where the remaining prime factors are collected together into a single integer m that is not divisible by 3 or 5. If we first focus on the possible values of r, we observe that since n is 5 times *a cube*, the exponent r must be a multiple of 3, and since n is 3 times a *5th power*, the number $r - 1$ has to be a multiple of 5. The smallest r that satisfies both these conditions simultaneously is $r = 6$. In the same way, the exponent s has to be a multiple of 5, while $s - 1$ has to be a mutiple of 3 and the least s that fits the bill is $s = 10$. To make n as small as possible, we take $m = 1$ and so $n = 3^6 \times 5^{10} = 3(3 \times 5^2)^5 = 3 \times 75^5$, so that n is indeed 3 times a 5th power and at the same time $n = 5(3^2 \times 5^3)^3 = 5 \times 1125^3$, and so n is also 5 times a cube.

An even more extreme example is the celebrated Cattle Problem, attributed to Archimedes (287–212 BC), the greatest mathematician of antiquity. It was not solved until the 19th century. The smallest herd of cattle that satisfies all the imposed constraints in the original 44-line poem is represented by a number with over 200,000 digits!

A warning to be gleaned from all this is that numbers do not display their full variety until we move into the realms of the very large. For that reason, the mere fact that there are no odd perfect numbers with fewer than 300 digits does not in itself give grounds for saying that they 'probably' do not exist. All the same, it is the case that some leading experts in the field would be astonished if one ever turned up.

Returning once again to the general behaviour of aliquot sequences, there are still simple questions that may be put that no one can answer. What possibilities are open to aliquot sequences? If the sequence hits a prime, it will immediately terminate thereafter at 1, and cannot do this in any other way. If this does not happen, the sequence could be cyclic and so represent a sociable number. There is, however, another related possibility that is revealed by calculating the aliquot sequence of 95:

$$95 = 5 \times 19 \rightarrow (1 + 5 + 19) = 25 = 5 \times 5 \rightarrow (1 + 5) = 6 \rightarrow 6 \rightarrow 6 \rightarrow \cdots .$$

What has happened here is that although 95 is not itself a sociable number, its aliquot sequence eventually hits a sociable number (or more precisely in this case, the perfect number 6) and then goes into a cycle.

There is conceivably one possibility remaining, that being that the aliquot sequence of a number never hits a prime nor a sociable number, in which case the sequence must be an unending series of different numbers, none of which are either prime or sociable. Is this possible? Surprisingly, no one knows. What is more surprising is that there are small numbers whose aliquot sequence remain unknown (and thereby remain candidates for having such an infinite aliquot sequence). The first of these mysterious numbers is 276, whose sequence begins:

$$276 \rightarrow 396 \rightarrow 696 \rightarrow 1104 \rightarrow 1872 \rightarrow 3770 \rightarrow 3790 \rightarrow$$
$$\rightarrow 3050 \rightarrow 2716 \rightarrow 2772 \rightarrow \cdots$$

but no one knows exactly where it ends up.

It might well be that the reader would like to explore a little on their own, in which case I should let you in on the secret of how to calculate the so-called *aliquot function* $a(n)$ from the prime factorization of n – take the product of all terms $(p^{k+1} - 1)/(p - 1)$, where p^k is the highest prime power of the prime p that divides n, and then subtract n itself. For example, $276 = 2^2 \times 3 \times 23$ and so

$$a(276) = \frac{2^3 - 1}{2 - 1} \times \frac{3^2 - 1}{3 - 1} \times \frac{23^2 - 1}{23 - 1} - 276 =$$
$$7 \times 4 \times 24 - 276 = 672 - 276 = 396$$

as indicated by the second term in the aliquot sequence for 276 listed above.

There is no end to the types of numbers that we can introduce by giving a name to the numbers n that bear a certain relationship to the aliquot function. As we have already mentioned, n is *perfect* if $a(n) = n$ and *abundant* if $a(n) > n$. A *semiperfect number* n is one that is the sum of some of its proper divisors (those less than n), so it follows from the definition that all semiperfect numbers are either perfect or abundant. For example, 18 is semiperfect as $18 = 3 + 6 + 9$. A number is called *weird* if it is abundant but *not* semiperfect, and the smallest weird number is 70.

One can take the view that the topic is becoming too miscellaneous in nature – bestowing names on rather arbitrarily defined classes of numbers does not of its own accord make them interesting. We should know when to stop. That said, it is worth appreciating that the underlying strategies used to tackle these new questions are yet reminiscent of what Euclid and Euler showed us in relation to perfect numbers. You will recall that what Euclid proved was that *if* a Mersenne number was prime *then* another number was even and perfect. Euler then proved conversely that all even perfect numbers arise from this approach. In the 9th century, the Persian mathematician Thabit ibn Qurra introduced for any number n a triple of numbers which, *if all prime*, allowed the construction of an amicable pair. Thabit's construction was generalized further by Euler in the 18th century, but even this enhanced formulation only seems to yield a few amicable pairs and there are many amicable pairs that do *not* arise from this construction. (There are now nearly 12 million known pairs of amicable numbers.) In modern times, a similar approach by Kravitz gives a construction of weird numbers from certain numbers should they happen to be prime, and this formula has successfully found a very large weird number with more than fifty digits.

These last two chapters have served to familiarize the reader with factors and factorization of the natural numbers, or *positive integers* are they are also known, illustrated through a variety of examples. This will stand you in good stead for the upcoming chapter, in which you will learn how those ideas are applied to contemporary cryptography, the science of secrets.

Chapter 4

Cryptography: the secret life of primes

The reader will now appreciate that the collection of counting numbers has, from the earliest times, been recognized as the repository of riddles and secrets, many of which have never been revealed to this day. For many of us, this is enough to justify the continued serious study of numbers but others may take a different attitude. Intriguing and difficult as these conundrums may be, it might be imagined that they have little bearing on the rest of human wisdom. But that would be a mistake.

Over the last few decades it has emerged that ordinary secrets, of the kinds we all indulge in from time to time, can be coded as secrets about numbers. This has now all been put into practice and our most precious secrets, whether they be commercial or military, personal or financial, political or downright scandalous, can all be protected on the Internet by masking them using secrets about ordinary counting numbers.

Secrets turned into numbers

How is all this possible? Any information, whether it be a poem or a bank statement, a blueprint for a weapon or a computer program, can be described in words. We may, however, need to augment the alphabet that is used to make up our words beyond the ordinary letters of the alphabet. We may include number symbols, punctuation symbols including special symbols for space between ordinary words, but it is nonetheless the case that all the information we wish to transfer, including instructions for producing pictures and diagrams, can be expressed using words from an alphabet of, let us say, no more than one thousand symbols. We can count these symbols and so represent each symbol uniquely as a number. Since numbers are cheap and inexhaustible, it may be convenient to use numbers all with the same number of digits for this purpose (so, for example, every symbol was represented uniquely by its own four-digit PIN). We could string the symbols together as required to give one big long number that told the entire story. We can even work in binary if we wish and so devise a way of translating any information into one long string of 0s and 1s. Every message we might ever want to send could then be coded as a binary string and then decoded at the other end by a suitably programmed computer, to be compiled in ordinary language that we can all comprehend. This then is the first realization: in order to send messages between one person and another, it is enough, both in theory and in practice, to be able to send numbers from one person to another.

Turning messages into numbers, however, is not the big idea. To be sure, the exact process by which all the information is digitized may be hidden from the general public, but nonetheless is not the source of protection from eavesdroppers. Indeed, from the point of view of cryptography, we may identify any message, the so-called *plaintext*, with the number that represents it and thereby think of that number as the plaintext itself, as it is assumed that anyone has access to the wherewithal that will allow one to be transformed into the other. Secrecy only comes on to the scene when we mask these plaintext numbers with other numbers.

Let me introduce you to the fictitious characters that populate the various scenarios of cryptography, which is the study of *ciphers* (secret codes). We imagine Alice and Bob, who want to communicate with each other, without being overheard by the eavesdropper, Eve. Instinctively, we might sympathize with Alice and Bob, picturing Eve as up to no good, but of course the reverse may be true, with Eve representing a noble policing authority striving to protect us all from the evil plots of Bob and Alice.

Whatever the moral standing of the participants, there is an age-old approach that Alice and Bob may employ to cut Eve out of the conversation even if Eve intercepts messages that pass between them. They can encrypt the data using a cipher key that is known only to Alice and Bob. What they may arrange to do is to meet in a secure environment where they exchange with one another a secret number (let us say 57) and then return home. When the time comes, Alice will want to send a message to Bob and, just to illustrate the point, suppose that message can be represented by a single digit between 1 and 9. On the big day, Alice wants to send the message '8' to Bob. She takes her message and adds the secret ingredient, that is to say she masks its true value by adding 57 and so sends the message to Bob, across an insecure channel, of 8 + 57 = 65. Bob receives this message and subtracts the secret number to retrieve Alice's plaintext 65 − 57 = 8.

The nefarious Eve, however, has a good idea what these two are up to and indeed does manage to intercept the enciphered message, 65. But what can she do with it? She may know, as we do, that Alice has sent one of the nine possible messages 1, 2, 3, · · · , 9 to Bob and also knows that she has encrypted it by adding a number to the message, which must therefore lie between 65 − 9 = 55 and 65 − 1 = 64. However, because she cannot tell which of these nine masking numbers has been used (she isn't in on the secret), she is none the wiser as to the actual plaintext message that Alice sent to Bob, which is still just as likely to be any one of the nine possibilities. All she knows is that Alice has sent a message to Bob but has no idea what it is.

It might seem that Alice and Bob are now impervious to the malice of Eve and can communicate with impunity using the magic number 57 to disguise all they have to say. That, however, isn't quite the case. They would be well advised to change that number, indeed they are better off using a new secret number every time because if they don't, the system will begin to leak information to Eve. For example, say in a future week Alice wants to send to Bob the same message number 8. Everything would run as before and once again Eve would intercept the mysterious number 65 from the airwaves, but this time it would tell her something. Eve would know that, whatever this message is, it is the same message that Alice sent to Bob in the first week – this is just the sort of thing Alice and Bob would not want Eve to know.

This, however, looks to be no big problem for Alice and Bob. When they first meet up to 'exchange keys', instead of agreeing on just one secret number, Alice could provide Bob with a long ordered list of thousands of secret numbers, to be used one after another, thus avoiding the possibility of meaningful coincidences in their publicly available communications.

And this is indeed what is done in practice. This kind of cipher system is known in the trade as a *one-time pad*. The sender and receiver mask their plaintext with a single-use number from the 'pad'. That leaf of the pad is then discarded by both the sender and receiver after the message has been sent and deciphered. The one-time pad represents a completely secure system in that the insecure message that travels in the public domain contains no information about the content of the plaintext. To decipher it, the interceptor needs to get hold of that pad in order to obtain the encryption–decryption key.

Keys and key exchange

It would seem then that the problem of secure communication is completely solved by the one-time pad and, in a way, that is true. The difficulty with ciphers like the one-time pad, however, is that they require the participants to exchange a key in order to use them. In practice, this takes a lot of effort. For high-level communications, such as those between the White House and the Kremlin, money is no object and the necessary exchanges are carried out under conditions of maximum security. In the everyday world on the other hand, all sorts of people and institutions need to communicate with one another in a confidential fashion. The participants cannot afford the time and energy required to secure key exchanges and, even if this were arranged by a trusted third party, it can be an expensive business.

The common drawback of all ciphers that had been used for thousands of years up until the 1970s was that they were all *symmetric ciphers*, meaning that the encryption and decryption keys were essentially the same. Whether it was the simple alphabet-shift cipher of Julius Caesar, or the complex Enigma Cipher of the Second World War, they all suffered from the common weakness that once an adversary learned how you were encoding your messages, they could decode them just as well as you. In order to make use of a symmetric cipher, the communicating partners needed to exchange the cipher key in a secure way.

It seemed to have been tacitly assumed that this was an unavoidable principle of secret codes – for a cipher to be used the partners needed, somehow or other, to exchange the key to the cipher and to keep it secret from the enemy. Indeed, this might be regarded as mathematical common sense.

This is the kind of assumption that makes a mathematician suspicious. We are dealing with what is essentially a mathematical situation, so one would expect such a 'principle' to be well founded and represented by some form of mathematical theorem. Yet there was no such theorem, and the reason that there was no such theorem was that the principle simply is not valid, as the following thought experiment reveals.

Transmission of a secure message from Alice to Bob does not in itself necessitate the exchange of the key to a cipher, for they can proceed as follows. Alice writes her plaintext message for Bob, and places it in a box that she secures with her own padlock. Only Alice has the key to this lock. She then posts the box to Bob, who of course cannot open it. Bob, however, then adds a second padlock to the box, for which he alone possesses the key. The box is then returned to Alice, who then removes her own lock, and sends the box for a second time to Bob. This time, Bob may unlock the box and read Alice's message, secure in the knowledge that the meddling Eve could not have peeked at the contents during the delivery process. In this way, a secret message may be securely sent on an insecure channel without Alice and Bob ever exchanging keys. This imaginary scenario shows that there is no law that says that a key *must* change hands in the exchange of secure messages. In a real system, Alice and Bob's 'locks' might be their own coding of the message rather than a physical device separating the would-be eavesdropper from the plaintext. Alice and Bob may then use this initial exchange to set up an ordinary symmetric cipher that would be used to mask all their future communication.

Indeed, this is the way a secure communication channel is often established in the real world. Replacing physical locking devices by personal codes is not, however, so easy to do. Unlike the locks, the encodings of Alice and Bob may interfere with one another, making the unscrambling (that is, the unlocking) that is carried out first by Alice and then by Bob unworkable. However, that this method can be effective was first publicly demonstrated by Whitfield Diffie and Martin Hellman in 1976.

A second related approach is the idea of *asymmetric* or *public key cryptography* in which everyone publishes their own public key that is then used to encipher messages meant for that person. However, each person also holds a private key, without which the messages enciphered using their own unique public key cannot be read. In terms of the padlock metaphor, Alice provides Bob with a box in which to place his plaintext message together with an open padlock (her public key) to which she alone holds the key (her private key).

A workable public key system might seem too much to ask for as the twin requirements of security and ease of use seem to conflict. Fast, safe encryption is, however, available to the general public on the Internet, even if they barely realize that it is there, safeguarding their interests. And it is all down to numbers, and prime numbers at that.

How secret primes protect our secrets

Remember that every plaintext message is regarded just as a single number, so it is natural to try to mask this number using other numbers. The most common way to do this is through employing the so-called RSA enciphering process, published in 1978 by its founders, Ron Rivest, Adi Shamir, and Leonard Adleman. In RSA, each person's private key consists of three numbers, p, q, and d, where p and q are (very large) prime numbers and the third ingredient d is Alice's secret deciphering number, the role of which will be explained in due course. Alice provides the public with $n = pq$, the product of her two secret primes, and an enciphering number e (which is an ordinary whole number, in no way related to the special constant called e mentioned in Chapter 2).

A simple example for the purposes of illustration would be for Alice to have the primes $p = 5$ and $q = 13$ so that $n = 5 \times 13 = 65$. If Alice sets her enciphering number to be $e = 11$, then her public key would be $(n, e) = (65, 11)$. To encrypt a message m, Bob only needs n and e. However, to decipher the encrypted message $E(m)$ that Bob transmits to Alice requires the deciphering number d, which in this case turns out to be $d = 35$, as we shall show a little further on. The mathematics that allows d to be calculated requires that the primes p and q are known. In this toy example, given that $n = 65$, anyone would soon discover that $p = 5$ and $q = 13$. However, if the primes p and q are *extremely* large (typically they are hundreds of digits in length), this task becomes a practical impossibility for almost any computer system, at least in a reasonably short time, such as two or three weeks. In summary, the RSA system of enciphering is based on the empirical fact that it is prohibitively difficult to find the prime factors of a very, very large number n. The clever part, which we shall explain in the remainder of the chapter, lies in devising a way that the message number m can be enciphered just using the publicly known numbers n and e but, in practice, deciphering requires possession of the prime factors of n.

Here is how it works. What Bob sends through the ether is not m itself but *the remainder* when m^e is divided by n. Alice can then recover m by taking this remainder r and similarly calculating the remainder when r^d is divided by n. The underlying mathematics ensures that the outcome for Alice is the original message m, which can then be decoded into ordinary plaintext by Alice's computer system. This is, of course, happening seamlessly behind the scenes for any real-life Alice and Bob.

It would seem that the only thing that Eve lacks that really matters is this deciphering number d. If Eve knew that, she could decipher the message just as well as Alice. It turns out that d is a solution of a certain equation. Solving this equation is computationally quite easy and relies on the Euclidean Algorithm, published in the Books of Euclid in 300 BC. That is not the difficulty. The trouble is that it is not possible to find out exactly what equation to solve unless you know at least one of the primes p and q, and that is the obstacle that stops Eve in her tracks.

We can explain more about how the numbers involved in all this work into the system. First, there is apparently quite a problem with Bob's initial task. The number m is big, the number n is monstrous (of the order of 200 digits) and even if e is not that large, the number m^e is going to be extremely large as well. After calculating it, we have to divide m^e by the number n to get the remainder r, which represents the enciphered text. It might seem that the calculations are too unwieldy to be practical. We should be aware that even though modern computers are extremely powerful, they yet have their limitations. When calculations involve very high powers, they can exceed the capacity of *any* computer system. We certainly cannot assume that any practical calculation that we set for a computer can be done in a short period of time.

The saving grace for Bob is that it is possible to find the required remainder r, without doing the long division at all. Indeed, the remainders just depend on remainders, and here is an example to illustrate the point. What are the final two digits of 7^{39}? (That is to say, what is the remainder when this number is divided by 100?) In order to answer this question, we might begin by calculating the first few powers of 7: $7^1 = 7, 7^2 = 49, 7^3 = 343$, $7^4 = 2,401, 7^5 = 16,807, \cdots$. It will soon become clear, however, that the sheer size of these numbers is going to become unmanageable well before we get anywhere near 7^{39}. On the other hand, as we calculate one power after another, we see a pattern emerging. The key observation is that, as we calculate succeeding powers, the final two digits of the answer depend only on the final two digits of the preceding number, as when we carry out the multiplication, digits in the hundreds column and beyond have no effect on what end up in the units and tens columns.

What is more, since 7^4 has 01 as the final digit pair, the next four powers will end in 07, 49, 43, and then 01 again. Hence, as we compute succeeding powers, the pattern of the last two digits will simply repeat this cycle of length four, over and over again. To return to the question in hand, since $39 = 4 \times 9 + 3$, we will pass through this four-cycle nine times and then take three more steps in calculating the final two digits of 7^{39}, which must therefore be 43.

And this works quite generally. In order to find the remainder when some power a^b is divided by n say, we need only take the remainder r when a is divided by n and keep track of the remainders as we take successive powers of r. When we work with the remainder r, which will be a number in the range from 0 to $n - 1$, mathematicians say that we are working *modulo n*, discarding any higher multiples of n that may arise, as they leave a remainder of 0 when divided by n, and so cannot contribute to the value of the final remainder r.

You might still suspect that I have rigged the evidence by choosing an example where a very small power left a remainder of 1 – in this instance 7^4 was 1 more than a multiple of $n = 100$. This, however, is only partly true. It turns out that, if we take any two numbers, a and n, whose highest common factor is 1 (we say such numbers are mutually *coprime*), then there is always a power t such that a^t equals 1 modulo n, that is to say leaves a remainder of 1 when divided by n. From this point, the remainders of successive powers follow a cycle of length t. It can, however, be hard to predict what is the value of t, but it is known that t must always equal or be a factor of a number traditionally written as $\phi(n)$, the value of the Euler *phi function*.

And so what is $\phi(n)$? It is defined as the count of the numbers up to n that are coprime with n. For example, if $n = 15$, then the set of numbers in question is $\{1, 2, 4, 7, 8, 11, 13, 14\}$, which lists all the numbers up to 15 that have no factor in common with 15 (except the inevitable factor of 1). Since this set has 8 members, we see that $\phi(15) = 8$. Fortunately there is a slicker way of finding $\phi(n)$ that does not entail explicitly listing all the integers coprime with n and then counting them up. As with most functions of this nature, the value can be expressed in terms of the prime factorization of n. Indeed, we only need know the prime factors of n, for $\phi(n)$ can be found by taking n and multiplying it by each of the fractions $(1 - \frac{1}{p})$ as p ranges over all the prime divisors of n. The prime factors of 15, for instance, are 3 and 5, so the answer in this case is

$$\phi(15) = 15 \times (1 - \frac{1}{3})(1 - \frac{1}{5}) = 15 \times \frac{2}{3} \times \frac{4}{5} = 8,$$

which is the same as the result that we obtained directly from the definition. Using this method, you might like to check yourself that $\phi(100) = 40$, and so, for instance, it then follows that 7^{40} equals 1 modulo 100. However, as we have already seen, the least power of 7 that yields a remainder of 1 is not 40 but its divisor 4.

All this serves to give an indication that the number sent by Bob to Alice, m^e modulo n, can indeed be calculated without too much effort on behalf of Bob's computer. All the same, the numbers involved are in practice mighty big, so more explanation is needed to show that they can be handled. The large powers involved in computing m^e can be dealt with in stages by a process known as *fast exponentiation*. Without going into detail, the method involves successive squaring and multiplying of powers to arrive at m^e modulo n with the binary form of e guiding the algorithm through to quickly find the required remainder in relatively few steps.

Euclid shows Alice how to find her deciphering number

The deciphering number is the receiver's magic wand that allows the message retrieval. This number d is chosen so that the product de leaves a remainder of 1 when divided by $\phi(n)$. Since $n = pq$ is a product of two distinct primes, the value of $\phi(n) = pq(1 - \frac{1}{p})(1 - \frac{1}{q}) = (p - 1)(q - 1)$. It turns out that there is always just one value for d in the range up to $\phi(n)$ that has the required property.

Alice's computer can find d using an algebraic tool that is over 2,300 years old, the Euclidean Algorithm, which will be explained in a moment. Eve's computer could of course do the same thing if it just knew which equation to solve. However, since p and q are private to Alice, so is $(p-1)(q-1)$ and Eve does not know where to begin.

The existence of d is only guaranteed if a certain mild restriction is placed on the (publicly declared) enciphering number e. Alice must ensure that e has no common prime factor with $\phi(n)$. This is quite easily done as Alice can test $\phi(n)$ for division by particular primes and so ensure that e meets these requirements without compromising the identity of p and of q. Indeed, the value of e often used in practice is the fourth so-called *Fermat prime* $e = 65537 = 2^{16} + 1$; this value, $2^{2^4} + 1$ has a particularly rare property, that being that it is possible to construct a regular polygon with e sides using a straightedge and compass. Its utility in cryptography, however, is due to it being a fairly large prime that exceeds a power of 2 by exactly 1, which lends well to the fast exponentiation process mentioned earlier.

Returning to the Euclidean Algorithm, this begins from the observation that it is possible to find the *highest common factor* (hcf) of two numbers $a > b$ by successive subtraction. (The hcf is also known as the gcd – *greatest common divisor*.) We just note that $r = a - b$ has the property that any common factor of any two of the three numbers a, b, and r will also be a factor of the third. For example, if c is a common factor of a and b, so that $a = ca_1$ and $b = cb_1$ say, we see that $r = a - b = ca_1 - cb_1 = c(a_1 - b_1)$, giving us a factorization of r involving the divisor c. In particular, the hcf of a and b is the same as the hcf of b and r. Since both these numbers are less than a, we now have the same problem but applied to a smaller number pair. Repetition of this idea then will eventually lead to a pair where the hcf is obvious. (Indeed, the two numbers in hand will eventually be the same, for if not we could proceed one more step; their common value is then the number we seek.)

For example, to find the hcf of $a = 558$ and $b = 396$, the first subtraction would give us $r = 558 - 396 = 162$, so our new pair would be 396 and 162. Since $396 - 162 = 234$, our third pair becomes 234 and 162, and as we continue the full list of number pairs is:

$$(558, 396) \to (396, 162) \to (234, 162) \to (162, 72) \to (90, 72) \to$$
$$\to (72, 18) \to (54, 18) \to (36, 18) \to (18, 18)$$

and so the hcf of 558 and 396 is 18.

It is possible to write down the hcf of a number pair from the prime factorizations of the numbers in question. In this example, $558 = 2 \times 3^2 \times 31$, while $396 = 2^2 \times 3^2 \times 11$; taking the common power of each prime entering into the factorizations, we obtain the hcf as $2 \times 3^2 = 18$. Nevertheless, for larger numbers it takes much less work to use Euclid's Algorithm as it is generally easier to perform subtractions than to find prime factorizations.

Another bonus of the Euclidean Algorithm is that it is always possible to work it backwards and in so doing express the hcf in terms of the original two numbers. To see this in action in the previous example, it is best to compress the calculation when the same number appears several times over in the course of the subtractions, representing this as a single equation as follows:

$$558 = 396 + 162$$
$$396 = 2 \times 162 + 72$$
$$162 = 2 \times 72 + 18$$
$$72 = 4 \times 18.$$

Beginning with the second to last line, we now use each little equation to eliminate the intermediate remainders, one at a time. In this example, by using first the penultimate equation, and then the one above that we obtain:

$$18 = 162 - 2 \times 72 = 162 - 2 \times (396 - 2 \times 162) = 5 \times 162 - 2 \times 396$$

and finally using the first equation we can eliminate the first intermediate remainder of 162:

$$= 5 \times (558 - 396) - 2 \times 396 = 5 \times 558 - 7 \times 396 = 18.$$

That we can perform this reverse procedure is important for both practical and theoretical reasons. In particular, to find Alice's deciphering number d, we want d to satisfy the condition that de leaves a remainder of 1 when divided by $\phi(n)$. (For brevity, we shall denote $\phi(n)$ by the single symbol k.) We can now see the reason why we insist on e and k being a coprime pair, as if their highest common factor is 1, when we act the Euclidean Algorithm on the pair e and k, the final remainder that appears is, of course, 1. By reversing the algorithm, we will eventually express 1 as a combination of e and k; in particular, we will find integers c and d such that $ck + de = 1$, or in other words $de = 1 - ck$, so that de will leave a remainder of 1 when divided by k.

This relatively simple process will yield Alice's deciphering number d: the initial value of d obtained from the equation may not lie in the range from 1 to k but if not, by adding or subtracting a suitable multiple of k, we will eventually find the unique number d in that range that has the magic property that de leaves a remainder of 1 when divided by k. (The uniqueness of d is easily proved, but we won't digress into further explanation here.) That is how the deciperhing number d is calculated as we can show by returning to the example given earlier where $p = 5$, $q = 13$, so that $n = pq = 5 \times 13 = 65$. We have $\phi(n) = (p-1)(q-1) = 4 \times 12 = 48$. Alice sets $e = 11$, and since 11 and 48 are coprime, this is within the rules of the game. The Euclidean Algorithm applied to $\phi(n) = k = 48$ and $e = 11$ then gives:

$$48 = 4 \times 11 + 4$$

$$11 = 2 \times 4 + 3$$

$$4 = 1 \times 3 + 1$$

confirming that the hcf of k and e is indeed 1. Reversing the algorithm we obtain:

$$1 = 4 - 3 = 4 - (11 - 2 \times 4) = 3 \times 4 - 11 = 3(48 - 4 \times 11) - 11$$
$$= 3 \times 48 - 13 \times 11.$$

This gives an initial value of $d = -13$ as the solution to the requirement that $11d$ leaves remainder 1 upon division by 48, so in order to get a positive value of d in the required range we add 48 to this number to get $d = 48 - 13 = 35$.

The reason why d works for Alice is all down to modular arithmetic and the fact that de leaves a remainder of 1 when divided by $k = \phi(n)$. Alice calculates $(m^e)^d = m^{de}$ modulo n. Now de has the form $1 + kr$ for some integer r. As explained before, m^k leaves a remainder of 1 when divided by n (this is often known as *Euler's Theorem*) and so the same is true of $(m^k)^r = m^{kr}$. Hence $m^{1+kr} = m \times m^{kr}$ leaves the remainder m when divided by n. (Detailed verification of this requires a little algebra, but that is what happens.) In this way, Alice retrieves Bob's message, m.

And in passing it is well to point out that the Euclidean Algorithm provides the missing link in our proof of the uniqueness of prime factorization as it allows us to verify the euclidean property that if a prime p is a factor of the product ab, so that $ab = pc$ say, then p is a factor of at least one of a and b. The reason for this is that if p is *not* a factor of a then, since p is prime, the hcf of a and p is 1. By reversing the Euclidean Algorithm when applied to the pair a and p, we can then find integers r and s say such that $ra + sp = 1$. This is enough to show that p is then a factor of b for, since $ab = pc$, we have:

$$b = b \times 1 = b(ra + sp) = r(ab) + psb = r(pc) + psb = p(rc + sb).$$

This is the required factorization of b that features the prime p as a factor.

In conclusion, the number theory underlying RSA enciphering makes the system sound, although various protocols that have not been explained here must be respected in order to safeguard the integrity of the system. There are issues of *authentification* (what if Eve contacts Alice pretending to be Bob?), *non-repudiation* (what if Bob pretends that it was Eve who sent his message to Alice?), and *identity fraud* (what if Alice abuses confidential identification sent to her by Bob and tries to impersonate him online?). Moreover, other weaknesses in the system can be exposed when predictable or repeated messages proliferate. However, these difficulties may potentially arise in any public key cryptosystem. They can be overcome and in the main are unrelated to the underlying mathematical techniques that ensure high quality and robust encyryption.

This chapter has demonstrated a major application of prime numbers and the theory of divisibility and remainders. The ancient mathematics of Euclid and the 18th-century contribution of Euler allows this to be explained, not only in broad principle, but in fine detail.

The first part of our book closes with Chapter 5 which introduces some special classes of integers associated with the enumeration of some naturally occurring groupings.

Chapter 5
Numbers that count

Numbers that arise of their own accord in counting problems are important and so have been extensively investigated. Here I will describe the binomial coefficients, and the numbers of Catalan, Fibonacci, and Stirling because they enumerate certain natural collections. But we first begin with some very fundamental number sequences.

Triangular numbers, arithmetic and geometric progressions

Since they will reappear when we look at binomial coefficients, I will take a moment to revisit the *triangular numbers*, the nth of which, denoted by t_n, is defined as the sum of the first n counting numbers. Its value, in terms of n, can be found by the following trick. We write t_n as the sum just mentioned and then again as the same sum but in the reverse order. Adding the two versions of t_n together:

$$t_n = 1 + 2 + 3 + \cdots + (n-2) + (n-1) + n$$
$$t_n = n + (n-1) + (n-2) + \cdots + 3 + 2 + 1;$$

the outcome is of course an expression for $2t_n$. However, the point of doing this is that we have paired 1 with n, 2 with $n-1$, 3 with $n-2$, etc. The sum of each of these pairs is the same value, $n+1$, and there are n pairs altogether. In conclusion, we infer that

$2t_n = n(n + 1)$, or in other words, the value of the nth triangular number is $\frac{1}{2}n(n + 1)$. For example, the sum of all the integers from 1 up to 1000 is therefore equal to $500 \times 1001 = 500, 500$.

Indeed, this formula allows us to find the rule for summing the first n terms of any *arithmetic* series, or *progression* as they are known, which is one of the form $a, a + b, a + 2b, a + 3b, \cdots$. We first take care of the change of scale. By multiplying through the expression for t_n by b we see that $b + 2b + 3b + \cdots + nb = \frac{b}{2}n(n + 1)$. To find the formula for the sum of the general arithmetic series, first note that the sum of the first $n - 1$ terms of the previous series is obtained by replacing n by $n - 1$ in the previous formula, to give $\frac{b}{2}n(n - 1)$. The general arithmetic series now comes from adding a to every term and including a as the first term as well. This means that we need to add na to the previous sum to give us the general formula for the sum of the first n terms of an arithmetic series:

$$a + (a + b) + (a + 2b) + \cdots + (a + (n - 1)b) = na + \frac{b}{2}n(n - 1).$$

For example, by taking $a = 1$ and $b = 2$, we see that the sum of the first n odd numbers is $n + n(n - 1) = n + n^2 - n = n^2$, the nth square.

If we replace addition by multiplication as the operation, we move from arithmetic series to *geometric series*. In an arithmetic series, each pair of successive terms is separated by a *common difference*, the number b in our notation. In other words, to move from one term to the next, we simply *add b*. In a geometric series, we once again begin with some arbitrary number, a as the first term and move from one term to the next by *multiplying* by a fixed number, called the *common ratio*, denoted by the symbol r. That is to say, the typical geometric series has the form $a, ar, ar^2, \cdots$ with the nth term being ar^{n-1}. As with arithmetic series, there is a formula for the sum of the first n terms of a geometric series:

$$a + ar + ar^2 + \cdots + ar^{n-1} = \frac{a(r^n - 1)}{r - 1}.$$

The quick way of seeing that this formula is right is to take the equivalent form that we obtain when we multiply both sides of this equation by $(r - 1)$ and multiply out the brackets. On the left-hand side we obtain:

$$(ar + ar^2 + ar^3 + \cdots + ar^n) - (a + ar + ar^2 + \cdots + ar^{n-1})$$

and the whole expression *telescopes*, meaning that nearly every term is cancelled by one in the other bracket: the only exceptions are $ar^n - a = a(r^n - 1)$, showing that our formula for the sum is correct. For example, putting $a = 1$ and $r = 2$ gives us the sum of powers of 2:

$$1 + 2 + 4 + \cdots + 2^{n-1} = 2^n - 1.$$

This formula is just what you need in order to verify Euclid's result from Chapter 3 on how to generate even perfect numbers from Mersenne primes.

Factorials, permutations, and binomial coefficients

As we have seen, the nth triangular number arises from summing all the numbers from 1 up to n together. If we replace addition by multiplication in this idea, we get what are known as the *factorial* numbers, which made their first appearance in Chapter 2.

Factorials come up constantly in counting and probability problems such as the chances of being dealt a certain type of hand in a card game like poker. For that reason, they have their own notation: the nth factorial is denoted by $n! = n \times (n - 1) \times \cdots \times 2 \times 1$. The triangular numbers grow reasonably quickly, at about half the rate of the squares, but the factorials grow much faster and soon pass into the millions and millions: for example $10! = 3,628,800$. The exclamation mark alerts us to this rather alarming rate of growth.

In particular, $n!$ is the number of recognizably different ways that you can arrange n objects, such as n numbered balls, in a row. This follows as you have n choices for which ball goes first, and for each such choice you have $n - 1$ balls remaining for the second place, $n - 2$ for the third, and so on. If we stop after selecting just r balls, and denote the corresponding number by $P(n, r)$, we see that there are $n \times (n - 1) \times (n - 2) \times \cdots \times (n - r + 1)$ *permutations*, as we say, of n balls, taking r at a time. This is also conveniently expressed as the ratio of two factorials: $P(n, r) = \frac{n!}{(n-r)!}$. For example, if you are dealt a poker hand, you pick up 5 cards from a deck of 52 and the number of ways this can happen is $P(52, 5) = 52 \times 51 \times 50 \times 49 \times 48$. However, a hand in a card game does not depend on the order in which you pick up the cards but only the collection of cards itself. For a poker hand, each set of 5 can itself be rearranged in $5! = 120$ ways so that the number of genuinely different 5-card hands is $P(52, 5)/120 = 2,598,960$, about two and a half million.

The most special class that emerges in counting problems, or *enumerations* as they are called, is that of the *binomial coefficients*, so named as they arise as the multipliers of powers of x when the binomial expression $(1 + x)^n$ is expanded. The binomial coefficient $C(n, r)$ is the number of different ways we may construct a set of size r from one of size n. For example, $C(4, 2) = 6$, as there are six pairs (taken without regard to order within a pair) that can be chosen from a group of four: for example, if we have four children, Alex, Barbara, Caroline, and David, there are six ways that we can select a pair from this group: AB, AC, AD, BC, BD, and CD.

The binomial coefficients can be calculated in two distinct ways. First, we can extend the argument above that we used to calculate $C(52, 5)$: in general we see that $C(n, r) = P(n, r)/r!$, which in turns gives us the useful expression:

$$C(n, r) = \frac{n!}{(n - r)!r!}.$$

A notable special case is when we let $r = 2$, which corresponds to the number of pairs that can be selected from a set of n objects.

The answer is $\frac{n!}{(n-2)!2!}$. Now all the factors in the $(n-2)!$ term in the denominator cancel with the corresponding factors in $n!$ and since $2! = 2$, the expression for $C(n, 2)$ simplifies to $\frac{n(n-1)}{2}$. In other words, the number of ways of choosing a pair from a collection of n objects is t_{n-1}, the $(n-1)$st triangular number. For instance, as we have already seen, $C(4, 2) = 6$, which is indeed the third triangular number.

This factorial-based formula for calculating binomial coefficients does give a nice algebraic hold on the binomial coefficients that allows us to demonstrate their many special properties. However, the evolution of these properties is often more transparent if we focus on a second way to generate these integers, which is by means of the *Arithmetic Triangle* (see Figure 2), also known as *Pascal's Triangle*, in honour of the 17th-century French mathematician and philosopher Blaise Pascal (1623–62). (The Arithmetic Triangle has been discovered and re-discovered throughout Persia, India, and China over the last 1,000 years: for example, it featured as the front cover of *The Precious Mirror* by Chu Shih-Chieh in 1303.)

Each number in the body of the triangle is the sum of the two above it. The triangle, which can be continued indefinitely, gives the full list of binomial coefficients. For example, to find the number of ways of selecting five people from a group of seven, proceed as follows. Number the lines of the triangle, beginning

$$
\begin{array}{ccccccccccccccccc}
& & & & & & & & 1 & & & & & & & & \\
& & & & & & & 1 & & 1 & & & & & & & \\
& & & & & & 1 & & 2 & & 1 & & & & & & \\
& & & & & 1 & & 3 & & 3 & & 1 & & & & & \\
& & & & 1 & & 4 & & 6 & & 4 & & 1 & & & & \\
& & & 1 & & 5 & & 10 & & 10 & & 5 & & 1 & & & \\
& & 1 & & 6 & & 15 & & 20 & & 15 & & 6 & & 1 & & \\
& 1 & & 7 & & 21 & & 35 & & 35 & & 21 & & 7 & & 1 & \\
1 & & 8 & & 28 & & 56 & & 70 & & 56 & & 28 & & 8 & & 1 \\
& & & & & & & & \vdots & & & & & & & & \\
\end{array}
$$

2. The Arithmetic Triangle

with 0 at the top. Similarly number the positions within each row from left to right, again starting with 0. Go down to the line numbered 7, and then go to the number on that line numbered 5 (remembering to start your count from 0): we see the answer is 21. You will note the symmetry of each row: for example, 21 is also the number of ways of choosing two people from a group of seven. This is explained by observing that when we choose the five from seven, we are simultaneously choosing two from seven as well – the two being the pair left behind. This symmetry argument of course applies to every row. This is also manifested in the formula on page 55, for it returns the same expression if we replace r by $n - r$, as the terms r and $n - r$ that we see in the denominator simply swap positions.

The reason that the pattern gives the right answers is not hard to see. Each row builds from the one above it. We can see easily that the first three rows are correct: for example, the 2 in the centre of the third row tells us that there are two ways of choosing a single person from a pair. The 1 that sits on top is saying that there is one way to choose a set of size zero from the empty set. In fact, there is one way of choosing a set of size zero from any set, which is why every row begins with 1. Let us focus on the example just given – there are 21 = 15 + 6 ways of selecting five from a group of seven people. The 21 quintets naturally split into two types. First, there are 15 ways to form a group of four from the first six people, to which we may add the seventh person to form our fivesome. If we don't include the seventh person, however, then we have to build a set of five from the first six, and there are six ways of doing this. This illustrates how one row leads to the next: each entry is the sum of the two above it, and this pattern propagates throughout the triangle. In symbols this rule takes the form:

$$C(n, r) = C(n - 1, r) + C(n - 1, r - 1).$$

The triangle is rich in patterns. For example, summing all the numbers in each successive row gives the doubling sequence

1, 2, 4, 8, 16, 32, $\cdots$: the sequence of powers of 2. In summing the row that begins 1, 8, 28, 56, $\cdots$ for instance, we are summing the number of ways of choosing a set of size 0, 1, 2, 3 etc. from a set of 8. In total, this gives us the number of ways of selecting a set of *any* size from a group of 8, which is equal to 2^8 as, in general, a set of size n contains 2^n subsets within it.

This last fact can be seen directly, for a subset of a set of size n can be identified by a binary string of length n in the following way. We consider the set in question in a specific order $\{a_1, a_2, \cdots, a_n\}$ say, and then a binary string of length n specifies a subset by saying that each instance of 1 in the string indicates the presence of the corresponding a_i in the subset in question. For example, if $n = 4$, the strings 0111 and 0000 stand respectively for $\{a_2, a_3, a_4\}$, and for the empty set. Since there are two choices for each entry in the binary string, there are 2^n such strings in all and therefore 2^n subsets within a set of size n.

Catalan numbers

Every second row in the Arithmetic Triangle has a number sitting in the middle: 1, 2, 6, 20, 70, 252, 924, $\cdots$. These numbers are divisible by the consecutive counting numbers 1, 2, 3, 4, 5, 6, 7, $\cdots$ and the numbers that come about as we carry out these divisions, 1, 1, 2, 5, 14, 42, 132 $\cdots$ are known as the *Catalan numbers*. In terms of these *central binomial coefficients*, the nth Catalan number can be expressed as $\frac{1}{n+1}C(2n, n)$ for $n = 0, 1, 2, \cdots$.

One of the simplest visual representations that gives rise to this number type is as the number of ways we can draw 'mountains' using n up strokes and n down strokes (see Figure 3)

Each mountain pattern has an interpretation, however, as a meaningful bracketing and so the number of meaningful ways of arranging a collection of n pairs of parentheses is the nth Catalan number. For example, (())() and ((())) are meaningful bracketings

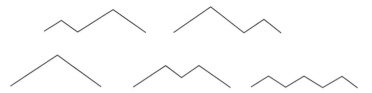

3. With three up and down strokes there are five mountain patterns

but ())(() is not: to be meaningful, the number of left brackets must never fall behind the number of right brackets as we count from left to right. This corresponds to the natural condition that our mountains must never dive underground. For instance, the first and last mountain patterns in Figure 3 correspond to the bracketing ()(()) and ()()() respectively.

The nth Catalan number also counts the number of ways that we can break up a regular polygon with $n + 2$ sides into triangles by means of diagonals that do not cross one another, and there are other interpretations along these lines. As with binomial coefficients, there are formulas relating Catalan numbers to smaller Catalan numbers, which makes them amenable to manipulation.

Fibonacci numbers

The Fibonacci sequence is one series of numbers that engenders wide fascination among the general public. The sequence runs as follows

$$1, 1, 2, 3, 5, 8, 13, 21, 34, 55, 89, 144, 233, 377, 610, \cdots$$

where each number after the pair of initial 1s is the sum of the two that come before. In this, there is a similarity with the binomial coefficients in that each term is the sum of two previous ones in the sequence, but the method of formation of the Fibonacci numbers is simpler:

$$f_n = f_{n-1} + f_{n-2}$$

where f_n denotes the nth Fibonacci number and we fix $f_1 = f_2 = 1$. We call such a formula that defines each member of a sequence in terms of its predecessors a *recursion* or a *recurrence relation*.

How does this sequence arise? It was first introduced in 1202 by Leonardo of Pisa, better known as Fibonacci, in the form of his celebrated Rabbit Problem. A female rabbit is born and after two months reaches maturity and thereafter gives birth to a daughter each month. The number of female rabbits we have at the beginning of each month is then given by the Fibonacci numbers, for there is 1 rabbit at the beginning of the first month, and the second, but at the start of the third month she gives birth to a daughter so we then have 2 rabbits. Next month she has another, giving 3 and the month after that we have 5 bunnies as both mother and her eldest daughter are now old enough to breed. In general, at the beginning of each month thereafter, the number of *newborn* daughters equals the number of females we had *two* months ago, as only they are old enough to breed. It follows that the number of females we have at the start of each subsequent month equals the total of the previous month (Fibonacci's rabbits are immortal) plus the number we had the month before that. Therefore the rule of formation of the Fibonacci numbers exactly matches the breeding pattern of his rabbits.

Despite the fact that real rabbits do not breed in this contrived fashion, Fibonacci numbers arise in nature in a variety of ways, including plant growth. The reasons for this are well understood but are related to more subtle attributes of the sequence connected to the so-called *Golden Ratio*, a number that we are about to introduce.

The simplest types of number progressions are the arithmetic and geometric progressions introduced in the first section. Although the Fibonacci sequence is neither of these, it does however have a surprising link with the latter type. If we form the sequence of differences of the Fibonacci sequence, because of the way the sequence is defined, we get $0, 1, 1, 2, 3, 5, 8, 13, \cdots$, that is we recover the Fibonacci sequence again except this time beginning at 0. This happens precisely because of the way the sequence is formed: the difference of two consecutive Fibonacci numbers is the one immediately preceding both in the sequence. (To see this algebraically, subtract f_{n-1} from both sides of the Fibonacci recurrence above.) Nor is the sequence a geometric progression as the ratio of consecutive Fibonacci numbers is not constant. All the same, when we look at the ratio of successive terms we see that it does seem to settle down to a limiting value. This near stable behaviour of the ratio comes about quite quickly, as we see as we divide each Fibonacci number by its predecessor:

$$\frac{34}{21} = 1 \cdot 6190, \ \frac{55}{34} = 1 \cdot 6176, \ \frac{89}{55} = 1 \cdot 6182, \ \frac{144}{89} = 1 \cdot 6180, \cdots$$

But what is the mysterious number, $1.6180\ldots$, which we see emerging? This number τ is known as the *Golden Ratio*, and it arises quite of its own accord in geometrical settings that look a world away from Fibonacci's rabbits. For example, τ is the ratio of the diagonal of a regular pentagon to its side (see Figure 4). Each diagonal meets another at a point that divides each into two parts that are themselves in the ratio $\tau : 1$. Pairs of intersecting sides and intersecting diagonals form the four sides of a rhombus (a 'square' parallelogram) *ABCD* as shown. Where diagonals cross, they form a smaller inverted pentagon.

A characteristic associated with the Golden Ratio is *self-similarity*, which means that objects such as the pentagon that involve τ often contain smaller copies of themselves within. This is seen in the rectangle with sides of lengths τ and 1, for it is unique in displaying the property that if we slice off the largest square we can (a square of side length 1) then the smaller rectangle that remains is a copy of the original. This figure is for that reason known as the *Golden Rectangle* (see Figure 4). The value of τ can be gleaned from the given property of the rectangle, for if we call the length of the longer side τ and make the shorter side one unit,

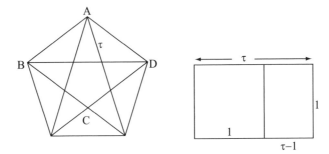

4. Pentagon and the Golden Rectangle

the similarity of the rectangles is captured by the equality $\frac{\tau}{1} = \frac{1}{\tau-1}$, which we obtain by equating the ratio of the longer to the shorter side of the rectangles. Cross-multiplying in this expression then yields the equation $\tau^2 - \tau = 1$. Using the standard formula to solve such a *quadratic equation* (one involving a square), we see that the positive root of this equation equals:

$$\tau = \frac{1 + \sqrt{5}}{2} = 1 \cdot 6180229 \cdots$$

Another way of retrieving this valuation of τ is through its so-called continued fraction, which ties τ directly to the Fibonacci numbers, and we shall explore this idea in Chapter 7.

In the long run, the Fibonacci sequence behaves like a geometric progression based on the Golden Ratio. It is this property, together with its simple rule of formation that causes the Fibonacci sequence to arise so persistently.

Stirling and Bell numbers

Like the binomial coefficients, the Stirling numbers often arise in counting problems and depend on two variables, n and r. The Stirling number $S(n, r)$ is the number of ways of partitioning a set of n members into r blocks (with no block empty, and the order of the blocks and within the blocks, is immaterial). (Strictly these are called Stirling numbers of the second kind. Those of the first kind, which are related, count something quite different, namely the number of ways we can permute n objects into r cycles.) For instance, the set with members a, b, c can be partitioned into three blocks in just one way: $\{a\}$, $\{b\}$, $\{c\}$, into two blocks in three ways $\{a, b\}$, $\{c\}$; $\{a\}$, $\{b, c\}$, and $\{a, c\}$, $\{b\}$, and into a single block in one way only: $\{a, b, c\}$; it follows that $S(3, 1) = 1$, $S(3, 2) = 3$ and $S(3, 3) = 1$. Since a set of n members can be partitioned in only one way into either 1 block or into n blocks, we always have $S(n, 1) = 1 = S(n, n)$. If we draw up the triangle of Stirling numbers after the fashion of Pascal's Triangle, we arrive at the array of Figure 5, and we now explain how the triangle is generated.

Once again, the numbers satisfy a recurrence relation, meaning that each can be related to earlier ones in the array. Indeed, as with the binomial coefficients, each Stirling number can be obtained from the two above it, but it is not simply the sum. What is more, the row symmetry we saw in the Arithmetic Triangle that generates the binomial coefficients is not present in Stirling's Triangle. For example, $S(5, 2) = 15$ but $S(5, 4) = 10$. The rule of recurrence is simple enough, however. The entry 90, for example, is equal to $15 + 3 \times 25$. This is indicative of the general situation: to find a number in the body of the triangle, take the two immediately above it, and add the first to the second *multiplied by the number of the position in the row you are at.* (This time, unlike the Arithmetic Triangle, start your row count at 1.) In a similar way, the entry $S(5, 4) = 10 = 6 + 4 \times 1$. It is only the part of the rule

```
                        1
                    1       1
                1       3       1
            1       7       6       1
        1      15      25      10      1
    1      31      90      65      15      1
1      63     301     350    140      21      1
                        ⋮
```

5. Stirling's Triangle

in italics that differs from that of the Arithmetic Triangle. That is enough, however, to make the study of Stirling numbers considerably more difficult to that of the binomial coefficients. For instance, we derived a simple explicit formula for each binomial coefficient in terms of the factorials. Similarly, there is a formula for the nth Fibonacci number in terms of powers of the Golden Ratio, but nothing of the kind exists for Stirling numbers.

The recurrence rule is not hard to explain. We argue similarly to that for the recursion for the binomial coefficients, and by doing so recover the recurrence outlined above that is identical in form except for a single multiplier. In order to form a partition of a set of size n into r non-empty blocks, we may proceed in two distinct ways. We may take the first $n - 1$ elements of the set and partition it into $r - 1$ non-empty blocks in $S(n - 1, r - 1)$ ways, and the final member of the set will then form the rth block. Alternatively, we may partition the first $n - 1$ elements of the set into r non-empty blocks, which can be done in $S(n - 1, r)$ ways, and then decide in which of the r blocks to place the final member of the set, giving a multiplier of r to that number. Hence we infer that

$$S(n, r) = S(n - 1, r - 1) + rS(n - 1, r) \text{ for } n = 2, 3, \cdots$$

Using this recursion formula, we may calculate each line of the Stirling Triangle from the one above it. For example, putting $n = 7$ and $r = 5$ we obtain:

$$S(7, 5) = S(6, 4) + 5S(6, 5) = 65 + 5 \times 15 = 65 + 75 = 140.$$

We can compute $S(n, 2)$ and $S(n, n - 1)$ directly from the definition as follows. An arbitrary partition of the n-set into a first set and a second set is described by a binary string of length n, where the presence of a 1 indicates presence in the first set and a 0 in the second (in a similar way to how we showed that the number of subsets of an n-set is 2^n). There are therefore 2^n such *ordered pairs* of sets. Since, however, there is no ordering of the blocks within a partition, we divide this number by 2 to find the number of partitions of the n-set into 2 sets, giving the number 2^{n-1}. Finally, we need to subtract 1 from this in order to exclude the case where one of the sets is empty; hence $S(n, 2) = 2^{n-1} - 1$. You can check that this represents the second diagonal line of numbers $1, 3, 7, 15, 31, 63, \cdots$ running from the top right to the bottom left in Figure 5.

At the other extreme, a partition of the n-set into $n - 1$ blocks is determined by a choice of the unique block of size 2. The number of ways of making this selection is $C(n, 2) = \frac{1}{2}n(n - 1)$, the $(n - 1)$st triangular number (see the second diagonal $1, 3, 6, 10, 15, 21, \cdots$ running from top left to bottom right in Figure 5).

The sum of any row of the Arithmetic Triangle gives the corresponding power of 2 –the number of subsets of a set of a given size. Similarly, summing the nth row of Stirling's Triangle gives the number of ways of breaking a set of n objects into blocks, and this is called the nth *Bell number*.

Partition numbers

If on the other hand, the n objects of the set to be partitioned are identical, and so cannot be distinguished from one another, the number of ways of splitting the whole collection up into blocks is a much smaller integer, known as the nth *partition number*. A particular partition corresponds to writing n as a sum of positive integers, without regard to order: for example, $1 + 1 + 1 + 1 + 1$ is one partition of 5 and there are six others, for we can also represent 5 as $1 + 1 + 1 + 2, 1 + 2 + 2, 1 + 1 + 3, 2 + 3, 1 + 4$, or simply as 5. Therefore the 5th partition number is 7 (that compares to the 5th Bell number, which from the Stirling Triangle is seen to be $1 + 15 + 25 + 10 + 1 = 52$). There is no simple exact formula for the nth partition number – there is a complex one, which is itself based on a beautiful approximation due to the Indian genius Srinivasa Ramanujan (1887–1920).

One simple symmetry regarding partitions is that the number of partitions of n into m parts is equal to the number of partitions of n in which the largest part is m. One way of seeing that this is true is through the *Ferrar's graph* (or *Young diagram*) of the partition, which is no more than the representation of the partition as a corresponding array of dots in which the rows are listed by decreasing size.

In the example shown in Figure 6 we have represented 17 partitioned as $5 + 4 + 4 + 2 + 1 + 1$. Note how the columns are also listed in decreasing order from left to right. If we reflect the array along the diagonal running from top left to bottom right, we recover a second Ferrar's graph as shown, which can be interpreted as the partition $17 = 6 + 4 + 3 + 3 + 1$. A similar reflection of the second graph returns you to the first and we say that the two corresponding partitions are *dual* to one another. This symmetry allows us to see that the numbers of partitions of two corresponding types are equal: the dual of a partition in which m, say, is the largest number (so the top row has m dots) is a partition with m rows, which corresponds to a partition into m numbers. For example, the number of partitions of 17 into 6 numbers therefore equals the number of partitions of 17 in which 6 is the largest number that occurs.

Mathematicians always have an eye out for these kind of symmetries that often arise in enumeration problems. Another example of this type occurs in relation to the Bertrand–Whitworth

6. Dual partitions of $17 = 5 + 4 + 4 + 2 + 1 + 1 = 6 + 4 + 3 + 3 + 1$

ballot problem where the votes for two electoral candidates are counted with the winner taking p votes and the loser q votes, say. A clever geometric argument using what is known as the *Reflection Principle* shows that the proportion of counts where the winner leads the counting throughout the night equals the winner's final margin of victory divided by the total number of votes cast: $\frac{p-q}{p+q}$. This in turn is equal to the proportion of counts where the eventual winning margin is never attained until the very last vote is counted. The reason why these two numbers must be equal is that the two types of count are dual to one another in that the reversal of the order of votes in a count of the first type gives a count of the second type, and vice versa.

Hailstone numbers

Although not a counting tool, the hailstone numbers are intriguing as they are also defined recursively but have more of a flavour of the aliquot sequences that we met in Chapter 3. The following question goes by several names, the *Collatz Algorithm*, the *Syracuse Problem*, or sometimes just the $3n + 1$-*problem*, and it is simply the observation that, beginning with any number n, the following process always seems to end with the number 1. If n is even, divide it by 2, while if n is odd, replace it by $3n + 1$. For example, beginning with $n = 7$ we are led by the rules through the following sequence:

$$7 \to 22 \to 11 \to 34 \to 17 \to 52 \to 26 \to 13 \to 40$$
$$\to 20 \to 10 \to 5 \to 16 \to 8 \to 4 \to 2 \to 1$$

And so the conjecture is true for $n = 7$, and indeed it has been verified for all n up beyond a million million. Things are different if you fiddle with the rules: for instance, replacing $3n + 1$ by $3n - 1$ results in a cycle:

$$7 \to 20 \to 10 \to 5 \to 14 \to 7 \to \cdots .$$

The sequences of numbers that arise from these calculations behave like hailstones in that they rise and fall erratically over a long period but eventually, it seems, always hit the ground. Of the first 1000 integers, more than 350 have a hailstone maximum height of 9232 before collapsing to 1. This will happen once you run into a power of 2, for they are exactly the numbers that cause you to fall straight down to ground level without encountering any more updrafts.

All sorts of intriguing features can be discerned in graphs and plots based on the hailstone sequences reminiscent of other chaotic patterns that arise in maths and physics. Typing 'hailstone numbers' into your favourite search engine will provide you with a wealth of information, often intriguing, sometimes speculative, but generally inconclusive.

Chapter 6
Below the waterline of the number iceberg

Introduction

The counting numbers, 1, 2, 3, $\cdots$ are just the tip of the number iceberg. This tip is of course the first part we discover, and for a time we might believe there is no more to the iceberg than the tip, especially if we remain reluctant to look below the waterline. In the course of this chapter, we first introduce the negative integers and coupling this extension with fractions, both positive and negative, gives the collection we call the set of *rational numbers*. This number collection is often pictured to lie along the *number line*, with the positive numbers lying to the right of zero, with their negatives forming the mirror image to the left. However, the number line turns out to be the home of other numbers that cannot be expressed as fractions, such as $\sqrt{2}$ and π, to take two examples. The set of *real numbers* is the name for the collection of all numbers on the number line, which are those that can be represented by decimal expansions of any kind, as shown in Figure 7.

However, one of the great achievements of the 19th century was the full realization that the true domain of number is not one-, but rather is two-dimensional. The plane of the complex numbers is the natural arena of discourse for much of mathematics. This has been brought home to mathematicians and scientists through

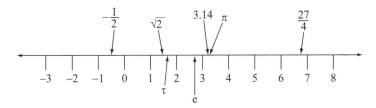

7. Central portion of the number line near 0

problem solving – to be able to carry out the investigations
required to solve real-world problems, many of which seem to be
only about ordinary counting numbers, it becomes necessary to
expand your number horizon. The explanation as to how this extra
dimension emerges will come towards the end of this chapter and
be explored further in Chapter 8.

Pluses and minuses

The *integers* is the name applied to the set of all whole numbers,
positive negative, and zero. This set, often symbolized by the letter
Z, is therefore infinite in both directions:

$$\{\cdots -4, -3, -2, -1, 0, 1, 2, 3, 4, \cdots\}.$$

The integers are often pictured as lying at equally spaced points
along a horizontal number line, in the order indicated. The
additional rules that we need to know in order to do arithmetic
with the integers can be summarized as follows:

(a) to add or subtract a negative integer, $-m$, we move m spaces to the
    left in the case of addition, and m spaces to the right for
    subtraction;

(b) to multiply an integer by $-m$, we multiply the integer by m, and
    then change sign.

In other words, the direction of addition and subtraction of
negative numbers is the opposite to that of positive numbers, while

multiplying a number by -1 swaps its sign for the alternative. For example, $8 + (-11) = -3$, $3 \times (-8) = -24$, and $(-1) \times (-1) = 1$.

You should not be troubled by this last sum. First, it is reasonable that multiplying a negative number by a positive one yields a negative answer: when a debt (a negative amount) is subject to interest (a positive multiplier greater than 1) the outcome is greater debt, that is to say a larger negative number. We are all well aware of this. That multiplication of a negative number by another negative number should have the opposite outcome, that is a positive result, would then appear consistent. The fact that the product of two negative numbers is positive can readily be given formal proof. The proof is based on the assumptions that we want our expanded number system of the integers to subsume the original one of the natural numbers, and that the augmented system should continue to obey all the normal rules of algebra. Indeed, the result on the product of two negatives follows from the fact that any number multiplied by zero equals zero. (This too is not an assumption but rather is also a consequence of the laws of algebra.) For we now have:

$$-1 \times (-1 + 1) = -1 \times 0 = 0;$$

if we then multiply out the brackets, we see that in order that the left-hand side equal zero, $(-1) \times (-1)$ must take the opposite sign to $(-1) \times 1 = -1$; in other words $(-1) \times (-1) = 1$.

Fractions and rationals

In a similar way that subtraction leads to the negative numbers, the operation of division also leads us out of the set of natural counting numbers into the larger realm of fractions. However, the nature of the new arithmetic we encounter is of a different character. When adding or subtracting, fractions with different denominators (bottom lines) are incompatible. The fractions in question need to be expressed with a common denominator before the sum can be completed. Multiplication is a comparatively simple process in that we only need to multiply the numerators (top lines) and denominators together in order to get the answer. Division is the inverse operation to multiplication so that division by n corresponds to multiplication by the reciprocal, $\frac{1}{n}$. In general, this carries over to fractions in that to divide by the fraction $\frac{m}{n}$ we multiply by its reciprocal, $\frac{n}{m}$, for that reverses the effect of multiplication by $\frac{m}{n}$.

The Ancient Egyptians were only happy with *unit fractions*, which are those that are simple reciprocals of whole numbers, $\frac{1}{2}, \frac{1}{3}, \frac{1}{4}$ etc. (although they retained a special symbol for $\frac{2}{3}$). A fraction such as $\frac{3}{4}$ was not thought of as a meaningful entity in its own right, and they would record this quantity as the sum of two reciprocals: $\frac{3}{4} = \frac{1}{2} + \frac{1}{4}$. (The notation for fractions used here is of course the modern European type, which has its origins in Greek mathematics.) It is not, however, obvious that it is necessarily possible to write any fraction as the sum of a number of *different* unit fractions, which is what they insisted on. It can, however, always be done and explaining this will allow you to brush up your skills on dealing with fractions.

If you wish to find an Egyptian decomposition of a fraction such as $\frac{9}{20}$, you need only subtract the largest unit fraction you can from the given number, and repeat this process until the remainder is itself a unit fraction. This will always work, and the number of fractions involved never exceeds the numerator of your original fraction. This is because, at each stage, the numerator of the fraction that still remains is always less than the previous one: not obvious but true. In this example the first stage will give:

$$\frac{9}{20} - \frac{1}{3} = \frac{27}{60} - \frac{20}{60} = \frac{7}{60};$$

next we find that the largest unit fraction less than $\frac{7}{60}$ is $\frac{1}{9}$. (To test this, compare the result of the cross-multiplication: $\frac{1}{9} < \frac{7}{60}$ because $1 \times 60 = 60 < 63 = 7 \times 9$.) Subtracting again, we see that

$$\frac{9}{20} - \frac{1}{3} - \frac{1}{9} = \frac{7}{60} - \frac{1}{9} = \frac{21}{180} - \frac{20}{180} = \frac{1}{180}$$

and so we recover the Egyptian decomposition:

$$\frac{9}{20} = \frac{1}{3} + \frac{1}{9} + \frac{1}{180}.$$

This greedy approach of always subtracting the largest unit fraction available does work but may not yield the shortest decomposition there is, as we can see even in this case as $\frac{9}{20} = \frac{1}{4} + \frac{1}{5}$. This two-fraction decomposition of $\frac{9}{20}$ can be found, however, through use of the technique of the Akhmim papyrus, a Greek parchment discovered at the city of Akhmim on the Nile and dated to AD 500–800. In modern notation, the trick can be expressed as the readily verified algebraic identity:

$$\frac{m}{pq} = \frac{m}{p(p+q)} + \frac{m}{q(p+q)}.$$

Applying this with $m = 9$, $p = 4$, $q = 5$ immediately gives us $\frac{9}{20} = \frac{9}{4\times9} + \frac{9}{5\times9} = \frac{1}{4} + \frac{1}{5}$.

It may well have been years since you last added even simple fractions together because nearly all practical arithmetic is now carried out in decimal format. The use of decimal fractions is found in ancient China and medieval Arabic nations but only came into widespread use in Europe in the latter part of the 16th century when serious efforts were made to improve practical methods of computation. There is a price to be paid, however, for this commitment to decimal forms. In normal base ten arithmetic we exploit the fact that any number can be written as a sum of multiples of powers of ten. When expressing a fraction as a decimal, we are attempting to write the number as a sum of powers of $\frac{1}{10} = 0.1$. Unfortunately, even for very simple fractions such as $\frac{1}{3}$, this cannot be done, and the decimal expansion goes on without end: $\frac{1}{3} = 0.333\ldots$. In practice, we appreciate that by truncating the decimal expansion after a certain number of places (depending on the accuracy we demand), we can get by with the resulting *terminating decimal* that approximates the exact fraction. Any inaccuracy is trivial in comparison with the convenience of carrying out all our number work in the standard base ten frame of reference. Decimal expansions can be thought of as the closest we can get to having a single common denominator for all fractions.

It is natural to ask, though, which fractions will have terminating expansions (and which will not)? The answer is, not very many. More often than not, the decimal expansion of a fraction goes into a recurring pattern: $\frac{3}{22}$ = 0.1363636... with the 36 part repeating forever. Every fraction generates a recurring decimal in one way or another, although in the case of a terminating decimal such as $\frac{1}{2}$ = 0.5, the recurring part is simply an unending string of zeros: $\frac{1}{2}$ = 0.5000···, and so is not explicitly mentioned. In any event, the length of the recurring block in a recurring decimal expansion is no longer than one less than the value of the denominator. This can be seen by considering what happens when we carry out the corresponding long division sum: if the denominator is n, then the remainder after each step in the division takes on one of the values $0, 1, ···, n-1$. If at some stage the remainder is 0, the division terminates and so does the decimal expansion: for example, $\frac{11}{40}$ is exactly equal to 0.275. Otherwise the division continues forever, but once a remainder is repeated, which is inevitable, we shall be forced into the same cycle of divisions once more, thus giving a recurring pattern whose block can be no longer than $n-1$. The expansion will terminate exactly when the denominator is a product of the prime factors 2 and 5 of our base 10 but not if there is any other factor involved. For example, fractions with denominators 16, 40, and 50 are terminating, but fractions like $\frac{1}{14}$ and $\frac{1}{15}$ will not terminate because the respective prime factors of 7 and 3 in their denominators force the expansion into a recurring cycle.

This does show, however, that whether or not a fraction's expansion terminates is not determined just by the number itself but rather depends on the relationship of the number to the base in which you are operating. If, for instance, we worked in *ternary* (base three) then 0.1 would represent $\frac{1}{3}$, as the 1 after the decimal point would stand for $\frac{1}{3}$, and not $\frac{1}{10}$, the way it does in decimal expansions.

The reverse process of turning a recurring decimal back into a fraction is also quite simple, showing that there is a one-to-one correspondence between fractions and recurring decimals, and we can use whichever representation best suits our current purpose. A simple example is as follows: let $a = 0.212121\cdots$. Since the length of the recurring block is 2, we can simplify this, as you will see, by multiplying by $10^2 = 100$ to obtain $100a = 21.212121\cdots$. This has been set up so that, upon subtraction, the recurring parts of the two numbers a and $100a$, being identical, will cancel, allowing us to infer that $99a = 21$, whence $a = \frac{21}{99} = \frac{7}{33}$.

This kind of trick is often used to simplify an expression that involves an infinite repeating process. For example, consider the following little monster:

$$a = \sqrt{2\sqrt{5\sqrt{2\sqrt{5}}}}\cdots$$

By squaring, and then squaring again, the left-hand side becomes a^4, while the expression on the right gives:

$$a^4 = 2^2 \times 5 \times \sqrt{2\sqrt{5\sqrt{2\sqrt{5}}}}\cdots$$

Since what follows the 5 is another copy of the expression for a, we infer that $a^4 = 20a$ so that $a^3 = 20$ or, if you prefer, a is the cube root of 20. We will call on this technique again in Chapter 7 when we introduce so-called continued fractions.

Does the class of fractions provide us with all the numbers we could ever need? As mentioned earlier, the collection of all fractions, together with their negatives, form the set of numbers known as the rationals, that is all numbers that result from whole numbers and the ratios between them. They are adequate for arithmetic in that any sum involving the four basic arithmetic operations of addition, subtraction, multiplication, and division will never take you outside the world of rational numbers. If we are happy with that, this set of numbers is all we require. However, we explain in the next section how numbers such as a above are not rational.

Irrationals

The word *irrational* applied to a number a means simply that the number is not rational, that is to say *cannot* be written as a fraction. Irrational numbers were first discovered a very long time ago, in ancient Greece. Pythagoras understood the irrational nature of $\sqrt{2}$. The Greeks did not think in terms of decimal expansions but were happy to recognize a length constructed in the geometry of straightedge and compass as representing a real quantity. In particular, Pythagoras' Theorem tells us that the longer side of a right-angled triangle whose shorter sides are each of length 1 unit is exactly equal to the square root of 2.

Pythagoras was able to prove that the square root of 2 was not equal to any fraction, thereby showing that irrational numbers truly exist. In particular, you cannot exactly measure the diagonal of a square with the same units with which you measure the side, for if you could the diagonal would be an exact fractional multiple of the side, in which case $\sqrt{2}$ would be equal to this fraction. The two lengths are however fundamentally incompatible, or *incommensurable* as they are described in the classical texts. The story is the same for π, which is approximately equal to the fraction $\frac{22}{7}$, but is different from it, and from any fraction that you care to nominate. (However, the easily remembered 'double 1, double 3, double 5' ratio: $355/113 = 3.1415929\cdots$ accurately approximates the value of π to better than one part in one million.)

Although it is very difficult to prove that π is irrational, the question for the square root of 2 can be settled easily by a simple contradiction argument. First, we note that for any number c, the highest power of 2 that is a factor of c^2, is twice the highest power of 2 that is a factor of c, and so in particular the highest power of 2 that divides any square must itself be an even number. For example, $24 = 2^3 \times 3$ while $576 = 24^2 = 2^6 \times 3^2$, and in this case the highest power of 2 dividing the number does indeed double from 3 to 6 when we take the square. This is always the case, and indeed applies not only to powers of 2 but to any prime factor of the original number.

Suppose now that $\sqrt{2}$ were equal to the fraction $\frac{a}{b}$. Squaring both sides of this equation allows us to deduce that $2 = \frac{a^2}{b^2}$, which gives $2b^2 = a^2$. By the previous observation, the highest power of 2 that divides the right-hand side of this equation is even, while the highest power that divides the left-hand side is odd (because of the presence of the extra 2). This shows the equation to be nonsense, and so it must not be possible to write $\sqrt{2}$ as a fraction in the first place. Like Pythagoras, we come face to face with the irrationals.

Arguments along these lines allow us to show that quite generally, when we take the square root (or indeed the cube or a higher root) of a number, the answer, if not a whole number, is always irrational, thus explaining why the decimal displays on your calculator never show a recurring pattern when asked to calculate such a root.

Pythagoras discovered that in order to do his mathematics, he required a wider field of numbers than mere fractions. The Greeks regarded a number to be 'real' if its length could be constructed from a standard unit interval using only a straightedge (not a marked ruler, just an edge) and compass. It turns out that although the square root operation does introduce irrationals, the full collection itself does not go very far beyond the rational. The set of euclidean numbers, as we shall refer to them, are all those that can be arrived at from the number 1 through carrying out any or all of the four operations of arithmetic and the taking of square roots, any number of times. For example, the number $\sqrt{7 - \sqrt{4/3}}$ is therefore a number of this kind. Even cube roots are beyond the grasp of the euclidean tools. This was the basis of perhaps the first great unsolved problem in mathematics. The first of the three Delian Problems as they were known was the call to construct the cube root of 2, using only straightedge and compass. Legend has it that this was the task set by the god when the citizens of Delos consulted the Oracle of Delphi to learn what they should do in order to banish the plague from Athens – the problem was put in the form of exactly doubling the volume of an altar that was a perfect cube.

This problem remained untouchable in classical times. That the cube root of 2 lies outside the range of the euclidean tools was only settled in 1837 by Pierre Wantzel (1814–48), as it requires a precise algebraic description of what is possible using the classical tools in order to see that the cube root of 2 is a number of a fundamentally different type. It does indeed come down to showing that you can never manufacture a cube root out of square roots and rationals. When put that way, the impossibility sounds more plausible. However, that in no way constitutes a proof.

Transcendentals

Within the class of irrationals lies the mysterious family of transcendental numbers. These numbers do *not* arise through the ordinary calculations of arithmetic and the extraction of roots. For the precise definition, we first introduce the complementary collection of *algebraic numbers*, which are those that solve some polynomial equation with integer coefficients: for example $x^5 - 3x + 1 = 0$ is such an equation. The *transcendentals* are then defined to be the class of non-algebraic numbers.

It is not at all clear that there are any such numbers. However, they do exist and they form a very secretive society, with those in it not readily divulging their membership of the club. For example, the number π is an instance of a transcendental but this is not a fact that it openly reveals. It will be explained in the next chapter when we explore the nature of infinite sets why it is that 'most' numbers are transcendental, in a sense that will be made precise.

For the time being, I will settle for introducing perhaps the most famous transcendental of all, the number $e = 2.71828\ldots$. This number arises constantly in higher mathematics and calculus: it is the base of the so-called natural logarithm, the function that tells you the area under the graph of the reciprocal function. It is also the limiting value of the sequence of numbers you get when you raise the ratio of two consecutive integers, $\frac{n+1}{n}$ ($= 1 + \frac{1}{n}$), to the power n. (Ask your calculator for the value of $(129/128)^{128}$ – you can 'fast exponentiate' this, just calculate $129/128$ and then square 7 times, as $2^7 = 128$.)

This sequence arises when we consider the problem of the limiting value of a compound interest rate as you reduce the interval of repayment shorter and shorter from annually, to monthly, to daily, and so on. To best illustrate the point, suppose that interest is paid at an annual rate of 100%, compounding in n instalments per year, which means that your initial investment is multiplied by the factor $(1 + \frac{1}{n})$, n times in all, throughout the course of the year. Your principal will then be multiplied by the factor $(1 + \frac{1}{n})^n$. The more often you are paid interest, the more you will earn as you begin to collect interest on your interest earlier and earlier as n becomes higher and higher. However, as n increases, the effective APR (Annual Percentage Rate) does not increase beyond all bounds but rather approaches a ceiling, an upper limit as mathematicians call it. This limiting multiplier that would apply to your principal in the continuous interest case is the limiting value, as n increases, of the number

$$\left(1 + \frac{1}{n}\right)^n \rightarrow e = 2.71828\ldots.$$

Another way in which the mysterious e arises is through the sum of the reciprocals of the factorials, and this gives a way of calculating e to a high degree of accuracy as this series converges rapidly because its terms approach zero very quickly indeed:

$$e = 1 + \frac{1}{1!} + \frac{1}{2!} + \frac{1}{3!} + \frac{1}{4!} + \cdots$$

This representation allows you to show by a relatively simple contradiction argument, outlined here, that e is an irrational number. We suppose that the preceding series for e equals a fraction $\frac{p}{q}$ and then we multiply both sides by $q!$. The left-hand side is then an integer but the right-hand side consists of terms that are integers followed by an infinite sequence of non-integral terms. By comparing to a simple geometric series, we deduce that this 'tail' sums to less than 1, and so the right-hand side cannot be a whole number, and therein lies the required contradiction. Showing that e is not just irrational, but transcendental, requires quite a bit more work.

The relationship of e with the factorials also manifests itself in a remarkable formula of the Scottish mathematician James Stirling (1692–1770), after whom Stirling numbers (see Chapter 5) are named. He showed that as n increases, the value of $n!$ is approximated better and better by the expression $\sqrt{2\pi n}(\frac{n}{e})^n$.

Since e crops up in a variety of distinct and fairly simple ways, it persistently appears throughout mathematics, often where you would not expect to meet it. For example, take two well-shuffled packs of playing cards, turn over the top card of each deck, and compare. Continue doing this until you have exhausted the packs. What are the chances that, at some stage, there is a perfect match? That is to say, on one turn or another the cards showing are exactly the same, be they the seven of clubs, queen of hearts, or whatever. It works out that the proportion of times this experiment yields at least one such match is as near as makes no difference to $\frac{1}{e}$, which is about 36.8%. This comes about through application of what is known as the *inclusion–exclusion principle*, which arrives at the solution through a sum of terms each of which represent alternating corrections and reverse corrections. In this example, the principle furnishes the series of reciprocals of the factorials but this time with alternating signs, which converges to $\frac{1}{e}$.

The real and the imaginary

The first five chapters of this *Very Short Introduction* dealt mainly with positive integers. We emphasized factorization properties of integers, which led us to consider numbers that have no proper factorizations, which are the primes, a set that occupies a pivotal position in modern cryptography. We also looked at particular types of numbers, such as the Mersenne primes, which are intimately connected with perfect numbers and took time to introduce some special classes of integers that are important in counting certain naturally occurring collections. Throughout all this, the backdrop was the system of integers, which are the counting numbers, positive, negative, and zero.

In this chapter we have gone beyond integers, first to the rationals (the fractions, positive and otherwise), then to the irrationals, and within the class of irrationals we have identified the transcendental numbers. The underlying system in which all this is taking place is the system of the *real numbers*, which can be thought of as the collection of all possible decimal expansions. Any positive real number can be represented in the form $r = n.a_1a_2\cdots$, where n is a non-negative integer and the decimal point is followed by an infinite trail of digits. If this trail eventually falls into a recurring pattern, then r is in fact rational and we have shown how to convert this representation into an ordinary fraction. If not, then r is irrational, so the real numbers come in those two distinct flavours, the rational and the irrational.

In our mathematical imaginations, we often picture the real numbers as corresponding to all the points along the number line as we look out from zero, to the right for the positive reals, and to the left for the negative reals. This leaves us with a symmetrical picture with the negative real numbers being a mirror image of the positive reals, and this symmetry is preserved when dealing with addition and subtraction – but not with multiplication. Once we pass to multiplication, the positive and negative numbers no longer have equal status as the number 1 is endowed with a property that no other number possesses, for it is the *multiplicative identity*, meaning that $1 \times r = r \times 1 = r$ for any real number r. Multiplication by 1 fixes the position of any number, but in contrast multiplication by -1 swaps a number for its mirror image on the far side of 0. Once multiplication enters the scene, the fundamental differences in the nature of positive and negative numbers are revealed. In particular, negative numbers lack square roots within the real number system because the square of any real number is always greater than or equal to zero.

This is the cue for imaginary numbers to make their entrance. This topic is one that we shall take up again in the final chapter; for the time being, we will just make some introductory comments.

These numbers arise through the search for solutions to simple polynomial equations. In particular, since the square of any real number is never negative, we can find no solution to the equation $x^2 = -1$. Undaunted, mathematicians invented one, denoted by i, which is endowed with that property, so that $i^2 = -1$. At first sight, this seems artificial and arbitrary but it is not too much different from the kind of behaviour we have indulged in before. After all, while recognizing that the counting numbers $1, 2, 3, \cdots$ are pre-eminent, in order to deal smoothly with general number matters we are led to the wider number system of the rationals, which is the collection of all fractions, positive, negative, and zero. We then find, however, that we have no solution to the equation $x^2 = 2$, as we have shown that the square of a rational number cannot exactly equal 2. To deal with this, we have to 'invent' $\sqrt{2}$. At this point we could take the alternative attitude and say that we have proved that the square root of 2 simply does not exist and that is the end of the matter. However, few would feel happy to haul up the drawbridge in this way. The ancient Greeks certainly were not content to let things stand at that, for they could construct a length representing $\sqrt{2}$ with compass and straightedge and so the number was, to their way of thinking, definitely real and any mathematical system that denied this was inadequate.

We might agree with Pythagoras for quite a different reason. We may react by saying that we can approximate $\sqrt{2}$ to any degree of accuracy via its decimal expansion: $\sqrt{2} = 1.414213\cdots$, and so $\sqrt{2}$ is the number that is represented exactly by the totality of this expansion. A modern person might find more force in this argument and so insist for this reason that the number system needs to be expanded beyond the rationals.

However, at first glance we might say that things are different when it comes to $\sqrt{-1}$ as there seems no immediate need to worry about its non-appearance among the collection of numbers that we habitually call 'real'. It transpires though that as our mathematics progresses a little further, the need for imaginary numbers becomes very pressing, and any initial reluctance to deal with them is dispelled as our understanding of things mathematical grows.

This first struck home in the 16th century when Italian mathematicians learnt how to solve cubic and fourth-degree polynomial equations in a fashion that extended that used to solve quadratic equations. The Cardano method, as it came to be known, would often involve square roots of negatives even though the solutions to the equations eventually turned out to be positive integers. By stages from this point, the use of *complex numbers*, which are those of the form $a + bi$, where a and b are ordinary real numbers, was shown to facilitate a variety of mathematical calculations. For example, in the 18th century Euler revealed and exploited the stunning little equation $e^{i\pi} = -1$, which cannot fail to surprise anyone on their first encounter.

Around the beginning of the 19th century, the geometric interpretation of complex numbers as points in the coordinate plane (the standard system of xy-coordinates), was investigated by Wessell and Argand, from which point the use of the 'imaginary' became accepted as normal mathematics. Identifying the complex number $x + iy$ with the point with coordinates (x, y) allows examination of the behaviour of complex numbers in terms of the behaviour of points in the plane, and this proves to be very illuminating. The theory of so-called *complex variables*, whose subject matter is represented by functions of complex numbers, rather than just real numbers, flourished spectacularly in the hands of Augustin Cauchy (1789–1857). It is now a cornerstone of mathematics, underpins much of electrical signal theory, and the entire field of X-ray diffraction is built on complex numbers. These numbers have proved to have real meaning, and moreover the system is complete in that *every* polynomial equation has its full complement of solutions within the system of complex numbers. We shall return to these matters in the final chapter. Before doing that, however, we shall in the next chapter look more closely at the infinite nature of the real number line.

Chapter 7
To infinity and beyond!

Infinity within infinity

It was the great 16th-century Italian polymath Galileo Galilei (1564–1642) who was first to alert us to the fact that the nature of infinite collections is fundamentally different from finite ones. As alluded to on the first page of this book, the size of a *finite* set is smaller than that of a second set if the members of the first can be paired off with those of just a portion of the second. However, infinite sets by contrast can be made to correspond in this way to subsets of themselves (where by the term *subset* I mean a set within the set itself). We need go no further than the sequence of natural counting numbers $1, 2, 3, 4, \cdots$ in order to see this. It is easy to describe any number of subsets of this collection that themselves form an infinite list, and so are in a one-to-one correspondence with the full set (see Figure 8): the odd numbers, $1, 3, 5, 7, \cdots$, the square numbers, $1, 4, 9, 16, \cdots$ and, less obviously, the prime numbers, $2, 3, 5, 7, \cdots$, and in each of these cases the respective complementary sets of the even numbers, the non-squares, and the composite numbers are also infinite.

The Hilbert Hotel

This rather extraordinary hotel, which is always associated with David Hilbert (1862–1943), the leading German mathematician of his day, serves to bring to life the strange nature of the infinite. Its

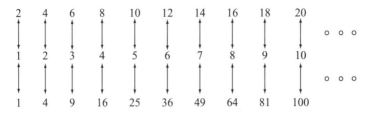

8. The evens and the squares paired with the natural numbers

chief feature is that it has infinitely many rooms, numbered
$1, 2, 3, \cdots$, and boasts that there is always room at Hilbert's Hotel.

One night, however, it is in fact full, which is to say each and every
room is occupied by a guest and much to the dismay of the desk
clerk, one more customer fronts up demanding a room. An ugly
scene is avoided when the manager intervenes and takes the clerk
aside to explain how to deal with the situation: tell the occupant of
Room 1 to move to Room 2 says he, that of Room 2 to move into
Room 3, and so on. That is to say, we issue a global request that
the customer in Room n should shift into Room $n + 1$, and this will
leave Room 1 empty for this gentleman!

And so you see, there *is* always room at the Hilbert Hotel. But how
much room?

The next evening, the clerk is confronted with a similar but more
testing situation. This time a spaceship with 1729 passengers
arrives, all demanding a room in the already fully occupied hotel.
The clerk has, however, learned his lesson from the previous night
and sees how to extend the idea to cope with this additional group.
He tells the person in Room 1 to go to Room 1730, that of Room 2
to shift to Room 1731, and so on, issuing the global request that
the customer in Room n should move into Room number $n + 1729$.
This leaves Rooms 1 through to 1729 free for the new arrivals, and
our clerk is rightly proud of himself for dealing with this new
version of last night's problem all by himself.

The final night, however, the clerk again faces the same situation – a full hotel, but this time, to his horror, not just a few extra customers show up but an infinite space coach with infinitely many passengers, one for each of the counting numbers $1, 2, 3. \cdots$. The overwhelmed clerk tells the coach driver that the hotel is full and there is no conceivable way of dealing with them all. He might be able to squeeze in one or two more, any finite number perhaps, but surely not infinitely many more. It is plainly impossible!

An infinite riot might have ensued except again for the timely intervention of the manager who, being well versed in Galileo's lessons on infinite sets, informs the coach driver that there is no problem at all. There is always room at Hilbert's Hotel for anyone and everyone. He takes his panicking desk clerk aside for another lesson. All we need do is this, he says. We tell the occupant of Room 1 to shift into Room 2, that in Room 2 to shift to *Room 4*, that in Room 3 to go to *Room 6*, and so on. In general the global instruction is that the occupant of Room n should move into Room $2n$. This will leave all the odd numbered rooms empty for the passengers of the infinite space coach. No problem at all!

The manager seems to have it all under control. However, even he would be caught out if a spaceship turned up that somehow had the technology to have one passenger for each point in the continuum of the real line. One person for every decimal number would totally overrun Hilbert's Hotel, and we shall see why in the next section.

Cantor's comparisons

All this may be surprising the first time you think about it, but it is not difficult to accept that the behaviour of infinite sets may differ in some respects from finite ones, and this property of having the same size as one of its subsets is therefore a case in point. In the 19th century, however, Georg Cantor (1845–1918) went much further and discovered that not all infinite sets can be regarded as having equally many members. This revelation was unexpected in nature but is not hard to appreciate once your attention is drawn to it.

Cantor asks us to think about the following. Suppose we have any infinite list L of numbers $a_1, a_2, \cdots$ thought of as being given in decimal form. Then it is possible to write down another number, a, that does not appear anywhere in the list L: we simply take a to be different from a_1 in the first place after the decimal point, different from a_2 in the second decimal place, different from a_3 in the third decimal place, and so on – in this way, we may build our number a making sure it is not equal to any number in the list. This observation looks innocuous but it has the immediate consequence that it is *absolutely impossible* for the list L to contain *all* numbers, because the number a will be missing from L. It follows that the set of all *real numbers*, that is all decimal expansions, cannot be written in a list, or in other words *cannot* be put into a one-to-one correspondence with the natural counting numbers, the way we saw in Figure 8. This line of reasoning is known as *Cantor's Diagonal Argument*, as the number a that lies outside the set L is constructed by imagining a list of the decimal displays of L as in Figure 9 and defining a in terms of the diagonal of the array.

There is some subtlety here, for we might suggest that we can easily get around this difficulty by simply placing the missing number a at the front of L. This creates an enlarged listing M containing the annoying number a. However, the underlying problem has not gone away. We can apply Cantor's construction again to introduce a fresh number b that is not present in the new list M. We can of course continue to augment the current list as before any number of times, but Cantor's point remains valid: although we can keep creating lists that contain additional numbers that were previously overlooked, there can never be one specific list that contains every real number.

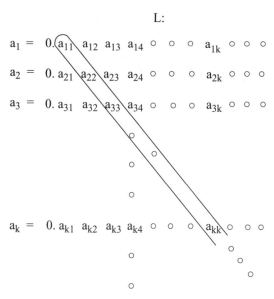

9. Cantor's number a differs from each a_k in the kth decimal place

The collection of all real numbers is therefore larger in a sense than the collection of all positive integers. Even though both are infinite, the sets cannot be paired off together the way the even numbers can be paired with the list of all counting numbers. Indeed, if we apply Cantor's Diagonal Argument to a putative list of all numbers in the interval 0 to 1, the missing number a will also lie in this range. Therefore, we likewise conclude that this collection will also defy every attempt at listing it in full. I mention this as we shall make use of that fact shortly.

Cantor's result is rendered all the more striking by the fact that many other sets of numbers can be put into an infinite list, including the Greeks' euclidean numbers. A little ingenuity is involved, but once a couple of tricks are learned, it is not hard to show that many sets of numbers are *countable*, which is the term we use to mean the set can be listed in the same fashion as the counting numbers. Otherwise an infinite set is called *uncountable*.

For example, let us take the set of all integers **Z**, which comes to us naturally as a kind of doubly infinite list. We can, however, rearrange it into a row with a starting point: 0, 1, −1, 2, −2, 3, −3, ⋯ by pairing each positive integer with its opposite, we create a list where every integer appears – none will escape. More surprisingly, we can also do the same with the rationals: start with 0, then list all the rationals that can be written using all numbers no more than 1 (which are 1 and −1), then those that involve no number higher than 2 (which are 2, −2, $\frac{1}{2}$, −$\frac{1}{2}$), then those that only use numbers up to 3, and so on. In this way, the fractions (positive, negative, and zero) can be arranged in a sequence in which they are all present and accounted for. The rationals therefore also form a countable set, as do the euclidean numbers, and indeed if we consider the set of all numbers that arise from the rationals through taking roots of any order, the collection produced is still countable. We can even go beyond this: the collection of all algebraic numbers (first mentioned in Chapter 6), which are those that are solutions of ordinary polynomial equations, form a collection that can, in principle, be arrayed in an infinite list: that is to say, it is possible to describe a systematic listing that sweeps them all out. (The proof is along the lines of the argument that works for the rationals.)

What we have allowed to happen in casually accepting any decimal expansion is to open the door to what are known as the transcendental numbers, those numbers that lie beyond those that arise through euclidean geometry and ordinary algebraic equations. Cantor's argument shows us that transcendental numbers exist and, in addition, there must be infinitely many of them, for if they formed only a finite collection, they could be placed in front of our list of algebraic numbers (the non-transcendentals), so yielding a listing of all real numbers, which we now know is impossible. What is striking is that we have discovered the existence of these strange numbers without identifying a single one of them! Their existence was revealed simply through comparing certain infinite collections to one another. The transcendentals are the numbers that fill the huge void between the more familiar algebraic numbers and the collection of all decimal expansions: to borrow an astronomical metaphor, the transcendentals are the dark matter of the number world.

In passing from the rationals to the reals, we are moving from one set to another of *higher cardinality* as mathematicians put it. Two sets have the same cardinality if their members can be paired off, one against the other. What can be shown using the Cantor argument is that any set has a smaller cardinality than the set formed by taking all of its subsets. This is obvious for finite collections: indeed, in Chapter 5 it was explained that if we have a set of n members then there are 2^n subsets that can be formed in this way. But how large is the set S of all subsets of the infinite set of natural numbers, $\{1, 2, 3, \cdots\}$? This question is not only interesting in itself but also in the manner in which we arrive at the answer, which is that S is indeed uncountable.

Russell's Paradox

Suppose to the contrary that S was itself countable, in which case the subsets of the counting numbers could be listed in some order $A_1, A_2, \cdots$. Now an arbitrary number n may or may not be a member of A_n – let us consider the set A that consists of all numbers n such that n is *not* a member of the set A_n. Now A is a subset of the counting numbers (possibly the empty subset) and so appears in the aforesaid list at some point, let $A = A_j$ say. An unanswerable question now arises: is j a member of A_j? If the answer were 'yes' then, by the very way A is defined, we conclude that j is *not* a member of A, but $A = A_j$, so that is self-contradictory. The alternative is no, j is not a member of A_j, in which case, again by the definition of A, we infer that j is a member of $A = A_j$, and once more we have contradiction. Since contradiction is unavoidable, our original assumption that the subsets of the counting numbers could be listed in a countable fashion must be false. Indeed, this argument works to show that the set of all subsets of any countable but infinite set is uncountable.

This particular self-referential style argument was introduced by Bertrand Russell (1872–1970) in a slightly different context that led to what is known as Russell's Paradox. Russell applied it to the 'set of all sets that are not members of themselves', asking the embarrassing question whether or not that set is a member of itself. Again, 'yes' implies 'no' and 'no' implies 'yes', forcing Russell to conclude that this set cannot exist.

In the 1890s, Cantor himself discovered an implicit contradiction stemming from the idea of the 'set of all sets'. Indeed, Russell acknowledged that the argument of his paradox was inspired by the work of Cantor. The upshot of all this, however, is that we cannot simply imagine that mathematical sets can be introduced in any manner whatsoever, but some restrictions must be placed on how sets may be specified. Set theorists and logicians have been wrestling with the consequences of this ever since. The most satisfactory resolution of these difficulties is provided by the now standard *ZFC Set Theory* (the Zermelo-Fraenkel set theory with the *Axiom of Choice*).

The number line under the microscope

There are different ways of looking at the size of infinite sets of numbers that are revealed if we look at the distribution of the various number types that knit together to bind the number line into a continuum. The rationals may only be a countable collection of numbers, but the collection is densely packed within the line in a way that the integers plainly are not. Given any distinct numbers, a and b, there is a rational number that lies between them. The average of the two numbers, $c = \frac{a+b}{2}$, certainly is a number lying between them, but it may be irrational. However, if c is irrational we can approximate it by a rational number d, with a terminating decimal expansion, by letting d have the same decimal representation as c up to a very large number of decimal places. For example, if we take $\sqrt{2} = 1.414\ldots$, we have that $\sqrt{2}$ differs from 1.414 by less than 0.001, and each time we take another decimal place we guarantee finding a rational number that approximates $\sqrt{2}$ more accurately (on average, ten times more accurately) than the previous one. If the number of initial places in which they agree is sufficiently large, then their difference will be so small that both c and d will lie between a and b. The number of places we need to take after the decimal place will depend on just how close a and b are to each other to begin with, but it is always possible to find a rational d that does the job (see Figure 10). We say that the set of rational numbers is *dense* in the number line for just this reason. Of course we can, by the same argument, show that there is another rational, splitting the interval from a to d, say, and, in this way, we arrive at the conclusion that infinitely many rational numbers lie between any two numbers, however small the difference between these two numbers might happen to be. In particular, there is no such thing as the smallest positive fraction, for, given any positive number, there is always a rational lying between it and zero.

Not to be outdone, the set of irrationals also forms a dense set. Before explaining this, I point out that once we have identified one irrational, the Pythagorean number $\sqrt{2}$ for example, the floodgates open and we can immediately identify infinitely more. When we add a rational to an irrational the result is always an irrational. For example, $\sqrt{2} + 7$ is irrational by dint of this fact. In a similar fashion, if we multiply an irrational number by a rational number (other than 0), the result is another irrational number.

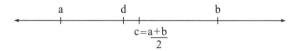

10. Rationals separate any given positions on the number line

(Simple contradiction arguments establish both these claims.)
In particular, we can find an irrational number of size as small as
we like: $t = \frac{\sqrt{2}}{n}$ is irrational for any counting number n and by
taking n larger and larger we can make t as close to 0 as we please.
As with the rationals, we therefore see that there is no smallest
positive irrational, and hence there is no such thing as the smallest
positive number.

Returning to our given numbers, a and b, once again let c be their
average. If c is irrational, we have a number of the required kind
(irrational). If on the other hand, c is rational, put $d = c + t$, where
t is the irrational number of the previous paragraph. By what has
gone before, d will also be irrational, and if we take n large enough,
we can always ensure that d is so close to the average c of the two
given numbers a and b that it lies between them. In this way, we
see that the irrational numbers too form a dense set and, as with
the rational numbers, we can infer that there are infinitely many
irrational numbers lying between any two numbers on the number
line.

And so the set of rationals and its complementary set of irrationals
are in one way comparable (they are both dense in the number
line) and in another not (the first set is countable, the second not).

Cantor's Middle Third Set

We now have a clearer idea as to how the rational and the
irrational numbers interlace to form the real number line. The
rational numbers form a countable set, yet are densely packed into
the number line. Cantor's Middle Third Set is, by way of contrast,
an uncountable subset of the unit interval that nevertheless is
sparsely spread. It is the result of the following construction.

We begin with the unit interval I, that is all the real numbers from
0 up to 1 inclusive. The first step in the formation of Cantor's set is
the removal of the middle third of this interval, that is all the

11. Evolution of Cantor's Middle Third Set to the 4th level

numbers between $\frac{1}{3}$ and $\frac{2}{3}$. The set that remains consists of the two intervals from 0 up to $\frac{1}{3}$ and from $\frac{2}{3}$ up to 1. At the second stage, we remove the middle third of these two intervals, at the third stage we remove the middle third of the remaining intervals, and so on. Cantor's Middle Third Set C then consists of all points of I that are *not* removed at any stage of this process.

The total length of the little intervals that remain as we pass from one stage of this process to the next is, by design, $\frac{2}{3}$ that of the previous stage; it follows that at the *n*th stage the total length of the surviving intervals is $\left(\frac{2}{3}\right)^n$. This expression approaches 0 as n increases and since the Cantor set C is the collection of all points that are left at the end of it all, it follows that the 'length', or *measure*, of C must be 0.

We might suspect that we have thrown the baby out with the bath water and that there are no points at all left in C. Is the Middle Third Set empty? The answer is a resounding no! There are infinitely many numbers left in C. This is best seen if we shift our representation of the numbers of the interval to base three 'decimals' known as *ternary*, as the whole construction is based on thirds. In base three decimals, the numbers $\frac{1}{3}$ and $\frac{2}{3}$ are respectively given by 0.1 and 0.2. By discarding the middle third of the unit interval, we have thrown away all those numbers whose ternary expansion begins with 0.1, and indeed the overall process weeds out exactly those numbers that have a 1 anywhere in their ternary expansions. The numbers in C are exactly those whose ternary expansions consist entirely of 0s and 2s. (For example, $\frac{3}{4}$ survives the infinite cull as in ternary it has the recurring expansion $0.202020\ldots$.)

Next we make an amazing observation. By taking the ternary expansion of any number c in C and replacing each instance of 2 by 1, we obtain the binary expansion of some number c' in the unit interval. This gives a one-to-one correspondence of C with the set of *all* numbers in I (written in binary). It follows that the cardinality of C is the same as that of I, and since the latter is an uncountable set (by Cantor's Diagonal Argument), it follows that the Cantor Middle Third Set is not only infinite but uncountable.

Therefore we have a set C that is in one sense negligible in size (has measure zero), but by another way of reckoning C is huge, as it has the same cardinality as I and hence of the whole real line.

What is more, far from being dense, C is *nowhere dense*. Recall that by saying that a set like the rationals is dense, we mean that whenever we take a real number a, there are rational numbers to be found in any little interval surrounding a, however small that interval might be. We say that any *neighbourhood* of a contains members of the set of rationals. The Cantor set has quite the opposite nature – numbers not in C might live their lives in the real line without ever coming across any members of C, provided they confine their experiences to a narrow enough locality around where they live. To see this, take any number a that is *not* in C, so that a has a ternary expansion that contains at least one 1: $a = 0 \cdot \ldots .1 \ldots$, with the 1 in the nth place, say. For a sufficiently tiny interval surrounding a, the numbers b in that interval have a ternary expansion that agrees with that of a up to places beyond the nth, and so *all* of them will also *not* be members of the strange set C as their ternary expansions will also contain at least one instance of 1.

On the other hand, any member a of the Cantor set will not feel too isolated, for when a looks out into any interval J that surrounds it in the number line, however small, a will find neighbours from the set C living alongside it (and numbers not in C as well). We can specify a member b of the given interval J that also lies in C by taking b to have a ternary expansion that agrees with a to a sufficiently large number of places, but with no entry being a 1. Indeed, there are uncountably many members of C in J.

In conclusion, the Cantor Middle Third Set C is as numerous as can be and, to the members of the C club, their brothers and sisters are to be seen all around them wherever they look. To the numbers not in C, however, C hardly seems to exist at all. Not one member of C is to be spotted in their exclusive neighbourhoods, and the set C itself has measure zero. To them, C is almost nothing.

Diophantine equations

Some of the principal sets of the number line may be characterized in the language of equations. The rational numbers, which form a countable set, are the numbers that arise as solutions of simple linear equations: the fraction $\frac{b}{a}$ is the solution to the equation $ax - b = 0$ (a and b are integers). Numbers like $\sqrt{2}$ that do not arise in this way are called irrational, and they form an uncountable collection that cannot be paired off with the counting numbers in the way that the rationals can. Within the set of irrationals there are the transcendentals, which are the numbers that never arise as the solutions of equations of these kinds even if we allow higher powers of x. It is known that π is an example of a transcendental number, but $\sqrt{2}$ is not, as it solves the equation $x^2 - 2 = 0$. The approach then is to define classes of numbers through the kinds of equations they solve.

An interesting line of study emerges, however, when we take the opposite tack and insist that not only the coefficients of our equations but their solutions have also to be integers. Here is a classic example.

A box contains spiders and beetles and 46 legs. How many of each kind of creature are there? This little number puzzle can be solved easily by trial, but it is instructive to note that first, it can be represented by an equation: $6b + 8s = 46$, and second that we are only interested in certain kinds of solutions to that equation, namely those where the number of beetles (b) and spiders (s) are counting numbers. In general, a system of equations is called *Diophantine* when we are restricting our solution search to special number types, typically integer or rational answers are what we are after.

There is a simple method for solving linear Diophantine equations such as this one. First, divide through the equation by the hcf of the coefficients, which are in this case 6 and 8 so their hcf is 2. Cancelling this common factor of 2 we obtain an equivalent equation, that is to say one with the same solutions: $3b + 4s = 23$. If the right-hand side were no longer an integer after performing this division, that would tell us that there were no integral solutions to the equation and we could stop right there. The next stage is to take one of the coefficients, the smaller one is normally the easiest, and work in multiples of that, in this case 3. Our equation can be written as $3b + 3s + s = (3 \times 7) + 2$; rearranging we obtain $s = (3 \times 7) - 3b - 3s + 2$. The point of this is that it shows that s has the form $3t + 2$ for some integer t. Substituting $s = 3t + 2$ into our equation and making b the subject, we get

$$3b + 4(3t + 2) = 23 \Rightarrow 3b = 15 - 12t \Rightarrow b = 5 - 4t.$$

We now have the complete solution in integers to the Diophantine equation: $b = 5 - 4t$, $s = 3t + 2$. Choosing any integral value for t will give a solution, and all solutions in integers are of this form.

Our original problem, however, was further constrained in that both b and s had to be at least zero, as negative beetles and spiders

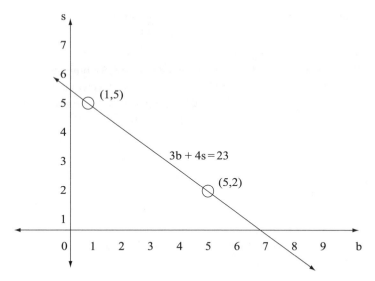

12. Lattice points on the line of a linear equation

do not exist. Hence there are only two feasible values of t, those being $t = 0$ and $t = 1$, giving us the two possible solutions of 5 beetles and 2 spiders, and 1 beetle and 5 spiders. If we interpret the puzzle as meaning that there is a plurality of both types of creature, we have the traditional solution: 5 beetles and 2 spiders.

This type of problem is called *linear* because the graph of the associated equation consists of an infinite line of points. The Diophantine problem then is to find the *lattice points* on this line, which are the points where both coordinates are integral or, if we only admit positive solutions, only lattice points in the positive quadrant will do.

However, once we allow squares and higher powers into our equations, the nature of the corresponding problems are much more varied and interesting. A classical problem of this type that has a full solution is that of finding all *Pythagorean triples*: positive integers a, b, and c such that $a^2 + b^2 = c^2$. A Pythagorean triple of course takes its name from the fact that it allows you to draw a right-angled triangle with sides of those integer lengths. The classic example is the $(3, 4, 5)$ triangle. Given any Pythagorean triple, we can generate more of them simply by multiplying all the numbers in the triple by any positive number as the Pythagorean equation will continue to hold. For example, we can double the previous example to get the $(6, 8, 10)$ triple. This, however, gives a similar triangle, one of exactly the same proportions, as the change is only a matter of scale and not of shape. Given the first triangle, we find the second Pythagorean triple simply by measuring the lengths of the sides in units that are half the size of the original units, thereby doubling the numerical size of the dimensions. There are, however, genuinely different triples such as those representing the $(5, 12, 13)$ and the $(65, 72, 97)$ right-angled triangles.

In order to describe all Pythagorean triples, therefore, it is enough to do the job for all triples (a, b, c) where the hcf of the three numbers is 1, as all others are merely scaled-up versions of these. The recipe is as follows. Take any pair of coprime positive integers m and n, with one of them even, and let m denote the larger. Form the triple given by $a = 2mn$, $b = m^2 - n^2$ and $c = m^2 + n^2$. The three numbers a, b, and c then give you a Pythagorean triple (the algebra is easily checked) and the three numbers have no common factor (also not difficult to verify). The three examples above arise by taking $m = 2$ and $n = 1$ in the first case, $m = 3$ and $n = 2$ in the second, while for the last triangle we have $m = 9$, $n = 4$. It takes more work to verify the converse: any such Pythagorean triple arises in this fashion for suitably chosen values of m and n, and what is more, the representation is unique so that two different pairs (m, n) cannot yield the same triple (a, b, c).

The corresponding equation for cubes and higher powers has no solution at all: for any power $n \geq 3$, there are no positive integer triples x, y, and z such that $x^n + y^n = z^n$. This is the famous *Fermat's Last Theorem*, which in future might be known as Wiles's

Theorem as it was finally proved in the 1990s by Sir Andrew Wiles. Even for the case of cubes, first solved by Euler, this is a very difficult problem. It is, however, relatively easy to show that the sum of two fourth powers is never a square (and so certainly not a fourth power). This is enough to reduce the problem to the case where n is a prime p (meaning that if we solved the problem for all prime exponents, the general result would follow at once), and indeed the problem was solved for so-called *regular* primes in the 19th century. However, the full solution was only realized as a consequence of Wiles settling a deep question called the Shimura–Taniyama Conjecture.

The most intensively investigated Diophantine equation is, however, the *Pell equation*, $x^2 - ny^2 = 1$, where n is a positive integer that is not itself a square. Its significance was appreciated very early, for it seems it was studied both in Greece and in India perhaps as far back as 400 BC, because its solution allows good rational approximations, $\frac{x}{y}$ of $\sqrt{n}$. For example, when $n = 2$, the equation has as one solution pair the numbers $x = 577$ and $y = 408$, and $(\frac{x}{y})^2 = 2.000006$. The equation is related to the geometric process of what the Greeks called *anthyphairesis* where one begins with two line segments and continues to subtract the shorter from the longer, a kind of analogue of the Euclidean Algorithm but applied to continuous lengths. Indeed, the Archimedes Cattle Problem mentioned in Chapter 5 leads to an instance of the Pell equation.

Versions of the Pell equation were studied by Diophantus himself around AD 150 but the equation was solved by the great Indian mathematician Brahmagupta (AD 628) and his methods were improved upon by Bhaskara II (AD 1150), who showed how to create new solutions from a seed solution. In Europe, it was Fermat who exhorted mathematicians to turn their attention to Pell's equation and the complete theory is credited to the reknowned French mathematician Joseph-Louis Lagrange (1736–1813) (the English appellation 'Pell' is an historic accident).

The general method of solution is based on the continued fraction expansion of $\sqrt{n}$.

Fibonacci and continued fractions

Recall the sequence of numbers, 1, 1, 2, 3, 5, 8, 13, 21, $\cdots$ discovered by Fibonacci and introduced in Chapter 5. Take a pair of successive terms in this sequence and write the corresponding ratio as 1 plus a fraction. If we now 'Egyptianize' this fraction by repeatedly dividing top and bottom by the numerator, a striking pattern emerges. Take, for instance

$$\frac{13}{8} = 1 + \frac{5}{8} = 1 + \frac{1}{1 + \frac{3}{5}} = 1 + \frac{1}{1 + \frac{1}{1 + \frac{2}{3}}} = 1 + \frac{1}{1 + \frac{1}{1 + \frac{1}{1 + \frac{1}{1}}}}$$

We obtain a multi-floored fraction consisting entirely of 1s, and each preceding ratio of Fibonacci numbers appears as we wind through the calculation. This must happen every time: by the very way these numbers are defined, each Fibonacci number is less than twice the next, and so the result of the division will leave a quotient of 1 and the remainder is the preceding Fibonacci number. You will recall that the ratio of successive Fibonacci numbers approaches the Golden Ratio, τ, and so this suggests that τ is the limiting value of the continued fraction consisting entirely of 1s.

As was shown in Chapter 5, the value of an infinite repeating process may be made the subject of an equation based on that process. If we call the value of the infinite fractional tower of 1s by the name a, we see that a satisfies the relation $a = 1 + \frac{1}{a}$, because what lies underneath the first floor of the fraction is just another copy of a. From this, we see that a satisfies the quadratic equation $a^2 = a + 1$, the positive root of which is $\tau = \frac{1+\sqrt{5}}{2}$.

The type of continued fractions that emerge from this process are intrinsically important. When we approximate an irrational number y by rationals we naturally turn to the decimal representation of y. This is excellent for general calculations but, being tied to a particular base, is not mathematically natural. Essential to the nature of y is how well our number y can be approximated by fractions with relatively small denominators. Is there any way to find a series of fractions that best deals with the conflicting demands of approximating y to a high degree of accuracy while keeping the denominators relatively small? The answer lies in the continued fraction representation of a number that does this through its truncations at ever lower floors.

Continued fractions look very awkward because of the many floors we have used in representing them. However, the inconvenience of writing all the floors of the division is easily side-stepped – since every numerator is 1, we need only record the quotients in the division to specify which continued fraction we are talking about. For instance, the representation for the fraction $\frac{25}{91}$ develops as follows:

$$\frac{25}{91} = 0 + \cfrac{1}{3 + \frac{16}{25}} = 0 + \cfrac{1}{3 + \cfrac{1}{1 + \frac{9}{16}}} = \cdots$$

that eventually yields a continued fraction specified by the list $[0, 3, 1, 1, 1, 3, 2]$. As we have seen, the Golden Ratio, τ has the continued fraction representation $[1, 1, 1, 1, \cdots]$. In a fashion reminiscent of repeating decimal notation, we write $\tau = [\overline{1}]$. The first instance of 3 in the continued fraction of $\frac{25}{91}$ comes from writing $91 = 3 \times 25 + 16$, which is the first line in the Euclidean Algorithm for the pair $(91, 25)$. Indeed, for this very reason there is one line in the continued fraction for every line of the algorithm when performed on the two numbers. In particular, starting with a *reduced fraction* in which the two numbers are coprime, the same will apply to each of the fractions that arise in the course of the calculation of the corresponding continued fraction.

The special example afforded by the Golden Ratio opens the door to the idea that we may be able to represent other irrational numbers not by finite continued fractions (which are obviously just rational themselves) but by infinite ones. But how is the continued fraction of a number a produced? The reader will need to tolerate a little algebraic trickery in order to see this in action, but here is how it goes.

There are two steps in the calculation of a continued fraction for a number $a = [a_0, a_1, a_2, \ldots]$. The number a_0 is the integer part of a, denoted by $a_0 = \lfloor a \rfloor$. (For example, the integer part of $\pi = 3.1415927 \cdots$ is given by $\lfloor \pi \rfloor = 3$.) In general, $a_n = \lfloor r_n \rfloor$, the integer part of r_n, where the remainder term r_n is defined recursively by $r_0 = a$, $r_n = \frac{1}{r_{n-1} - a_{n-1}}$. Applying this for example to $a = \sqrt{2}$ and employing the algebraic device of rationalizing the denominator (with which some readers may be familiar) we obtain, since $\lfloor \sqrt{2} \rfloor = 1$:

$$a = r_0 = \sqrt{2} = 1 + (\sqrt{2} - 1) \text{ so that } a_0 = 1;$$

$$r_1 = \frac{1}{r_0 - a_0} = \frac{1}{\sqrt{2} - 1} = \frac{\sqrt{2} + 1}{(\sqrt{2} - 1)(\sqrt{2} + 1)} = \sqrt{2} + 1, a_1 = \lfloor r_1 \rfloor = 2;$$

Next we get

$$r_2 = \frac{1}{r_1 - a_1} = \frac{1}{(\sqrt{2} + 1) - 2} = \frac{1}{\sqrt{2} - 1} = \frac{\sqrt{2} + 1}{(\sqrt{2} - 1)(\sqrt{2} + 1)} = \sqrt{2} + 1,$$

so that $r_1 = r_2 = \cdots = \sqrt{2} + 1$, $a_1 = a_2 = \cdots = 2$, and so $\sqrt{2} = [1, \overline{2}]$.

Indeed, the numbers that have recurring representations as continued fractions are rational numbers (which are exactly the ones whose representations terminate) and those that arise from quadratic equations such as τ, which we saw above is one solution of the equation $x^2 = x + 1$, and $\sqrt{2} = [1, \overline{2}]$, which satisfies $x^2 = 2$. Some other examples showing the rather unpredictable nature of the recurrences are $\sqrt{3} = [1, \overline{1, 2}]$, $\sqrt{7} = [2, \overline{1, 1, 1, 4}]$, $\sqrt{17} = [4, \overline{8}]$ and $\sqrt{28} = [5, \overline{3, 2, 3, 10}]$. There is nevertheless one very particular and remarkable facet to the pattern of the expansion of the continued fraction of an irrational square root. The expansion begins with an integer r, and the recurrent block consists of a palindromic sequence (a sequence of numbers that reads the same in reverse) followed by $2r$. This can be seen in all the preceding examples: for instance for $\sqrt{28}$ we see that $r = 5$, the palindromic part of the expansion is 3, 2, 3, which is followed by $2r = 10$. For $\sqrt{2}$ and $\sqrt{17}$, the palindromic part is empty, but the pattern is still there, albeit in a simple form. It can be shown that the continued fraction representation of a number is unique – two different continued fractions have different values.

The importance of continued fractions in approximation of irrationals by rationals is due to the so called *convergents* of the fraction, which are the rational approximations of the original number that result from truncating the representation at some point and working out the corresponding rational number. These represent the best approximation possible to the number in question in the sense that any better approximation will have a larger denominator than that of the convergents. The convergents of the Golden Ratio are the Fibonacci ratios. Since every term in the continued fraction representation of τ is 1, the convergence of these ratios is retarded as much as it possibly could be. For that reason, there is no more difficult number than τ to approximate by rationals and the Fibonacci ratios are the best you can do.

If the denominator of a convergent of a continued fraction is q, then the approximation is always within $\frac{1}{\sqrt{5}q^2}$ of the true value of the number and the convergents of a continued fraction alternately underestimate and overestimate the value to which they approach. It is, however, the euclidean numbers such as τ and $\sqrt{2}$ that are the worst when it comes to rational approximation. Some particular transcendentals, whose nature may seem the farthest removed from the rational world, may yet be approximated very closely and have convergents that home in on the target number with great rapidity.

The connection with Pell's equation, $x^2 - ny^2 = 1$, mentioned at the close of the previous section, now comes about as the solution (x, y) to the equation with the minimum possible positive value of x exists and is to be found among the convergents of the continued fraction representation of $\sqrt{n}$. For example, when $n = 7$ the sequence of convergents of $\sqrt{7}$ begins with $2/1,\ 3/1, 5/2, 8/3, \cdots$ and it is $x = 8,\ y = 3$ that provides this smallest so called *fundamental solution* of the Pell equation $x^2 - 7y^2 = 1$. The fundamental solution, however, sometimes does not turn up at all early in the expansion: for example, the smallest positive solution to $x^2 - 29y^2 = 1$ is $x = 9801$ and $y = 1820$. Once this fundamental solution (x, y) has been located, however, all other solutions arise by taking successive powers of the expression $(x + y\sqrt{n})^k$ $(k = 1, 2, 3, \cdots)$ and extracting the coefficients of the corresponding rational and irrational parts of the expanded expression. In this way, the full solution set of the Pell equation is realized through the continued fraction representation of $\sqrt{n}$.

Chapter 8
Numbers but not as we know them

Real and complex numbers

The construction of the complex numbers is much simpler and goes much more smoothly than the construction of the real numbers. The first stage in producing the reals is development of the rationals, at which point we have to explain what is meant by a fraction. A fraction, such as $\frac{2}{3}$ is just a pair of integers, which we represent in this familiar but peculiar manner. The idea of fractional parts is not difficult to understand, although the corresponding arithmetic takes real effort to master. Along the way your teachers explain in passing that such fractions as $\frac{2}{3}, \frac{4}{6}, \frac{6}{9}$ etc. are 'equal' – they are not the same number pairs but they do represent equal slices of pie. This is not hard to accept but it does draw our attention to the fact that a rational number is in reality an infinite set of equivalent fractions, each represented by a pair of integers. This sounds intimidating and we might prefer not to think too much about this, for the prospect of manipulating infinite collections of pairs of integers might leave us feeling uneasy. There is one saving grace in that any fraction has a unique reduced representation where the numerator and denominator are coprime, which can be got by cancelling any common factors in the fraction with which you originally began. Nonetheless, once you are familiar with the properties of fractions and the rules for using them, nothing should go wrong even though closer examination reveals that, as you do your sums, you are implicitly manipulating infinite collections of integer pairs.

However, things get worse at the next stage when we try to pin down what real numbers truly are. Let's begin with Pythagoras' problem – he found that there was no fraction equal to $\sqrt{2}$, so we can introduce a new symbol r, endow it with the property that $r^2 = 2$, and form a new 'field' of numbers from the rationals together with the new number r. This works in that the set of all numbers of the form $a + br$, where a and b are rational obey all the normal rules of algebra – we can even divide because the reciprocal of a number of this form retains the form, as can be seen through a little fancy algebraic footwork known as rationalizing the denominator.

The new numbers r and $-r$ furnish the two solutions of the equation $x^2 = 2$, but what about $x^2 = 3$? It seems that we need to adjoin yet another new number in order to solve this equation as it is easy to check that no number of the form $a + br$ will square to give 3. (A simple contradiction argument suffices here: assuming that $(a + br)^2 = 3$, allows you to deduce the false statement that at least one of $\sqrt{2}$ or $\sqrt{3}$ is rational after all.)

It is tempting to cut through all this fretting about particular equations and simply declare that we already know what the real numbers are – they are the collection of all possible decimal expansions, both positive and negative. These are very familiar, in practice we know how to use them, and so we feel on safe ground. At least until we ask some very basic questions. The main feature of numbers is that you can add, subtract, multiply, and divide. But, for example, how are you supposed to multiply two infinite non-recurring decimals? We depend on decimals being finite in length so that you 'start from the right-hand end', but there is no such thing with an infinite decimal expansion. It can be done, but it is complicated both in theory and in practice. A number system where you struggle to explain how to add and multiply does not seem satisfactory.

And there are other little pitfalls. When you multiply $\frac{1}{3}$ by 3, the answer is 1. When you multiply $0.333\cdots$ by 3, the answer is surely $0.999\cdots$. It is indeed the case that two different decimal expansions can represent the same number: $1.000\cdots = 0.999\cdots$. In fact, this happens with any terminating decimal, for example $0.375 = 0.374999\cdots$. Hence it can't be quite right to say that decimals and real numbers are one and the same, as we see that two different decimal expansions can equal the same number. Moreover, the numbers with non-unique decimal expansions will change if we work in another base, and that raises another complication. If we define real numbers by decimals, we are making the construction depend on an arbitrary choice (base ten). If we do the same construction in binary, will the set of 'real numbers' be the same? And what do we mean by 'the same' in any case?

You may find the foundational questions raised above interesting or you may grow impatient with all the introspection as we seem to be making trouble for ourselves when previously all was smooth sailing. There is a serious point, however. Mathematicians appreciate that, whenever new mathematical objects are introduced, it important to construct them from known mathematical objects, the way, for instance, fractions can be thought of as pairs of ordinary integers. In this way, we may carefully build up the rules that govern the new extended system and know where we stand. If we neglect foundations completely, it will come back to haunt us later. For example, the rapid development of calculus, which was born out of the study of motion, led to spectacular results, such as prediction of the movement of the planets. However, manipulation of infinite things as if they were finite sometimes provided amazing insights and at other times patent nonsense. By putting your mathematical systems on a firm foundation, we can learn how to tell the difference. In practice, mathematicians often indulge in 'formal' manipulations in order to see if some sparkling new theorem is in the offing. If the outcome is worthy of attention, the result can be proved rigorously by going back to basics and by invoking results that have been properly established earlier.

This is why Julius Dedekind (1831–1916) took the trouble of formally constructing the real number system based on his idea that is now referred to as *Dedekind cuts* of the real line. The first mathematician, however, to successfully deal with the dilemma caused by the existence of irrational numbers was Eudoxus of Cnidus (fl 380 BC) whose *Theory of Proportions* allowed Archimedes to use the so-called *Method of Exhaustion* to rigorously derive results on areas and volumes of curved shapes before the advent of calculus some 1,900 years later.

The final piece of the number jigsaw – the imaginary unit

The introduction of a new symbol i that squares to -1 is staggeringly successful as it resolves at a stroke not only the problem of providing a solution to one equation but allows solution of *all* polynomial equations and much more besides. We certainly have two square roots of any negative number, $-r$, as both the numbers $\pm i\sqrt{r}$ square to $-r$ by virtue of the property that $i^2 = -1$ and the assumption that, as with ordinary arithmetic, multiplication *commutes* meaning that $zw = wz$ for any numbers z and w. Indeed, if we continue on the basis that the system of complex numbers $a + bi$ should subsume that of the reals (which correspond to the case where $b = 0$) and that all the normal rules of algebra should continue to be respected, we meet with no difficulties and many pleasant surprises. The set of complex numbers, denoted by **C** is a 'field' which, among other things, guarantees that division is also possible. To see how it all works out, however, it is best to leave the monorail of the real line and look at life in two dimensions.

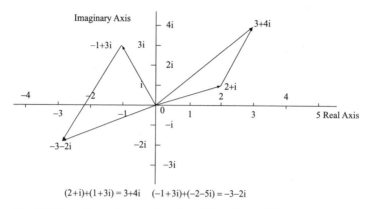

$(2+i)+(1+3i) = 3+4i$ $(-1+3i)+(-2-5i) = -3-2i$

13. Addition of complex numbers by adding directed line segments

The arithmetic of complex numbers presents itself very nicely in the *complex plane*. We think of the complex number $a + bi$ as being represented by the point (a, b) in the coordinate plane. When we add two complex numbers $z = (a, b)$ and $w = (c, d)$, we simply add their first and second entries together, to give us $z + w = (a + c, b + d)$. If we make use of the symbol i, we have for example $(2 + i) + (1 + 3i) = 3 + 4i$.

This corresponds to what is known as *vector addition* in the plane, where directed line segments (*vectors*) are added together, top to tail (see Figure 13). We begin at the *origin*, which has coordinates of $(0, 0)$, and in this example we lay down our first arrow from there to the point $(2, 1)$. To add the number represented by $(1, 3)$, we go to the point $(2, 1)$, and draw an arrow that represents moving 1 unit right in the horizontal direction (that is the direction of the *real axis*), and 3 units up in the direction of the vertical (the *imaginary axis*). We end up at the point with coordinates $(3, 4)$. In much the same way, we can define subtraction of complex numbers by subtracting the real and imaginary parts so that, for example, $(11 + 7i) - (2 + 5i) = 9 + 2i$. This can be pictured as starting with the vector $(11, 7)$, and subtracting the vector $(2, 5)$, to finish at the point $(9, 2)$.

Multiplication is another matter. Formally it is easy to do: we multiply two complex numbers together by multiplying out the brackets, remembering that $i^2 = -1$. Assuming the *Distributive Law* continues to hold, which is the algebraic rule that allows us to expand the brackets in the usual way, then multiplication proceeds as follows:

$$(a + bi)(c + di) = a(c + di) + bi(c + di) =$$
$$ac + adi + bci + bdi^2 = (ac - bd) + (ad + bc)i$$

Division, on the other hand, can be calculated by means of the *complex conjugate*. In general, the conjugate of $z = a + bi$ is denoted by $\bar{z}$ and is $a - bi$, in other words, $\bar{z}$ is the reflection of z in the real axis. The multiplication rule applied to $z\bar{z}$ gives $a^2 + b^2$, which is just a real number as the imaginary part turns out to be zero. This equals the square of the distance of z from the origin, which is denoted by $|z|$. In symbols $z\bar{z} = |z|^2$. We may now divide one complex number by another by multiplying top and bottom by the conjugate of the divisor in order to make the division one by a purely real number. This is analogous to the standard technique of rationalizing the denominator that is used to remove square roots in the bottom line, which we used to calculate the continued fraction for $\sqrt{2}$. For example:

$$\frac{15 + 16i}{2 + 3i} = \frac{(15 + 16i)(2 - 3i)}{(2 + 3i)(2 - 3i)} = \frac{30 - 45i + 32i - 48i^2}{2^2 - 6i + 6i - 3^2i^2}$$

$$= \frac{(30 + 48) - (45 - 32)i}{2^2 + 3^2} = \frac{78 - 13i}{13} = 6 - i.$$

By using general rather than specific complex numbers we can, in the same way, find the outcome of a general division of complex numbers in terms of their real and imaginary parts as we have done above for general complex multiplication. However, as long as the technique is understood, there is no pressing need to produce and to memorize the resulting formula.

Multiplication has a geometric interpretation that is revealed if we alter our coordinate system from the ordinary rectangular

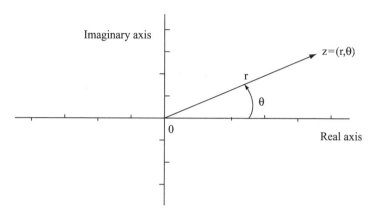

14. The position of a complex number in polar coordinates

coordinates to *polar coordinates*. In this system, a point z is once again specified by an ordered pair of numbers, which we shall write as (r, θ). The number r is the *distance* of our point z from the origin O (called in this context the *pole*). Therefore r is a non-negative quantity and all points with the same value of r form a circle of radius r centred at the pole. We use the second coordinate θ to specify z on this circle by taking θ to be the *angle*, measured in an anti-clockwise direction, from the real axis to the line Oz. The number r is called the *modulus* (plural moduli) of z, while the angle θ is called the *argument* of z.

Suppose now that we have two complex numbers, z and w, whose polar coordinates are (r_1, θ_1) and (r_2, θ_2) respectively. It turns out that the polar coordinates of their product zw take on a simple and pleasing form. The rule of combination can be expressed neatly in ordinary language: the modulus of the product zw is the product of the moduli of z and w, while the argument of zw is the *sum* of the arguments of z and w. In symbols, zw has polar coordinates $(r_1 r_2, \theta_1 + \theta_2)$. The multiplication of the real numbers is subsumed under this more general way of looking at things: a positive real number r, for instance, has polar coordinates $(r, 0)$, and if we multiply by another $(s, 0)$, the result is the expected $(rs, 0)$, corresponding to the real number rs.

Much more of the character of the multiplication of complex numbers is revealed through this representation. The polar coordinates of the complex unit i are given by $(1, 90°)$. (Normally, angles are not measured in degrees in such circumstances but in the natural mathematical unit of the *radian*: there are 2π radians in a circle, so that a turn of one radian corresponds to moving one unit along the circumference of the unit circle, centred at the origin. One radian is about $57.3°$.) If we now take any complex number $z = (r, \theta)$ and multiply by $i = (1, 90°)$, we find that $zi = (r, \theta + 90°)$. That is to say, *multiplication by i corresponds to rotation through a right angle about the centre of the complex plane*. In other words, the right angle, that most fundamental geometric idea, can be represented as a number.

Indeed, the effect of adding or multiplying by a complex number z on all the points in a given region of the complex plane can be pictured geometrically. Imagine any region you fancy in the plane. If we *add z* to every point inside your region, we simply move each point the same distance and direction determined by the arrow, or vector as we often call it, represented by z. That is to say we *translate* the region to some other position in the plane so that the shape and size are exactly maintained, as is its attitude, by which we mean the region has not undergone any rotation or reflection. Multiplying every point in your region by $z = (r, \theta)$ has two effects, however, one caused by r and the other by θ. The modulus of each point in the region is increased by a factor r, so all the dimensions of the region are increased by a factor of r also (so its area is multiplied by a factor of r^2). Of course, if $r < 1$ then this 'expansion' is better described as a contraction as the new region will be smaller than the original. The region will, however, maintain its shape – for instance, a triangle is mapped on to a similar triangle with the same angles as before. The effect of θ, as we have explained above, is to rotate the region through an angle

θ, anticlockwise about the pole. The net effect then in multiplying all points of your region by z is to expand and rotate your region about the pole. The new region will still have the same shape as before but will be of a different size, determined by r, and will be lying in a different attitude as determined by the rotation angle θ.

Further consequences

The polar version of complex numbers is particularly suited to the taking of powers and roots for to raise $z = (r, \theta)$ to some positive power n, we simply raise the modulus to that power, and add θ to itself n times, to give $z^n = (r^n, n\theta)$. The same formula applies to fractional and negative powers. Division can be comprehended in polar form as well. As with real numbers, division by a complex number z means multiplication by its reciprocal $w = \frac{1}{z}$, but what number is this w? Given that $z = (r, \theta)$ the number w is the one with the property that $zw = (1, 0)$, the number 1. This shows us that we must take $w = (\frac{1}{r}, -\theta)$, for then $zw = (r, \theta)(\frac{1}{r}, -\theta) = (r\frac{1}{r}, \theta - \theta) = (1, 0)$, as we require. This gives an alternative to the rectangular approach to division that makes use of complex conjugation.

There are a host of applications of complex numbers, even at the elementary level. The interplay between rectangular and polar representations brings trigonometry into play in a surprising and advantageous way. For instance, a standard exercise for students is the derivation of important identities that now arise very naturally by taking arbitrary complex numbers of unit modulus (i.e. $r = 1$), and calculating powers using both rectangular and then polar coordinates. Equating the two forms of the answer then reveals a trigonometric equation.

A point with polar coordinates $(1, \theta)$ has, by elementary trigonometry, the rectangular coordinates $(\cos \theta, \sin \theta)$. If we now multiply two such complex numbers $z = \cos \theta + i \sin \theta$ and $w = \cos \phi + i \sin \phi$ in rectangular coordinates we obtain:

$$zw = (\cos\theta\cos\phi - \sin\theta\sin\phi) + i(\cos\theta\sin\phi + \sin\theta\cos\phi)$$

while the same in polar coordinates gives:

$$zw = (1, \theta)(1, \phi) = (1, \theta + \phi) = \cos(\theta + \phi) + i\sin(\theta + \phi);$$

equating the real and imaginary parts of the two versions of this one product then painlessly yields the standard angle sum formulas of trigonometry:

$$\cos(\theta+\phi)=\cos\theta\cos\phi-\sin\theta\sin\phi, \;\; \sin(\theta+\phi)=\cos\theta\sin\phi+\sin\theta\cos\phi.$$

Alternatively, the polar form for complex multiplication can be derived using these trigonometric formulas. Indeed, the rule that we have stated here, without proof, for multiplication in polar form is usually first derived from the rectangular form by using trigonometric formulas.

Much more comes quite easily now as the use of complex numbers reveals a connection between the exponential or power function, and the seemingly unrelated trigonometric functions. Without passing through the portal offered by the square root of minus one, the connection may be glimpsed, but not understood. The so-called *hyperbolic functions* arise from taking what are known as the even and odd parts of the exponential function. To every trigonometric identity there corresponds one of identical form, except perhaps for sign, involving these hyperbolic functions. This can be verified easily in any particular case, but then the question remains as to why it should happen at all. Why should the behaviour of one class of functions be so closely mirrored in another class, defined in so different a manner, and of such different character? Resolution of the mystery is by way of the formula $e^{i\theta} = \cos\theta + i\sin\theta$, which shows that the exponential and trigonometric functions are intimately linked, but only through use of the imaginary unit i. Once this is revealed (for it is surprising and is by no means obvious), it becomes clear that results along the lines described are inevitable through performing calculations using the two alternative representations offered by this equation and then equating real and imaginary parts. Without the formula, however, it all remains a mystery.

Complex numbers and matrices

Let us examine some consequences of the revelation that multiplication by i represents a rotation through a right angle about the centre of the coordinate plane. If $z = x + iy$, we have through expanding the brackets and reordering multiplications that $i(x + iy) = -y + ix$, so that the point (x, y) is taken to $(-y, x)$ under this rotation; see Figure 15. In this way, multiplication by i can be regarded as operating on points in the plane. This operation enjoys the special property that for any two points z and w and any real number a, we have $i(z + w) = iz + iw$, and $i(aw) = a(iw)$.

Moreover, if we multiply a real number a by a complex number $x + iy$, we get $a(x + iy) = ax + i(ay)$. In terms of points in the

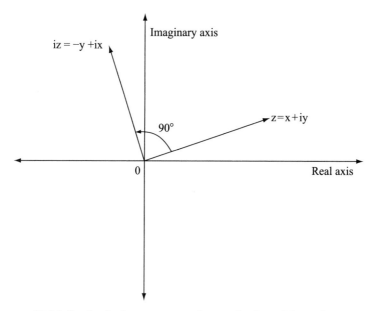

15. Multiplication by i rotates a complex number by a right angle

complex plane, we have that (x, y) is moved to (ax, ay), or to write it another way, $a(x, y) = (ax, ay)$.

The kinds of operations that enjoy these two properties are known as *linear* and are of paramount importance throughout all mathematics. Here, I wish only to draw to your attention to the fact that the effect of such an operation L is determined by its action on the two points $(1, 0)$ and $(0, 1)$, for let us suppose that $L(1, 0) = (a, b)$ and $L(0, 1) = (c, d)$. Then for any point (x, y) we have $(x, y) = x(1, 0) + y(0, 1)$, and so using the properties of a linear operation we obtain:

$$L(x, y) = L(x(1, 0) + y(0, 1)) = xL(1, 0) + yL(0, 1) =$$
$$= x(a, b) + y(c, d) = (ax, bx) + (cy, dy) = (ax + cy, bx + dy).$$

This information may be summarized by what is known as a *matrix equation*:

$$(x, y) \begin{pmatrix} a & b \\ c & d \end{pmatrix} = (ax + cy, bx + dy).$$

Here we have drawn out an example of matrix multiplication, which indicates how that operation is carried out in general. A *matrix* is just a rectangular array of rows and columns of numbers. Matrices, however, represent another kind of two-dimensional numerical object and, what is more, they pervade nearly all of higher mathematics, both pure and applied. They represent a whole corpus of algebra, and much of modern mathematics strives to represent itself through matrices, so useful have they proved to be. Two matrices with the same number of rows and the same number of columns as each other are added entry-to-entry: for example, to find the entry in the second row and third column of the sum of two matrices, we simply add the correspondingly placed entries in the two matrices in question. It is matrix multiplication, however, that gives the subject a new and important character, and how it is conducted has emerged of its own accord in the previous example – each entry in the product matrix is formed by taking the *dot product* of a row of the first matrix with a column of the second, meaning that the entry is the sum of the corresponding products when the row of the first matrix is placed on top of the column of the second.

Matrices follow all the usual laws of algebra except commutativity of multiplication, meaning that for two matrices A and B it is *not* generally true that $AB = BA$. However, matrix multiplication is *associative*, meaning that products of any length may be written unambiguously without the need for bracketing.

Linear transformations of the plane are typically rotations about the origin, reflections in lines through the origin, enlargments and contractions about the origin, and so called *shears* (or *slanting*), which move points parallel to a fixed axis by an amount proportional to their distance from that axis in a manner similar to the way the pages of a book can slide past one another. Any sequence of these transformations can be effected by multiplying all of the relevant matrices together to reveal a single matrix that has the same net effect as all those transformations acting in turn. The rows of the resultant matrix are simply the images of the two points $(1, 0)$ and $(0, 1)$, as we saw above, known as *basis vectors*.

It is now natural to look at the matrix J that represents an anticlockwise rotation of a right angle about the origin as it should mimic the behaviour we see when we multiply by the imaginary unit i. Since the point $(1, 0)$ is taken onto the point $(0, 1)$ by the rotation and similarly the point $(1, 0)$ moves to $(-1, 0)$, these two vectors form the rows of our matrix J. The result of squaring J will be a matrix that has the geometric effect of rotating points through $2 \times 90° = 180°$ about the origin. We calculate this below by matrix multiplication. To find, for example, the bottom right entry of J^2 we take the dot product of the second row and second column, which gives $(-1) \times 1 + 0 \times 0 = -1 + 0 = -1$. The complete calculation has the following outcome:

$$J^2 = \begin{pmatrix} 0 & 1 \\ -1 & 0 \end{pmatrix} \begin{pmatrix} 0 & 1 \\ -1 & 0 \end{pmatrix} = \begin{pmatrix} -1 & 0 \\ 0 & -1 \end{pmatrix} = -I.$$

The matrix I with rows $(1\,0)$ and $(0\,1)$ is the *identity matrix*, so called as it acts like the number 1 in that when multiplied by another matrix A the result is A. The matrix $-I$, which represents a full half turn rotation about the origin, does behave like -1 in that $(-I)^2 = I$. The upshot of all this is that the matrices $aI + bJ$, where a and b are real numbers, faithfully mimic the complex numbers $a + bi$ with respect to addition and multiplication, and so give a matrix representation of the complex number field. The matrix corresponding to the typical complex number $a + bi$ is

$$\begin{pmatrix} a & b \\ -b & a \end{pmatrix}.$$

The matrices that represent the complex numbers do commute with one another but, as was mentioned above, this does not generally apply to all matrix products and another way in which matrices can misbehave is that not all of them can be 'inverted'. For most square matrices A (a matrix with equal numbers of rows and columns), we may find a unique *inverse matrix B* such that $AB = BA = I$, the identity matrix. The existence of the inverse matrix however depends upon a single number associated with a square matrix known as its *determinant*. In general, this is a certain sum of signed products formed by taking one entry from each row and column of the array. For the typical 2×2 matrix array as introduced on page 118, the determinant is the number $\Delta = ad - bc$. Determinants have many uses and agreeable properties. For instance, Δ represents the area scale factor of the corresponding matrix transformation: a shape of area a will be transformed into one of area Δa when undergoing a transformation by that matrix (and if Δ is negative, the shape also undergoes a reflection, reversing the original orientation). What is more, the determinant of the product of two square matrices is the product of the determinants of those matrices. A square matrix A will have an inverse B except in the case where $\Delta = 0$, in which case it will not. A zero determinant corresponds geometrically to a *degenerate* transformation where areas are collapsed by the matrix to figures of zero area such as a line segment or even a single point.

For the matrix of a complex number $z = a + bi$, we note that $\Delta = a^2 + b^2$, which is never zero except when $z = 0$ – but of course the number 0 never had a reciprocal before, and that remains the case in the wider arena of the complex numbers. This does confirm however that every *non-zero* complex number possesses a multiplicative inverse.

We stand here on the edge of the vast worlds of linear algebra, representation theory, and applications to multi-dimensional calculus, and this is not the place to go further. However, the reader should be aware that matrices apply to three dimensions and indeed to n-dimensional space, typically through $n \times n$ matrices. Although the arrays become larger and more complicated, the matrices themselves yet remain two-dimensional numerical objects.

Numbers beyond the complex plane

The field **C** of all complex numbers is *complete* in two important ways. An infinite sequence of complex numbers in which the terms cluster into ever smaller circles of radius that approaches 0 is called *convergent*. Any convergent sequence of complex numbers approaches a limiting complex number. This is also true of the real numbers, but not of the rationals – the successive decimal approximations to any irrational number represent a sequence of rational numbers that approach a limit outside of the rationals. Moreover, **C** is complete (or *closed*) in the algebraic sense that it can be shown that any polynomial equation
$p(z) = a + bz + cz^2 + \cdots + z^n = 0$ has n (complex) solutions,
$z_1, z_2, \cdots, z_n$, which then allows $p(z)$ itself to be fully factorized as
$p(z) = (z - z_1)(z - z_2) \cdots (z - z_n)$.

This and other stunning successes of the complex numbers largely obviate the need to expand the number system further beyond the complex plane. Indeed, it is not possible to construct an augmented number system that contains C and also retains all the normal laws of algebra. Moreover, there are only two extended systems that retain much algebraic structure at all, these being the *quaternions* and the *octonions*. Although their use is not nearly so widespread as that of the complex numbers, the *quaternions* are put to work, for example, in three-dimensional computer graphics. The octonions, which can be thought of as pairs of quaternions, lack not only the commutative property but also the associative property of multiplication.

A quaternion is a number of the form $z = a + bi + cj + dk$, where the first part $a + bi$ is an ordinary complex number and the two *quaternion units* j and k also satisfy $j^2 = k^2 = -1$. In order to do multiplication with quaternions, we need to know how the units multiply with one another and this is determined by the rules $ij = k$, $jk = i$, $ki = j$ but the reversed products carry the opposite sign, so that, for example, $ji = -k$ (indeed, all these products may be derived from the single additional equation: $ijk = -1$). The quaternions then form an enhanced algebraic system that satisfies all the laws of algebra except for commutativity of multiplication, due to the sign changes mentioned above in the reversed products. The consistency of the system can also be demonstrated through representation by 2×2 matrices, but this time we allow complex rather than just real entries. The number 1 is once more identified with I, the identity matrix but the units i, j, and k have as their matrix counterparts:

$$i = \begin{pmatrix} i & 0 \\ 0 & -i \end{pmatrix} \quad j = \begin{pmatrix} 0 & 1 \\ -1 & 0 \end{pmatrix} \quad k = \begin{pmatrix} 0 & i \\ i & 0 \end{pmatrix}$$

while the typical quaternion z has as its matrix:

$$z = \begin{pmatrix} a + bi & c + di \\ -c + di & a - bi \end{pmatrix}.$$

This representation of the quaternions by matrices is not unique, however, and indeed the representation of the complex numbers by matrices also has equivalent alternatives. Moreover, it is possible to represent the quaternions without employing complex numbers but only at the expense of using larger matrix arrays: the quaternions can be represented by certain 4×4 matrices with only real number entries.

New kinds of numbers and the extensions of old systems have come about through the need to perform calculations the outcome of which could not be accommodated by the number system as it stood. Every civilization begins with the counting numbers, but calculations involving fragments lead to fractions, those involving debt lead to negatives, and as Pythagoras discovered, those involving lengths lead to irrational numbers. Although a very ancient revelation, the fact that not all numerical matters could be dealt with using whole numbers and their ratios was a subtle discovery of a deeper kind. As science became more sophisticated, the number systems required have needed to mature in order to deal with these advances. Scientists do not generally look to create new numbers systems in a whimsical fashion. On the contrary, they are introduced often reluctantly and hesitatingly at first, to deal with research problems. For example, although first introduced in the 19th century, matrices arose irresistibly in quantum mechanics in the early 20th century when physicists encountered a quantity of the form $q = AB - BA$ that was nevertheless not zero. In any commutative system of numbers, q would of course be 0, so the numerical objects needed here were not of a kind they had met before: they were matrices.

It seems now that the world of mathematics and physics has enough number types. Although there are kinds of numbers not mentioned in this book, the number types that are commonly used throughout mathematics and science have not needed to change a great deal since the first half of the 20th century.

These observations, however, bring our mathematical balloon ride to its conclusion. We began at ground level and have ascended to where I hope the reader can gaze down upon a view of the rich and mysterious world of numbers.

Further reading

Two other books in the OUP VSI series that complement and expand on the current one are *Mathematics* by the Field's medallist Timothy Gowers and *Cryptography* by Fred Piper and Sean Murphy. Probability and statistics, fields that were neglected here in *Numbers*, are the subject of the *VSI Statistics* by David J. Hand.

An insight into the nature of numbers can be read in David Flannery's book, *The Square Root of 2: A Dialogue Concerning a Number and a Sequence* (Copernicus Books, 2006). This leisurely account is in the Socratic mode of a conversation between a teacher and pupil. *One to Nine: The Inner Life of Numbers* by Andrew Hodges (Short Books, 2007) analyses the significance of the first nine digits in order. Actually it uses each number as an umbrella for examining certain fundamental aspects of the world and introduces the reader to all manner of deep ideas. This contrasts with Tony Crilly's *50 Mathematical Ideas You Really Need To Know* (Quercus Publishing, 2007), which does as it says, digesting each of 50 notions into a four-page description in as straightforward a manner as possible. The explanations are mainly through example with a modest amount of algebraic manipulations involved, rounded off with historical details and timelines surrounding the commentary. A particularly nice account on matters concerned with binomial coefficients is the paperback of Martin Griffiths, *The Backbone of Pascal's Triangle* (UK Mathematics Trust, 2007), in which you will read proofs of Bertrand's Postulate and Chebyshev's Theorem, giving bounds for the number of primes less than *n*.

Elementary Number Theory by G. and J. Jones (Springer-Verlag, 1998) gives a gentle but rigorous introduction and goes as far as aspects of the famous Riemann Zeta Function and Fermat's Last Theorem. The classic book *An Introduction to the Theory of Numbers*, by G. H. Hardy and E. M. Wright, 6th edn (Oxford University Press, 2008) assumes little particular mathematical knowledge but hits the ground running. The author's book *Number Story: From Counting to Cryptography* (Copernicus Books, 2008) has more in the way of the history of numbers than this *VSI* and includes mathematical details in the final chapter. *The Book of Numbers* by John Conway and Richard Guy (Springer-Verlag, 1996) is full of history, vivid pictures, and all manner of facts about numbers. Quite a lot of the history and mystery surrounding complex numbers is to be found in *An Imaginary Tale: The Story of $\sqrt{-1}$* (Princeton University Press, 1998) by Paul J. Nahin. Paul Halmos's *Naive Set Theory* (Springer-Verlag, 1974) gives a quick mathematical introduction to infinite cardinal and ordinal numbers, which were not introduced here.

A popular account of the Riemann Zeta Function is the book by Marcus du Sautoy, *The Music of the Primes, Why an Unsolved Problem in Mathematics Matters* (HarperCollins, 2004), while Carl Sabbagh's, *Dr Riemann's Zeros* (Atlantic Books, 2003) treats essentially the same topic.

There are two accounts of the solution to Fermat's Last Theorem, those being *Fermat's Last Theorem: Unlocking the Secret of an Ancient Mathematical Problem* by Amir D. Aczel (Penguin, 1996) and *Fermat's Last Theorem* by Simon Singh (Fourth Estate, 1999). The best popular book on the history of coding up to the RSA cipher is also an effort of Simon Singh: *The Code Book* (Fourth Estate, 2000). The unsolvability of the quintic (fifth-degree polynomial equations) was not explained in our text here but is the subject of an historical account: *Abel's Proof: An Essay on the Sources and Meaning of Mathematical Unsolvability* (MIT Press, 2003) by Peter Pesic.

Websites

A very high-quality web page that allows you to dip into any mathematical topic, and is especially rich in number matters, is Eric Wolfram's *MathWorld: mathworld.wolfram.com*. For mathematical history topics, try *The MacTutor History of Mathematics archive* at St Andrews University, Scotland: *www-history.mcs.st-andrews.ac.uk/history.index.html*. Web pages accessed 8 October 2010. Wikipedia's treatment of mathematics by topic is generally serious and of good quality, although the degree of difficulty of the treatments is a little variable. For example, Wikipedia gives a good quick overview of important topics such as matrices and linear algebra.

Index

认准读客熊猫

读客所有图书，在书脊、腰封、封底和前后勒口都有"**读客熊猫**"标志。

两步帮你快速找到读客图书

1. 找读客熊猫

2. 找黑白格子

马上扫二维码，关注"**熊猫君**"

和千万读者一起成长吧！